Globalization of Japan

Globalization of Japan

Japanese *Sakoku* Mentality and U.S. Efforts to Open Japan

Mayumi Itoh

St. Martin's Press
New York

Globalization of Japan

ISBN 0-312-17708-9

Library of Congress Cataloging-in-Publication Data

Itoh, Mayumi, 1954–
   Globalization of Japan : Japanese *Sakoku* mentality and U.S. efforts
to open Japan: a manuscript / by
Mayumi Itoh.
      p. cm.
   Includes bibliographical references and index.
   ISBN 0-312-17708-9
   1. Japan—Foreign relations—1868–   2. Japan—Civilization—1868–
3. National characteristics, Japanese.   4. United States—Foreign
relations—1865–   I. Title.
DS881.96.I865   1998
327.52073—dc21   93-26784
                                                                              CIP

Internal design and typesetting by Letra Libre

First edition: May, 1998
10   9   8   7   6   5   4   3   2   1

Contents

Acronyms

APEC	Asia Pacific Economic Cooperation forum
ASEAN	Association of Southeast Asian Nations
DPJ	Democratic Party of Japan
GATT	General Agreement on Tariffs and Trade
HC	House of Councillors
HR	House of Representatives
ICJ	International Commission of Jurists
IMF	International Monetary Fund
JCP	Japan Communist Party
JDA	Japan Defense Agency
JNP	Japan New Party
JSP	Japan Socialist Party
LDP	Liberal Democratic Party
MFA	Ministry of Foreign Affairs
MITI	Ministry of International Trade and Industry
MNF	Multinational Forces
MOF	Ministry of Finance
NFP	New Frontier Party (*Shinshintô*)
NHK	*Nippon Hôsô Kyôkai*
NPS	New Party Sakigake (*Shintô Sakigake*)
ONUMOZ	United Nations Operation in Mozambique
PKF	Peacekeeping Force
PRC	People's Republic of China
ROC	Republic of China
ROK	Republic of Korea
SC	Security Council
SCAP	Supreme Commander of Allied Powers
SDF	Self-Defense Forces
SDPJ	Social Democratic Party of Japan
SII	Structural Impediments Initiative
UN	United Nations
UNSC	United Nations Security Council
UNAMIR	United Nations Assistance Mission in Rwanda
UNDOF	United Nations Disengagement Observer Force
UNPKO	United Nations Peacekeeping Operations
UNTAC	United Nations Transitional Authority in Cambodia

List of Figures

List of Tables

Acknowledgments

I acknowledge with gratitude the advice and assistance that I have received during the course of completing this manuscript. First, I would like to thank Tsuneo Akaha, Erika Engstrom, Chalmers Johnson, and Donald S. Zagoria for their valuable advice and comments on the earlier versions of the manuscript. I also would like to thank Shirley Davis, Pansy McDowell, Juline Haworth, Dawn Pomento, and Greg Rewoldt for their help in preparing this manuscript. I am grateful to the University of Nevada, Las Vegas (UNLV), for granting me a faculty development leave for the year 1995–1996, which enabled me to complete this manuscript.

Earlier versions of parts of this book were published previously. Chapter 1 was originally published as an article, "American Efforts to Open up Japan and Japanese Market: A Historical Perspective," *Halcyon*, Vol. 17 (1995), pp. 95–107. Chapters 2 and 6 are from "Japan's Abiding *Sakoku* Mentality," *Orbis*, Vol. 40, No. 2 (Spring 1996), pp. 235–245. Chapter 3 originated with "Japanese Perceptions of the United States," *Asian Survey*, Vol. XXXIII, No. 12 (December 1993), pp. 1122–1135. Chapter 4 is taken from "Japanese Politicians' 'Attitudinal Prism': Racial Superiority Complex Toward Asia," *Popular Culture Review*, Vol. 7, No. 2 (August 1996), pp. 87–98. Chapter 8 is based on "*Kome Kaikoku* and Japanese Internationalization," *Asian Survey*, Vol. XXXIV, No. 11 (November 1994), pp. 991–1001. Chapter 10 was first published as "Expanding Japan's Role at the United Nations: Peacekeeping Operations and the Security Council," *Pacific Review*, Vol. 8, No. 2 (1995), pp. 283–302.

I would like to thank the following publishers for permission to reproduce the above articles: Foreign Policy Research Council *(Orbis)*, Routledge *(Pacific Review)*, the Regents of the University of California *(Asian Survey)*, Nevada Humanities Committee and University of Nevada Press *(Halcyon)*, and Far West Popular and American Culture Associations *(Popular Culture Review)*.

Finally, I would like to thank Karen Wolny, Elizabeth Paukstis, Ruth Mannes, and Donna Cherry for their herculean editorial work; my parents, Shigeru and Asako Itoh, and my sister, Yayoi Itoh, for their tireless help in sending books and other materials from Japan. Although the publication of this book was not possible without the help of the people mentioned above, all responsibility for its contents rests with me.

—*Mayumi Itoh*

A Note on the Text

The English translations of the Japanese sources were made by the author. Direct translations of the Japanese into English sometimes do not make sense in English. Therefore, the English translations were made in such a way that they best make sense in English or were paraphrased from the original Japanese. The English translations that are not exact translations of the Japanese are not put into quotation marks.

Strictly speaking, the word "Japan" is an inactive noun referring to a nation. Unless specified otherwise, however, this book uses the term as an active noun referring to the members of public policy decision-making groups that make up the Japanese government.

For positions and titles of the people cited in the text, the book uses those held at the time of the event or situation in which the person is cited, instead of the present one, unless specified otherwise.

Introduction

In August 1995, Japan's Prime Minister Tomiichi Murayama decided to dispatch Self-Defense Forces (SDF) personnel to the Israeli-held Golan Heights, at the border of Israel and Syria, to participate in the United Nations Disengagement Observer Force (UNDOF). The Japanese personnel were to replace a Canadian contingent engaged in logistical operations for food transport, road maintenance, and other daily necessities for UNDOF. The actual dispatch of the Japanese mission did not occur until late January 1996, more than a year and a half after the then-UN secretary-general Boutros Boutros-Ghali had requested Prime Minister Tsutomu Hata to send such a mission in June 1994. The Hata coalition cabinet sent an investigation team to Syria to study the feasibility of the mission and considered dispatching an SDF contingent to UNDOF as early as fall 1994. The mission did not materialize, however, because of the change in the government in late June 1994. The Hata cabinet collapsed en masse 59 days after its inception. A new coalition cabinet led by socialist Tomiichi Murayama replaced it in July 1994.[1]

The Murayama cabinet comprised an unprecedented coalition of the conservative Liberal Democratic Party (LDP); the Social Democratic Party of Japan (SDPJ), the LDP's archenemy; and the New Party *Sakigake* (harbinger) (NPS), a splinter of the LDP. The SDPJ, which had a platform of unarmed neutrality, was opposed to the mission. Party officials were concerned with the possibility that the SDF personnel might get involved in armed conflict and thought the dispatch might violate Japan's 1992 Law Concerning Cooperation for United Nations Peacekeeping Operations and Other Operations (the International Peace Cooperation Law). The law allowed the SDF to participate only in logistical operations and froze participation in peacekeeping forces (PKF) until a future review. The law provided for review of the feasibility of removing the freeze on the SDF's participation in PKF in three years. The law also limited the use of weapons to self-defense. In essence, the Japanese Parliament repeated the same futile debate as in the case of previous missions to Cambodia (UNTAC) and Mozambique (ONUMOZ). The Diet debated whether the mission might violate the International Peace Cooperation

Law and whether the group should be equipped with one machine gun or two.[2]

Under these circumstances, the Japanese government delayed the dispatch, despite eager calls from the United Nations and foreign governments requesting that Japan play a more active role in the maintenance of international peace and security commensurate with its economic power. The delay was all the more embarrassing because Japan was not participating in any United Nations Peacekeeping Operations (UNPKO) after the completion of a mission in Mozambique in December 1994. The Murayama cabinet did not review the International Peace Cooperation Law in August 1995, as was stipulated in the law, and thus kept the ban on participation in PKF intact. Prime Minister Murayama finally decided to send an SDF contingent to UNDOF on the condition that SDF personnel would not participate in PKF in principle. He also decided to equip the 45-man group with two machine guns and 32 automatic rifles. The SDF personnel could not even participate in UNDOF's military training. Murayama left unresolved the issues of weapons and ammunition transport and the use of weapons in the event that SDF personnel were caught in an armed conflict. The actual SDF dispatch was preceded by the collapse of the Murayama cabinet in early January 1996.[3]

The Murayama cabinet's reluctance to send the SDF to the Golan Heights and the Diet's futile debate concerning Japan's participation in UNDOF demonstrated the parochial mind-set and the lack of "international awareness" (the recognition of one country's roles and responsibilities in the international community commensurate with its global standing) on the part of the Japanese government and its people (see Chapter 10).

Compensation for Former Comfort Women

Japan's parochialism and anachronistic attitudes are evident not only in its reluctance to play an active role in the maintenance of international peace and security but also in its attitude toward its neighbors in Asia. In June 1995, the late Michio Watanabe, a leading LDP member who served as deputy prime minister and foreign minister, denied Japan's colonial rule of Korea during 1910–1945 by stating that Japan's annexation of Korea was made in an amicable manner. Watanabe's assertion infuriated the South Korean government and its people. The South Korean Foreign Ministry spokesman called Watanabe's remark "outrageous" and "paranoiac." Watanabe's gaffe did not cost him his political life, since he was not holding any ministerial position at that time. Three months later, in September 1995, he died without achieving his political ambition of becoming prime minister. It was not the first time that a Japanese politician denied Japan's acts of aggression toward Asia during

World War II; several leading cabinet members of the ruling LDP had made similar remarks in the past. In each case, the incumbent minister apologized and withdrew his statement, but he ended up resigning from his post. Nonetheless, other cases have occurred even after Watanabe's statement.[4]

Given this attitude of ruling politicians, it is not surprising that the Japanese government has ignored the individual compensation of Asian victims of World War II for more than fifty years. The controversy over "comfort women," who were conscripted into wartime brothels for the Imperial Japanese Army, highlighted the demand for individual compensation issue in recent years. The comfort women were mainly Korean, Filipino, and Taiwanese. Korean comfort women who had remained silent about their shameful experiences began to speak out and demanded individual compensation in the late 1980s.[5]

To commemorate the fiftieth anniversary of the end of World War II, the Murayama cabinet set up the "Army's Comfort Women Issue Subcommittee" as part of the "Project Team for Postwar Fifty Years' Issues" in 1994. The subcommittee initially tried to establish a state fund to pay official compensation to the Korean comfort women. Its efforts were in vain due to LDP opposition. Conservative politicians have had a hard time admitting any of Japan's wrongdoing during the war. With the failure of the state fund, the subcommittee recommended the creation of a private fund at the Japan Red Cross to collect contributions for the compensation. At the government's request, Japanese volunteers managed to establish a private fund, the "Asia Peace and Friendship Fund for Women," in August 1995. The fund was originally expected to collect $3 million by the end of 1995 and pay temporary compensation to former victims. The fund had collected only $700,000 by the end of November 1995, however, and failed to pay temporary compensation in 1995.[6]

International legal experts criticized the Japanese government for its refusal to pay official compensation to the former comfort women. The International Commission of Jurists (ICJ), located in Geneva, stated that by establishing a private fund, the Japanese government intended to evade formal compensation as well as responsibility toward individual victims. The ICJ also said that neither the Japan-South Korean Basic Relations Treaty of 1965 nor the Japan-Philippine Compensation Agreement of 1956 should prevent former comfort women from claiming individual compensation. It further recommended that the Japanese government pay $40,000 per victim as a provisional remedy.[7]

In addition, a UN Human Rights Commission researcher urged the Japanese government to pay the official compensation to the former comfort women. Radhika Coomaraswamy, a Sri Lankan jurist who was assigned by the UN commission in March 1994 to investigate the issue, compiled a report in February 1996. Her report determined that the forced conscription of the women represented "sex slavery," which was banned under international law, including the Geneva Convention. It also stated that while the private fund should be hailed as a means to fulfill Japan's moral responsibilities, it allowed the government to avoid acknowledging its legal responsibilities. The report, among other things, called for the Japanese government to accept its legal responsibilities, pay compensation to former comfort women, and punish those who were involved in the conscription.[8]

In April 1996, with international criticism and exposure of the issue, the new prime minister, Ryutaro Hashimoto, decided to pay a temporary compensation—approximately $20,000—through the private fund to about 300 former victims. Yet he insisted that the state compensation had already been legally settled. As of July 1997, only 25 former victims received the compensation.[9] The lack of willingness to resolve the issue through official channels epitomizes Japan's insincere attitude toward its Asian neighbors. It is yet another example of the shortsightedness and lack of international awareness on the part of the Japanese government and its people (see Chapter 4).

Key Questions

The above two examples illustrate the wide gap between the international community's expectations for Japan to assume global responsibilities and the awareness of those responsibilities on the part of Japan; the Japanese government and its people lack international awareness of their global role as the world's second-largest economy. Whereas the expectation by foreign governments for Japan to play a more active role in the international community commensurate with its economic power has grown, Japan has kept a low-key profile on military and political issues and has continued to flood the world with its manufactured goods. In this context, the Japanese have earned for themselves the derogatory epithet of "economic animals," and Japan itself is referred to as a "faceless nation." As recently as April 1996, *Time* magazine mistook former Japanese ambassador to the United States Nobuo Matsunaga for former senator Spark Matsunaga (Hawaii), who had died of cancer, and erroneously carried the ambassador's picture in an obituary.[10]

The economic animals achieved the economic miracle in the 1970s. As Japan's exports expanded and its trade surplus grew, trade friction with other advanced capitalist countries intensified. The U.S. and European governments criticized Japan for unfair trade practices and for closing its economic markets to foreign goods and services. They demanded that Japan open its markets and liberalize its economic system. The economic friction has spilled over to security issues, most notably the "free-ride" arguments concerning the U.S.-Japan Security Treaty. The U.S. government (the U.S. Trade Representatives in particular) argued that Japan was able to divert its national resources fully to economic recovery and achieved its economic miracle because the United States provided free national security under the security treaty; however, Japan's new economic status no longer warranted such free protection by the United States. The polarity escalated in the 1970s, with the U.S. government demanding that Japan contribute to the "equal burden sharing" cost of maintaining the security arrangement.

As the *gaiatsu* (foreign pressure) for Japan to open its markets and play a more active role in the maintenance of international peace and security intensified during the 1980s, the word *kokusaika* (internationalization) became a popular slogan in Japan. It is difficult to define the term clearly, for it involves complex phenomena in diverse fields. Past attempts to define *kokusaika* ranged from "the expansion of the movement across national boundaries of goods, capital, information, people, and culture as the totality of all these" (by Japan's Economic Planning Agency) to "a process of opening Japan's heart to the outside world" (by Ryuhei Hatsuse of Kobe University). Yet *kokusaika* is not a mere "expansion of the movement" or "opening of a nation's heart"; it involves changes in domestic systems, rules, and regulations.[11]

This book emphasizes the internal dimension of *kokusaika* (inward *kokusaika*) rather than the external one (outward *kokusaika*), because the former represents a genuine and qualitative phenomenon, whereas the latter is nationalistic and superficial. It is important to distinguish the two dimensions of *kokusaika*. The outward *kokusaika* took place mainly in the realm of the economy, compelled by Japan's national interest and its global market strategy. The exodus of Japanese tourists to U.S. and European destinations, another aspect of the outward *kokusaika*, reflects a superficial *kokusaika* in the absence of a real understanding of foreign cultures. In contrast, a genuine inward *kokusaika* refers to the assimilation of the Japanese mind to foreign values and the transformation of Japan's domestic systems to meet internationally accepted norms and standards.[12]

It may be argued that the necessity for an inward *kokusaika* grew out of the very success of the nationalistic and superficial outward *kokusaika*. As Japanese economic power increased and trade surpluses accumulated, foreign pressure for Japan to open its markets and change its systems escalated. Economically, an inward *kokusaika* refers to a change in the traditional Japanese way of doing business in general, and deregulation and liberalization in particular. Politically, *kokusaika* involves political reforms that would make the Japanese election system more democratic (such as reducing the gap in voting power between urban and rural districts) and eradicate political corruption. Socially, *kokusaika* concerns the opening of Japanese society to foreigners and eliminating discrimination against foreigners, minorities, and women at home. Finally, and more important, *kokusaika* also entails a substantial contribution to the global community, or what is referred to as *kokusaikôken* (international contribution) in Japanese. The ubiquity of Japanese goods in the world is not matched by the presence of Japanese working for the world. A real *kokusaika* requires Japan to play a more active global role commensurate with its economic power, instead of simply pursuing its national interest.[13]

Japan embarked on *kokusaika* in the 1980s primarily to alleviate the foreign pressure to open its markets to foreign goods and services. Former prime minister Yasuhiro Nakasone made *kokusaika* an official policy when he declared the creation of a *kokusai kokka Nihon* ("an international country Japan") at the ninety-seventh session of the Japanese Parliament in February 1984. At the National Diet, Nakasone said that the creation of a *kokusai kokka Nihon* was necessary in that Japan's peace and prosperity could not exist without world peace and prosperity in today's deeply interdependent international society. He also said that Japan should become a *kokusai kokka* due to its rising status in international society and foreign countries' growing demands and expectations toward it.[14]

More than ten years after Nakasone's declaration, however, progress on *kokusaika* has been superficial at best, amounting only to modest relaxations of the barriers against certain foreign imports. The *gaiatsu*-concession nexus (whereby Japan grudgingly changes its policies inch by inch, yielding to foreign pressure) has been repeated. Even though the volume of particular Japanese imports has increased substantially, criticism of Japan has not stopped. Japanese resistance to trade liberalization is so strong and the process is so painstakingly slow, as exemplified by automobile, "beef and oranges," and semiconductor negotiations, it has exasperated foreign trade negotiators. As a result, foreign governments' complaints against Japanese economic practices and systems have intensified further, culminating in the Structural Impediments Initiative (SII) under the Bush administration and the Economic Framework Talks under the Clinton administration.

The progress of *kokusaika* in terms of *kokusaikôken* has been painstakingly slow as well, even though the word *kokusaikôken* has become a cliché in Japan. The slow progress of Japan's *kokusaikôken* is most evident in its contribution to the maintenance of international peace and security. Notwithstanding the strong requests by foreign governments, for example, Japan did not participate in the Multinational Forces (MNF) during the Gulf War, again using the pretext of constitutional limitations. Eventually succumbing to *gaiatsu,* the Japanese government made an enormous financial contribution ($13 billion) to the MNF by levying special taxes on its citizens. Yet the contribution was ridiculed as "checkbook diplomacy." When Japan belatedly sent minesweepers to the Persian Gulf after the war to help clean up the gulf, this gesture was regarded as "too little too late."

Furthermore, until December 1995, Japan was the only major advanced industrialized country that had not ratified the International Convention on the Elimination of All Forms of Racial Discrimination. The UN General Assembly adopted the treaty in 1965, and 146 countries had already ratified it. Japan ratified the treaty in December 1995, only after the United States did so in October 1994. Japan's ratification marked the end of decades of wrangling over Article 4 of the convention, which calls for countries to make activities or the dissemination of ideas promoting discrimination a criminal offense. Some Japanese politicians and bureaucrats, particularly in the Ministry of Justice, had argued that the article could violate constitutional rights of free speech, association, and assembly. Japan ratified the treaty under the condition that Article 4 would not be applied in violation of the Japanese constitution.[15]

This book addresses several key questions: Why is Japan so staunchly resistant to liberalizing its markets? Why is Japan so reluctant to participate in the maintenance of international peace and security, even in UNPKO? Why is Japan so hesitant to ratify an internationally recognized treaty? Finally, why is Japan so reluctant to launch *kokusaika*? Is it because of cultural, economic, or political reasons, or a combination of these three?

A Theoretical Framework

To answer the key questions posed above, this book establishes a theoretical framework on the role of perceptions in foreign policy. Theoretically, this book examines correlations among perceptions, national interest, and foreign policy. Specifically, this book explores in how the psychological predispositions of foreign policy decision makers (input), such as their individual beliefs, ideology, and other cultural, societal, and national characteristics, affect the decision makers' views of national interest and the formation of foreign policy (output). This book is also interested in how foreign policy elites' perceptions or views of a country (such as their dislike of that country) affect foreign policy toward that country. It is necessary to note here that this book does not analyze the foreign policy decision-making process per se but rather examines correlations between the input (decision makers' predispositions and perceptions) and the output (foreign policy).

Robert Jervis contributed to the study of perceptions in international politics by stressing the prime importance of decision makers' perceptions in the formation of foreign policy. Refuting the realist's assumption of rational policy making, in which actors are presumed to see a situation accurately, Jervis argued that elites perceive a situation differently and that not all decision makers respond the same way to a given situation. Jervis maintained that irrational factors, such as the values, beliefs, goals, and motivations of decision makers, affect decision makers' perceptions of their environments, which in turn affect foreign policy outputs.[16]

Richard Snyder and Michael Brecher, among others, developed conceptual models of foreign policy decision-making processes. These models extend the pioneering work on the "man-milieu relationships" postulated by Harold and Margaret Sprout. The Sprouts hypothesized that the milieu (environment) affects human behavior in two ways: first, the milieu can influence decisions only if decision makers perceive factors in the milieu; second, the milieu can limit the outcome of decisions when they were made on the basis of erroneous perceptions of factors in the milieu. In essence, Sprouts proposed that decisions are based on the decision maker's perceptions of the milieu and that the results of these decisions are limited by the objective nature of the milieu. In doing so, they distinguished the *psychomilieu* (the environment perceived by the decision maker) from the operational milieu (the real environment in which policy will be carried out). This distinction marked a departure from the realist school, which assumed that foreign policy decision makers perceive the operational environment correctly.[17]

Building on Sprouts's conceptualization of the man-milieu relationship, Richard Snyder and his colleagues developed a model of foreign policy decision making (hereafter "Snyder's model"). Snyder et al. construed foreign policy decision making as a process of input-output conversion of variables and postulated that the way decision makers define a situation is the key factor in foreign policy behavior. Snyder's model identified three sources of stimuli by which decision makers define a situation: the "decision-making process" (influence from within the governmental organizations that produce the decision itself); the "internal setting" (influence from the nongovernmental aspects of the society for which the decisions are being made); and the "external setting" (influence from outside that society). Snyder's model is significant because it offered a comparable operational model of the role of domestic, external, and organizational variables as sources of foreign policy behavior in terms of how they impact decision making.[18]

Brecher's Model

Michael Brecher, Blema Steinberg, and Janice Stein elaborated Snyder's model and created a well-defined model of foreign policy behavior ("Brecher's model"). First, Brecher's model clearly distinguishes the psychological environment from the operational environment and illustrates how the former affects the latter. Second, the model identifies two key elements in the psychological environment: attitudinal prism and elite image. An attitudinal prism comprises the psychological predispositions of decision makers, which include societal factors (such as ideology and tradition) and personality factors (the idiosyncratic qualities of decision makers). Brecher and his colleagues argue that these factors are critical,. because they "constitute the screen or prism through which elite perceptions of the operational environment are filtered." The elite image, in turn, is the environment perceived by decision makers; it plays a pivotal role in that "decision-makers act in accordance with their perception of reality, not in response to reality itself." In short, Brecher's model postulates that the attitudinal prism distorts the way foreign policy elites see the operational environment. Thus, elites' image of reality may be widely disparate from the real one, which results in unsuccessful foreign policy.[19]

This book primarily employs Brecher's model. Its conceptualization of attitudinal prism is instrumental in analyzing how Japanese foreign policy elites' predispositions and perceptions of other nations affect Japan's foreign policy toward these nations. For instance, if Japanese foreign policy elites do not like South Koreans for cultural or ethnic reasons, they might not be attentive to the South Korean government's requests (such as giving individual compensation to the former comfort women), even if meeting such requests would better serve Japan's long-term national interest and improve its bilateral relations.

This book further postulates that public perceptions play an important role in foreign policy decision making. For instance, elites cannot ignore the public perceptions of other countries when making foreign policy, nor can they neglect public opinion concerning highly political diplomatic issues, such as the SDF's overseas engagement. Thus, this book extends Brecher's model to public attitudes and examines correlations between perceptions of the public and foreign policy.

This book does not argue that perceptions are the only important determinants of foreign policy decision making; structures of the international system as well as of the domestic system also play important roles. The focus here is on perceptions because there has been little study of Japanese foreign policy makers' predispositions, their perceptions of other countries, and the effect on contemporary Japanese foreign policy. Therefore, this book primarily analyzes perceptions but also examines other factors that affect Japanese foreign policy decision making.

Literature Review

Despite the importance of the subject, the literature is scanty, partly because of the vast scope and complexity of the subject. Japan's *kokusaika* encompasses much more than the globalization of its economic activities. It involves the transformation of Japan's economic, political, and social systems and, what is more important, opening of the Japanese mind to the outside world and to other peoples.

Several Japanese scholars studied the subject in the 1980s. For example, Toru Yano at Kyoto University examines the subject in term of cultural compatibility. Yano defines *kokusaika* as "an effort to place a nation that has its own identity and unique culture in the framework of international compatibility with least friction." According to Yano, this process involves a total transformation of a nation through spiritual assimilation with the outside world, as well as the adaptation of norms and rules commonly accepted by international society. Yano says that Japan was obliged to take up *kokusaika* in 1985 when the international community recognized Japan's economic power and reevaluated the yen.[20] In contrast, Yasuaki Onuma at Tokyo University discusses Japanese identity and culture in the age of *kokusaika,* as well as Japanese prejudice against Asians and minority groups in Japan, from a more negative standpoint. Onuma reveals reservations about *kokusaika* when he says that it destroys Japan's cultural traditions through the imposition of European modernization and that it subjects the Japanese to a form of cultural colonialism.[21]

There are few English-language publication of the subject. Of the several books in English on Japan's internationalization, most deal with a single aspect of *kokusaika*—outward economic expansion.[22] One of the earlier exceptions is an edited work by Hiroshi Mannari at Kwansei Gakuin University and Harumi Befu at Stanford University, of proceedings of a conference held at Kwansei Gakuin University, Nishinomiya, Hyogo, Japan, in 1981. The contributors analyze cultural, economic, and social aspects of *kokusaika* in the late 1970s and early 1980s.[23]

One of the most comprehensive analyses of Japan's *kokusaika,* published in the 1990s, is an edited work by Glenn Hook and Michael Weiner, both at the University of Sheffield. This book is an outcome of the Silver Jubilee Conference of the Centre for Japanese Studies at the University of Sheffield, held in 1989. Both the Japanese and the Western contributors examine such aspects of *kokusaika* as economic policy, national and local politics, labor markets, and education. Yet the book's focus is on the positive aspects of *kokusaika* and does not delve into fundamental problems. Also, little is said about Japan's foreign policy, which is an essential part of Japan's internationalization.[24] In contrast, this book examines several important issues concerning Japan's foreign policy, including its changing role in the international community and its bilateral relations with the United States and East Asia. It also analyzes the fundamental impediments to *kokusaika* that still exist in the 1990s.

These impediments to Japan's *kokusaika* include cultural, economic, and political barriers. Cultural impediments comprise the Japanese way of thinking and behavior, which are deeply rooted in its tradition and customs. Economic barriers consist of the Japanese corporate structure and the Japanese way of doing business, whereas political barriers comprise the Japanese decision-making system, bureaucratic politics, and individual policy makers' decision-making style. This book argues that cultural barriers constitute the foremost impediments to Japan's *kokusaika*. Even if *gaiatsu* pressure forces Japan to remove economic and political impediments to liberalization, it cannot eliminate cultural impediments, because that would entail compelling the Japanese to change their way of thinking and behavior, and such change must come from within. Despite the apparent glut of foreign goods in Japan and the phenomenal exodus of Japanese tourists to overseas destinations (a superficial outward *kokusaika*), *kokoro no kokusaika* (the internationalization of the mind) has not taken root in the heart of the Japanese. Soseki Natsume, a famous novelist, said in 1911 that Japan's *kaika* (opening)—the first attempt at *kokusaika* in the Meiji era—was caused by external stimuli, not internal ones, and therefore was unreal and superficial. It is almost as though Natsume is referring to contemporary Japan's *kokusaika*.[25]

Nihonjinron and Kokusaika

The theme of this book is closely related to *Nihonjinron* (discourse on the Japanese national character) because *kokusaika* in many ways challenges traditional Japanese values. As Tamotsu Aoki, an anthropologist at the University of Tokyo, pointed out, Japanese were faced with an identity crisis three times in the past. The first was when Japan was striving for modernization and Westernization in the Meiji era. Meiji leaders were awestruck by advanced Western technology and tried to catch up with the West. Yukichi Fukuzawa, a leading educator in the Meiji era and a founder of Keiô University, called on the nation to adopt *Wakon Yôsai* ("Japanese soul, Western knowledge"), to acquire Western knowledge while retaining the Japanese mentality. It was this superficial adoption of the Western way of living by the Japanese that Soseki Natsume lamented.[26]

The second identity crisis came with defeat in World War II. Japanese went through a drastic change in their mental state, from overconfidence (represented by the *kamikaze* spirit and the deity of the emperor) to a loss of confidence (symbolized by the atomic bombings and the emperor's "human declaration"). As a backlash response, Japan made a 180-degree turn and strove to Americanize, taken by the chocolates and chewing gum of the American occupation forces. The Japanese became *haibei* (reverent toward the United States) and downplayed Japanese culture and identity. The

Japanese have seemingly gone from one extreme to another, from overconfidence to a loss of confidence.[27]

With the success of Japan's economy in the 1970s and 1980s, the Japanese regained their confidence. The *Nihonjinron* in Japan reflected such overconfidence. Aoki identified the period 1964–1983 as the period of "recognition of Japan's positive uniqueness." According to Aoki, the first phase of the period (1964–1976) began with Chie Nakane's study of Japanese collectivism and vertical society, Keiichi Sakuta's reexamination of the Japanese "culture of shame," and Kunio Odaka's work that positively evaluated the Japanese management system. The second phase (1977–1983) was marked by Eshun Hamaguchi's '*Nihon rashisa' no saihakken* (rediscovery of "Japaneseness") and a collaborative study of Japanese *ie* (house) society by Yasusuke Murakami, Shumpei Kumon, and Seizaburo Sato. Added to this was Ezra Vogel's *Japan as Number One*, which stirred Japanese confidence.[28]

In this context, some scholars pointed out a negative and rather ironical aspect of *kokusaika* during this confident cycle. Harumi Befu defined Japan's *kokusaika* first as an economic phenomenon and second as processes that resulted from economic *kokusaika*. Befu stated that the primary goal of Japan's internationalization was to enhance its national economic interest, and thus the more Japan became internationalized *(kokusaika),* the more nationalistic *(kokusuika)* it became. Although the two notions were antithetical to each other, they were inseparable in the Japanese case; the two Japanese words were also barely distinguishable. Thus, Befu argued that Japan can continue to pursue neonationalism with impunity under the banner of *kokusaika.*[29] Here, one finds a close link between *Nihonjinron* and Japan's *kokusaika.* Chalmers Johnson also noted in this period that the conservative tide of *Nihonjinron* was using *kokusaika* to its advantage; the term *kokusaika* was "merely the latest code word" for *Nihonjinron,* in that the former used the cultural explanation to legitimize the Japanese economic miracle and economic systems.[30]

The so-called revisionist school of *Nihonjinron* abroad surged in reaction to this confident cycle of the *Nihonjinron* in Japan. Chalmers Johnson's study of the Ministry of International Trade and Industry (MITI), among others, analyzed how Japanese systems were inherently different from Western systems. So-called Japan bashers, such as James Fallows and Karel van Wolferen, escalated their criticisms. A study by Richard J. Samuels at Massachusetts Institute of Technology (MIT), which reviews the controversies involving the "Chrysanthemum Club" school and the revisionist school, is one of the most comprehensive studies of the *Nihonjinron* abroad.[31]

Since the 1980s, Japanese have been faced with a third identity crisis in the midst of their country's drive for internationalization. Aoki identifies this stage as the period "from the unique to the universal" (1984–present) in *Nihonjinron.* Odaka, who had defended the anachronistic Japanese management system twenty years ago, deplored in 1984 that the myth of the superiority of the Japanese management system was created among foreigners as well as the Japanese, who failed to see the demerits of the system.[32] Masaru Tamamoto at American University in Washington, D.C., states that the proliferation of *Nihonjinron* attests to the ambiguous nature of the Japanese national identity and to the need of Japanese to tell the outside world who they are. The world's second-largest economic power lacks an articulate national consciousness. In the face of the foreign pressure for *kokusaika,* Japan is a power without purpose, which does not know where it is going.[33]

To sum up, according to Bruce Stronach, who studied *kokusaika* in terms of identity and nationalism, *kokusaika* is irreconcilable with nationalism by nature: in Japan, genuine *kokusaika* has progressed only at a superficial and pragmatic level and has not substantially changed domestic systems to conform to world standards or to accept foreigners. *Kokusaika* has been a mere coerced Westernization, and it is not clear with which region Japan identifies itself—Asia or the West.[34] Thus, the Japanese are pressured by the U.S. and European governments as well as revisionist scholars to change their systems and adopt Western ways. Here again, the recurring question is whether it is possible for Japan to adopt Western systems while preserving the Japanese identity. As Natsume asked 86 years ago, will the Japanese be able to adopt Western systems only superficially because things Japanese and those Western are intrinsically irreconcilable?

Thesis: The *Sakoku* Mentality

In acknowledging the *Nihonjinron* of the past, this book takes a cultural approach to understanding Japanese behavior. It postulates that the *sakoku* ("secluded nation") mentality constitutes the core of Japan's barriers to *kokusaika.* Nevertheless, this book does not intend to justify cultural factors as a pretext for the slow pace of *kokusaika.* The pervasive Japanese attitude of exclusiveness and parochialism stems from two powerful roots: (1) the country's geographic isolation as an island nation; and (2) the Tokugawa Shôgunate's policy of seclusion *(sakoku)* from 1639 to 1868. That combination of natural and voluntary isolation created a uniquely homogeneous culture and parochial mentality. The *sakoku* mentality still lingers and underlies the modern Japanese way of thinking and behaving. This mind-set is not only ubiquitous in the business sector but is also prevalent in Japan's cultural, educational, and societal systems. Under the surface of the modern way of living adopted by the Japanese, traditional characteristics of insularity and parochialism are still preserved. Not all

Japanese hold the *sakoku* mentality; but those who advocate Japan's *kokusaika* remain a minority.[35]

Hypotheses for Japanese Foreign Policy

This book postulates that the *sakoku* mentality constitutes the core of Japanese foreign policy decision makers' attitudinal prism. It argues that this exclusionist mind-set has prevented Japanese policy makers from formulating an open-door policy and from promoting *kokusaika*. Notably, Japanese resistance to opening its markets to foreign goods and services has created serious trade friction with the United States and Europe. This protectionist policy has obliged Japanese consumers to purchase commodities such as beef, oranges, and rice at uncompetitive prices for decades. Nonetheless, the Japanese government resists full liberalization of its domestic markets. Japanese policy makers demonstrated the *sakoku* mentality at the APEC (Asia Pacific Economic Cooperation forum) meeting in Osaka in November 1995, when they tried to protect a minor agricultural interest at the expense of Japan's larger national interest.

This book also postulates that the *sakoku* mentality is accountable for Japan's reluctance to participate in the maintenance of international peace and security. Japan's natural geographic isolation forged a sense of pacifism in the minds of Japanese. The "peace constitution," adopted during the Allied occupation, renounced war as a right of the nation and relinquished any possession of force, thereby reinforcing pacifism. The parochial mentality is most evident in Japan's hesitation to take part in UNPKO. As seen earlier, the majority of Japanese are reluctant to send the SDF even on peacekeeping missions. This attitude also prevents Japan from establishing an equal partnership with the United States in the maintenance of regional peace and the security of East Asia.

Further, this book hypothesizes that ethnocentric prejudice is another aspect of the *sakoku* mentality. It is most evident in Japan's attitudes toward its Asian neighbors, especially Korea and China. This study argues that the feeling of Japanese racial superiority directed at other Asians is a backlash from their inferiority complex toward Western Caucasians. Moreover, Japan's high-handed attitude toward other Asians has kept Japanese leaders from constructing positive relationships with their neighbors. This arrogant attitude accounts for Japanese policy makers' reluctance to fully admit Japan's acts of aggression toward Asia during World War II and give individual compensation to Asian victims of the war for more than fifty years.

Finally, this book posits that Japan's xenophobia is another manifestation of the *sakoku* mentality. This xenophobic attitude accounts for discrimination against foreigners in Japanese society, which in turn prevents *gaijin* (foreigners) from being assimilated into Japanese society and entering Japanese labor markets, in both nonprofessional and professional sectors. Those policies, clouded by myopic attitudes and biases, are bound to fail eventually. They neglect how other nations perceive Japan and ignore regional and international systemic constraints.

In summary, the book hypothesizes that Japanese exclusionişm, protectionism, racial prejudice, and xenophobia, all derived from the *sakoku* mentality, constitute the attitudinal prism of Japanese foreign policy decision makers (as well as of the public), which has retarded Japan's liberalization and internationalization even today.

Real *kokusaika* is extremely difficult to achieve; it not only involves a tangible liberalization of Japanese systems but also the intangible liberalization of the Japanese mentality. Genuine inward *kokusaika* cannot be achieved without fundamental changes in the Japanese way of thinking and behaving. Unless the Japanese open their minds and overcome the *sakoku* mentality, Japan's *kokusaika* will remain mere *e ni kaita mochi* (pie in the sky). Yasushi Akashi, one of the first Japanese career staffers at the United Nations since Japan's admission in 1956, recently said, "Japan is still a *shimaguni* (insular country) not only in terms of physical geography but also in terms of psychological makeup."[36] He further stated that Japan does not know how to contribute to the international community. Akashi successfully supervised the UNPKO in Cambodia and, more recently, was the UN secretary-general's special envoy to Bosnia-Herzegovina. He was appointed deputy secretary-general of the UN Humanitarian Issues Bureau in March 1996.

Japan's Foreign Policy Decision-Making System

The Japanese foreign policy decision-making system is another structural impediment to Japan's *kokusaika*. First, the nature of postwar Japanese diplomacy, being "passive and reactive" and "minimalist and risk-avoidance," has prevented *kokusaika* from taking off in earnest.[37] According to Hisashi Owada, ambassador to the United Nations (and ex-administrative vice-foreign minister, the highest career position in the Ministry of Foreign Affairs [MFA]), there were two critical determinants for the formation of postwar Japanese foreign policy: the San Francisco Peace Treaty and the U.S.-Japan Security Treaty. The conclusion of the San Francisco Peace Treaty in 1951 was the watershed of Japan's postwar diplomacy. Prime Minister Shigeru Yoshida's decision to make peace with 48 Allied powers, excluding the Soviet bloc, laid down the basic course of postwar Japanese foreign policy. It incorporated Japan into the Western "freedom" camp in the Cold War era. The U.S.-Japan Security Treaty, signed simultaneously with the peace treaty, articulated the content of Japan's foreign policy and made Japan dependent on the United States for its national security.[38]

Under the aegis of the United States, Japan was able to focus on economic reconstruction and later on foreign trade, eventually achieving the "economic miracle." Meanwhile, Japan followed the U.S. lead in military and political foreign policy decision making. For instance, Japan established diplomatic relations with Communist China in 1972, only after the United States did so with President Nixon's historic visit in 1971. Officials at the MFA endorse the minimalist foreign policy. Minoru Tamba, deputy vice-foreign minister, said that "it was a natural choice for Japan to make 'partial peace' with the Allied Powers excluding the Soviet bloc, instead of 'total peace' with all the Allied Powers. The choice was inevitable because U.S. forces were occupying Japan and Japan wanted to regain independence as soon as possible."[39]

In contrast, critics of mainstream diplomacy argue that Japan has avoided making important foreign policy decisions and call Japan's diplomacy "dependent diplomacy on the United States."[40] Others believe that Japan has no foreign policy except for economic diplomacy and think that Japan's foreign policy lacks principles.[41] To these criticisms, Shinsaku Hogen, a retired administrative vice-foreign minister, responded that "it is wrong to think that Japan's postwar diplomacy lacks initiative. The U.S.-Japan Security Treaty is a prime example of Japan's 'autonomous diplomacy.' Japan made that decision."[42]

In essence, the basic framework of postwar Japan's diplomacy, defined by the San Francisco Peace Treaty and the U.S.-Japan Security Treaty under the Pax Americana, made the nature of Japanese foreign policy passive and reactive. It was an irony that U.S. efforts to open Japan politically, through demilitarization and the institution of democracy, were also instrumental to the formation of Japan's minimalist diplomacy. In the absence of its own initiative, *gaiatsu* (foreign pressure), especially that of the United States, has been the only effective way of forcing Japan to change its foreign policy.

A specific decision-making style, *kotonakareshugi* (problem-avoidance principle), also has discouraged bureaucrats from drafting and implementing new policies toward *kokusaika*. The status quo mentality, caused by bureaucratic inertia, is generally observed in bureaucratic politics and is not unique to Japan. In the case of Japan, however, *kotonakareshugi* is deeply rooted in decision making in every sector because it derives from conflict avoidance and consensus building, both of which are inherent in Japanese culture. This standard operating procedure discourages decision makers from taking the initiative and making innovative policies. Thus, bureaucratic inertia serves as another structural impediment to *kokusaika*. This is not to say that all the foreign policy makers suffer from the *sakoku* syndrome, but they are obliged to work in the confines of the systemic limitations described above.

Japanese Domestic Politics

Recent upheavals in Japanese domestic politics have further plagued the progress of *kokusaika*. The end of the Cold War critically weakened the power base of the conservative LDP, which had dominated postwar Japanese politics for nearly four decades. The Japan New Party (JNP), a splinter group of the LDP led by Morihiro Hosokawa, formed an anti-LDP coalition cabinet comprising seven parties and a political group in August 1993. This event marked the end of the 38-year-long monopoly of power by the LDP since 1955. The Hosokawa cabinet called for an end to political corruption and advocated political reforms. The cabinet collapsed in April 1994, however, with Hosokawa's resignation over a financial scandal. Tsutomu Hata, a leader of the Renewal Party, another LDP splinter group, formed a new coalition. The Hata cabinet resigned en masse after 59 days in June 1994, when the SDPJ withdrew from the coalition, reducing the coalition cabinet to a minority in Japan's Parliament.

Then, in July 1994, the LDP, the SDPJ, and NPS formed an unprecedented coalition cabinet. It was unusual because the LDP and the SDPJ had been archenemies with the latter the leading opposition in Parliament. A socialist, Tomiichi Murayama, the head of the SDPJ, led the cabinet. Yet Prime Minister Murayama resigned in January 1996 because of the decline of his party's power in Parliament. Subsequently, Ryutaro Hashimoto, the new head of the LDP, replaced Prime Minister Murayama and formed yet another coalition cabinet. In all, four cabinets were formed in two and half years. The problem the present political parties in Japan face is that none of them can form a cabinet alone, as the LDP had done in the past four decades. Thus they are obliged to form coalitions with parties that do not share similar platforms. As seen earlier, Japan delayed its participation in UNDOF because of the reluctance of the SDPJ and NPS. For the same reason, the Murayama cabinet did not review the International Peace Cooperation Law concerning the SDF's participation in peacekeeping forces.

Thus, Japanese policy decision makers are incapacitated by domestic affairs and show little interest in Japan's *kokusaika*. Bureaucrats have been caught up in unprecedented corruption scandals (notably one at the Ministry of Finance) as well as traditional bureaucratic inertia. Politicians are struggling to survive in the face of successive cabinet turnovers and financial scandals. Under these circumstances, the Japanese government has no zeal for *kokusaika* and is reluctantly taking it up only due to *gaiatsu*. As a result, *gaiatsu* has been the only effective means for foreign governments to force Japan to move toward genuine inward *kokusaika*.

Part I of this book examines the origin and evolution of the *sakoku* mentality, which constitutes a cultural and psychological impediment to Japan's *kokusaika*. Chapter 1 provides the historical background for Japan's *sakoku* and *kokusaika*. It reviews three *kaikoku* (open-door policies) Japan has undertaken and analyzes how and why the United States was deeply involved in each. Chapter 2 examines various aspects of the *sakoku* mentality, such as exclusiveness, parochialism, racial prejudice, and xenophobia. It also studies how the Japanese perceive *kokusaika* and Japan's role in the international community.

Part I then looks into Japan's perceptions of other nations and how the *sakoku* mentality affects Japanese views of other countries. Chapter 3 examines Japan's perceptions of the United States. It analyzes the tension between the inferiority complex and the superiority complex toward the United States on the part of the Japanese. It also focuses on the role of the mass media in shaping Japan's perceptions of the United States. Chapter 4 studies Japanese perceptions of China and South Korea. In particular, it investigates how Japanese racial biases have affected Japan's foreign policy toward these nations. Chapter 5 then examines Japanese perceptions of ASEAN and Japan's economic diplomacy in the region. It also looks at ASEAN's perceptions of and economic policy toward Japan. By so doing, the chapter analyzes the correlation between perceptions and foreign policy.

Part II shifts to specific case studies of Japan's *sakoku*-minded policy, both domestic and foreign. Chapter 6 examines Japan's immigration and labor policies and looks at discrimination against foreign workers. Thereby, it considers societal impediments to Japan's globalization. Chapter 7 analyzes Japanese policy toward Okinawa and issues involving the U.S. military bases. It examines how the *sakoku* mentality has affected Japanese views of Okinawa and Japan's policy toward Okinawa. Chapter 8 covers the partial opening of the Japanese rice market, which was a landmark for Japan's agricultural liberalization. The chapter also discusses the complex bargaining at international (the Uruguay Round of GATT negotiations), bilateral (U.S.-Japan negotiations), and domestic levels (Agricultural Ministry and Agricultural Cooperatives).

Chapter 9 assesses changing Japanese attitudes toward the constitution. The revision of Article 9 of the constitution is an important move toward expanding Japan's contribution to international security. Earnest Japanese participation in the maintenance of international security hinges on this constitutional revision. Chapter 9 also shows how the *sakoku* mentality accounts for Japan's resistance to the constitutional revision and impedes the country's active participation in international security arrangements. Chapter 10 looks further into Japan's expanding role in international security and discusses how participation in UNPKO has evolved in the 1990s. In addition, the chapter examines Japan's bid for a permanent seat on the UN Security Council and the United Nations's efforts to reform the Security Council. The concluding chapter gives an overview of Japanese *sakoku* policies and ends with the prospects for Japan's successful internationalization and transformation in the twenty-first century.

PART ONE

The Japanese Sakoku *Mentality*

CHAPTER ONE

Historical Background

J apan has adopted an open-door policy *(kaikoku)* twice in its modern history, once in the nineteenth century and again after World War II. Although Japan pursued open-door policies earlier in its history, notably when the country sent the *Kentôshi* missions to China (630–894), this book limits its scope to the modern history because of its primary interest in the U.S.-Japan relations. Japan embarked on a third *kaikoku* through its negotiations with the Reagan, Bush, and Clinton administrations on trade liberalization. U.S. Commodore Matthew Perry's first visit to Japan in 1853 triggered the first *kaikoku;* William Perry, a descendent of Commodore Perry, took part in the third *kaikoku,* as the defense secretary in the Clinton administration.[1] This chapter examines why and how Americans have played a crucial role in each of these three processes and emphasizes the problems encountered by President Clinton in the current debate over trade barriers.

First *Kaikoku*

The roots of the *kaikoku* movement lie in the mid-nineteenth century. The first *kaikoku* occurred in reaction to the 1853 visit of U.S. Commodore Matthew Perry to Japan with a letter from President Millard Fillmore requesting diplomatic relations with Japan. Japan had been under self-imposed seclusion *(sakoku)* from the rest of the world for more than two hundred years. In the age of steam power, American ships needed Japan as a coal refueling stop on the route to China, and Perry, with his four warships, tried to force the Japanese to open their ports. Perry revisited Japan in 1854 with seven ships and coerced the Tokugawa Shôgunate government into signing the Treaty of Amity. The pact required Japan to open two ports, supply American ships with fuel and food, rescue wrecked American ships and their crews, allow the establishment of an American consulate, and award the United States most-favored nation status. Later the same year, Japan signed similar treaties with Great Britain, Russia, and the Netherlands, effectively ending its isolation. Subsequently in 1858, Townsend Harris, the first U.S. consul-general to Japan, forced Japan to conclude the Treaty of Commerce with the United States. The treaty was unequal in that Japan could neither fix customs on its imports by itself nor revise the treaty unilaterally. Japan concluded similar treaties with the Netherlands, Russia, Britain, and France in the same year.[2]

In the aftermath of these developments, the Tokugawa government collapsed, and a new government emerged with the reinstitution of the power of the emperor (Meiji Restoration) in 1868. The Meiji government set forth the objectives of the first *kaikoku:* modernizing Japanese industry and gaining economic and military parity with the West. The new leaders mobilized the nation to achieve these goals under the slogan of *Fukoku Kyôhei* (rich nation, strong army). Catching up with and surpassing the West became a national goal. The Meiji government mobilized the Japanese into "military technonationalism," by which Japan developed technology to enhance national security. In 1871, Tomomi Iwakura, a cabinet member of the Meiji government, led a mission of 48 members to inspect the West at first hand and persuade foreign powers to revise the unequal treaties concluded by the Tokugawa Shôgunate. Although the Iwakura mission's negotiations to annul the unequal treaties were unsuccessful, the trip enlightened the new Meiji leaders and made them realize the enormous gap between the Western powers and Japan.[3]

Given the small land mass of the Japanese home islands, the Meiji leaders decided to pursue an expansionist policy toward Asia to make the nation self-sufficient in raw materials, industry, and markets, and to gain economic and military parity with the West. Protectionist policies adopted by the Americans and Europeans in the late nineteenth century, which restricted foreign access to their markets, only accentuated Japan's drive for territorial expansion. The Japanese desire to catch up with the West and become an imperial power was so strong that it fostered the rise of nationalism and an imperialistic policy toward East Asia. The Meiji government adopted *Datsuaron* (discourse on exiting Asia), envisaged by Yukichi Fukuzawa, a philosopher and ideologue in the Meiji era, to promote Japan's national interest. Thus, under the banners of *Datsua Nyûô* (exit Asia, enter West) and *Wakon Yôsai* (Japanese soul, Western knowledge), Japan separated itself from the tributary system centering on China and attempted to adopt Europe's balance-of-power system. In contrast to its subservient posture toward Western powers, Japan displayed high-handed attitudes toward other Asian countries, demanding their *kaikoku* to Japan and imposing unequal treaties on them.[4]

In this context Meiji leaders undertook aggressive foreign policies in the Korean campaign (1873) and the Taiwan expedition (1874). Aggression was also a solution to quell the *samurai* class, who had lost their position in the Shôgunate government. Moreover, Japan waged war with Asian countries. Wars with China (1894) and Russia (1904–1905) gave Japan the Liaodong Peninsula (where the strategic naval base of Port Arthur was located), Formosa (Taiwan), the southern half of Sakhalin Island, and suzerainty over Korea. Annexation of Korea came in 1910. In the 1930s, Japan seized Manchuria in Northeast China, renamed it Manchukuo, and invaded Southeast Asia to create a "Greater East Asia Coprosperity Sphere." Then, in 1940, it joined with Nazi Germany and Fascist Italy to form the Axis alliance. In 1941, Japan attacked Pearl Harbor, which led to the massive American air and naval operations against Japan that ultimately destroyed the Japanese economy and empire. In essence, the expanded military spending and aggressive foreign policy of the Meiji mobilization went too far and led to the disasters of World War II. The cultural and economic opening of Japan during the first *kaikoku* resulted in the military opening of Japan.[5]

Second *Kaikoku*

Japan's defeat in World War II and the onset of the Cold War forced America to pursue different policies in its effort to keep Japan open to foreign influence. The second *kaikoku,* initiated in 1945, was a reaction to both Japanese militarism and to the success of the first *kaikoku.* The primary goal of the second *kaikoku* was to "undo" the first. Thus, to demilitarize and democratize Japan became the Truman administration's main objectives in promoting the second *kaikoku.* The execution of these goals entailed political reform. The occupation forces, led by General Douglas MacArthur, demobilized the Japanese Army completely and drafted a new Japanese constitution, which renounced war as a sovereign right of the nation and relinquished the maintenance of land, sea, and air forces. The occupation forces also democratized Japan through revision of the election law, which granted universal suffrage to men and women. The first Yoshida cabinet emerged in 1946 as a result of the first postwar general elections to the House of Representatives of the Japanese Parliament. Under Prime Minister Shigeru Yoshida, who was a strong pro-U.S. leader, Japan signed the San Francisco Peace Treaty in 1951 and regained its independence. Japan simultaneously concluded the U.S.-Japan Security Treaty, which allowed the stationing of U.S. armed forces within its territory. In effect, the United States became Japan's protector.[6]

The outbreak of the Korean War in 1950 decisively transformed Japan from a former enemy to a key American ally. Japan's strategic location provided a valuable base for America's containment policy against the Soviet

Union and Communist China. Even though Japan was placed under the U.S. nuclear umbrella, the Truman administration saw a need for Japan to rearm. Responding to American requests, Japan created the *Keisatsu Yobitai* (National Police Reserves) in 1950, reorganized it into the *Hoantai* (National Security Forces) in 1952, and upgraded it into the *Jieitai* (Self-Defense Forces) in 1954. Thus, the second *kaikoku* succeeded in incorporating Japan into the "free world camp" led by the United States.[7]

Despite playing a subordinate role vis-à-vis the United States, Japan greatly benefited from this relationship in the 1950s and 1960s: By guaranteeing Japan's security, the United States allowed the Japanese government to keep defense spending to a minimum and divert most of its resources to economic recovery. Having learned a lesson from the failure of the military technonationalism during the first *kaikoku*, the Japanese geared themselves toward the development of commercial technology and industry. Paradoxically, as in the first *kaikoku*, the U.S. policy of opening Japan (politically in the second *kaikoku*) made Japan a major competitor to the United States (an economic one this time) resulting in strained relations between the two. Thus the United States' very success led to another policy change—the third *kaikoku*, which is in progress today.

Third *Kaikoku*

Japan embarked on the third *kaikoku* in the late 1980s, when it began yielding to U.S. pressure to open its markets to foreign goods and investment. Thus, at first, the third *kaikoku* entailed the economic opening of Japan. The major objectives of the Reagan and Bush administrations in promoting the third *kaikoku* were to liberalize and internationalize Japanese markets by reducing trade restrictions and increasing the volume of overseas transactions. Both measures aimed at reducing America's chronic trade imbalances with Japan.[8]

To accomplish this, the United States supported import liberalization, which assumed that the elimination of import barriers (notably tariffs) imposed by Japan would lower the prices and thereby increase the volume of goods imported by that country. Japan had been liberalizing its markets to imports since joining the General Agreement on Tariffs and Trade (GATT) in 1955. Indeed, the record of Japanese import liberalization is quite impressive: Japan reduced the total number of items under import restrictions from 1,443 in 1960 to 79 in 1981. Also, the Japanese import burden ratio (the ratio of total tariff revenues to the total value of imports) decreased from 5.8 percent in 1961 to 2.5 percent in 1983, whereas that of the U.S. decreased from 6.7 percent to 3.5 percent during the same period. Yet, the U.S. trade imbalance with Japan did not diminish.[9]

The United States also adopted monetary liberalization to raise the value of the yen. The assumption was that the appreciation of the yen would make American exports to Japan cheaper and thus increase their volume, while conversely making Japanese exports to the United States more expensive. In 1971, during the Nixon Administration, the International Monetary Fund (IMF) replaced the previous fixed exchange system with a flexible exchange system. Under the new international monetary regime, the yen's exchange rate vis-à-vis the dollar shifted from ¥360 in 1971 to ¥210 by 1977. The sudden appreciation of the yen, dubbed the "Nixon shock," caused a stir among Japanese businessmen and politicians. After a decade of relative stability, the yen further appreciated to ¥169 to the dollar in 1986 and then to a record high of ¥111 in 1993. The 100 yen to the dollar mark was finally reached in June 1994.[10]

The yen's sharp appreciation severely damaged Japanese manufacturing industries. Nonetheless, U.S. trade deficits with Japan did not fall because other factors restricted Japanese importation of U.S. products. Searching for the reasons, American trade negotiators argued that Japanese markets were in effect closed to foreign goods, owing to unique Japanese economic structures. They asserted that traditional Japanese ways of doing business, such as exclusionary business practices by familylike, tightly knit corporate affiliations called *keiretsu,* indirectly restricted trade, constituting nontariff barriers (NTBs). The Bush administration called these traditional Japanese ways of limiting foreign access "structural impediments" to open markets and demanded that they be eliminated.[11]

In return, the Japanese government responded to the U.S. demand by listing the problems with the U.S. economy that contributed to the U.S. trade deficits, such as federal budget deficits, the lack of savings, the over-valued U.S. dollar, and the lack of a global corporate strategy. Simultaneously, reacting to greater U.S. pressure, the Japanese government had begun to evaluate its options for reducing the trade imbalance. The Study Group on Economic Structural Adjustments for International Cooperation, created as a private advisory group for then-prime minister Nakasone in 1985, issued the so-called Maekawa Report the following year. Named for the head of the group, Haruo Maekawa, a former president of the Bank of Japan, the Maekawa Report anticipated that foreign demands to open Japanese markets could escalate and recommended that Japan transform itself into a *yunyû taikoku* ("import giant") and a *seikatsu taikoku* ("living-standard giant"). Among other things, the report suggested that Japan revise the tax system so as to replace incentives for savings with incentives for spending. It also suggested that Japan import more agricultural products.[12]

The advisory group issued a second report (referred to as the new Maekawa Report) in 1987 with more concrete policy recommendations.

The new Maekawa Report proposed a reduction in the average working hours to 1,800 per year, which was designed to encourage workers to take more leisure time and spend more money. The new report also recommended a revision of tax laws to end the preferential taxation on agricultural land in urban areas in order to encourage landowners to sell for residential development, thereby increasing public spending for housing. In essence, the two Maekawa reports responded to U.S. and Western European calls to reduce Japan's trade surpluses, to open Japanese markets, and to increase domestic and public spending.[13]

The reports showed foresight and presaged the third *kaikoku*, but the Japanese government did not take their recommendations seriously. In hindsight, had the government acted on the reports, the U.S.-Japan "verbal war" over nontariff trade barriers could have been avoided and the third *kaikoku* could have taken off smoothly. Instead, the trade conflict, which had simmered for decades, finally escalated in the late 1980s to become a major issue in American politics. Pressured by Chrysler chairman Lee Iacocca and a loose coalition of unions, President Bush prodded Japanese leaders to begin negotiations for a "Structural Impediments Initiative" (SII) in September 1989.[14]

The primary objective of the SII talks was to remove the structural impediments that prevented the liberalization and internationalization of Japanese markets. U.S. trade officials considered the SII the last resort for ending U.S. trade imbalances with Japan to avoid invoking the "Super 301" article of the Omnibus Trade Act, which allows the United States to identify nations with unfair trade practices and apply sanctions. At the outset, American negotiators listed more than 200 items they regarded as Japanese structural impediments, including the *keiretsu*'s exclusionary business practices, rigid pricing mechanisms, inefficient distribution systems, inadequate enforcement of antimonopoly laws, high saving rates, shortage of social investment, high land prices and irrational land use, and lack of acceptance of intellectual property rights.[15]

In return for addressing these concerns, Japanese trade representatives, no longer playing the traditional role of subordinate, insisted that the United States reform its own structures. Specifically, they demanded commitment to increased productivity in manufacturing sectors, increased corporate investment, higher rates of saving, a reduced federal deficit, and improvements in the education system as the price for beginning Japanese reforms.[16]

The SII negotiations concluded in June 1990, with both sides agreeing to make substantial changes. At the follow-up review in February 1992, however, U.S. negotiators found no visible changes in Japan's economic structure. They viewed Japan's unfulfilled promise as merely a ploy to buy time. The United States once again requested that Japan remove certain structural barriers, especially the *keiretsu,* governmental regulations, and the multilayer distribution system. Unfortunately, there was no improvement in the situation by the end of the Bush administration in January 1993. On the contrary, U.S. trade deficits with Japan had increased from $38.2 billion in 1991 to $43.6 in 1992. The increase was nominal, however, largely due to the substantial appreciation of the yen.[17]

After twelve years of Republican leadership, President Bill Clinton brought a fresh, more aggressive approach to the debate in 1993. The Clinton administration renamed the U.S.-Japan bilateral trade negotiations "economic framework talks." Exasperated by the continuing trade deficits with Japan, President Clinton, in his first U.S.-Japan summit talks with Prime Minister Kiichi Miyazawa in April 1993, insisted on establishing specific targets to measure the success of Japanese market-opening moves. Miyazawa objected to Clinton's plan, denouncing it as "managed trade." In response, the Clinton administration suggested that Japan cut its trade surplus by as much as one half in the next three years. It also urged Japan to set a target for purchases by Japanese automobile manufacturers of U.S. automobile parts in and beyond fiscal 1995, even though the Japanese automobile industry had already volunteered to buy as much as $19 billion worth of automobile parts from U.S. suppliers in fiscal 1994, as part of the 1992 Bush-Miyazawa summit agreements.[18]

In the meantime, domestic events in Japan threatened the Clinton efforts. The July 1993 general elections to the House of Representatives of the Japanese Parliament gave birth to a new cabinet in August, ending a 38-year monopoly of power by the conservative Liberal Democratic Party (LDP). This dramatic political shift reflected Japanese voters' disgust with the LDP's politics after long condoning rampant corruption and acquiescing in the collusion of power among the LDP, the bureaucracy, and big business, known as the "iron triangle." Voters had condoned the corruption in the iron triangle as an unavoidable byproduct or *umi* (pus) of a rotten political system that enhanced Japanese economic success. But the tide of reform that swept Europe and Asia with the Cold War's end, combined with discontent with sluggish economic growth, impelled voters to drive the LDP out of power. In the political revolution of the summer of 1993, Japanese voters dramatically ended the LDP's reign and entrusted Prime Minister Morihiro Hosokawa with a mandate to carry out sweeping political reforms.[19]

Prime Minister Hosokawa, a former LDP member, had created the Japan New Party (JNP) to carry out anticorruption reforms. His cabinet differed greatly from its predecessors in being a coalition of seven ideologically diverse parties and a political group, including the Renewal Party, another splinter of the LDP, and the Social Democratic Party of Japan (SDPJ). But the Hosokawa cabinet's foreign policy was no different from the LDP's; it refused the Clinton administration's request to set "numerical criteria" to evaluate the openness of Japanese markets. The U.S. trade deficit with Japan for 1993 reached $50.2 billion, a 15.2 percent increase from the previous year. In February 1994, the U.S.-Japan summit talks between President Clinton and Prime Minister Hosokawa ended in a stand-off, putting the U.S.-Japan economic framework talks in a stalemate.[20]

Two months later came another destabilizing blow, when Prime Minister Hosokawa abruptly resigned over a scandal involving illegal campaign contributions. Even the self-proclaimed reformer was not immune to corruption in Japanese politics. The difficulty of managing the coalition government that included the socialist party, formerly the perpetual opposition on the left, contributed to his resignation. Subsequently, Tsutomu Hata, a former LDP member who had created the Renewal Party, replaced Hosokawa, but the departure of the socialists in a dispute over the cabinet's formation left Hata heading a minority government. This situation was unprecedented in Japanese politics.[21]

At the end of May 1994, Prime Minister Hata resumed the U.S.-Japan economic framework talks, which had been stalled for more than three months, and promised to open Japanese markets in three priority sectors: government procurement, insurance, and motor vehicles and motor vehicle parts. This concession came after U.S. trade representative Mickey Kantor demanded that Japan make a concerted effort to liberalize its markets for specific industries.[22]

The unprecedented domestic turmoil in Japanese politics is not the only serious obstacle that faces the current *kaikoku*. There is an even more fundamental problem with the third *kaikoku*. The economic reforms envisaged in Bush's SII and Clinton's economic framework talks will be extremely difficult to achieve because they involve changes in Japanese thinking. The way the Japanese conduct business is deeply rooted in tradition and in a unique corporate culture. American businessmen such as H. Ross Perot have condemned Japanese business practices for being closed, exclusive, and discriminatory against outsiders. This "mind cartel," widespread among Japanese business corporations, impedes foreign access to Japanese markets and is a formidable obstacle to changes sought by the United States.[23]

Military *Kaikoku*

The third *kaikoku* has assumed a new dimension—military opening—to strengthen cooperation and form an equal bilateral partnership with the United States, a departure from the unilateral dependence on U.S. security protection. While Japan enjoyed the economic miracle of the 1970s, rising

Japanese prosperity bred American discontent, and Americans were no longer willing to be lenient with Japan. American politicians, faced with growing deficits worsened by Cold War defense spending, objected strongly to financing the protection of Japan. Presidential spokesmen and congressmen increasingly demanded that Japan pay more toward its security, based on the equal partnership concept. In response, Japan began to raise its defense budget in the 1980s. It also increased the so-called *omoiyari yosan* ("host-nation support") to cover the payroll and the overhead cost of Japanese personnel at U.S. bases in Japan (see Chapter 9).[24]

During this period, sentiment grew in Japan to reduce postwar reliance upon the United States in favor of a more independent course. Proponents of this view became vocal in response to mounting U.S. demands on Japan to liberalize its markets and increase defense burden sharing. Shintaro Ishihara, a conservative member of the Japanese Parliament, argued that the United States had taken advantage of Japan's weaker position in the postwar years and used his nation to achieve American ends in containing communism in Asia. Therefore, it was wrong to portray Japan as the sole beneficiary of the U.S.-Japan relationship. Ishihara argued that for Japan to be an equal partner, it should have equal say. In short, Ishihara insisted that Japan should no longer be a passive subordinate of the United States. In addition, Chalmers Johnson and E. B. Keehn argued that continued U.S. commitment to Japan's defense would prolong Japan's dependence on the United States and prevent it from becoming an "ordinary" country. Yet mainstream policy makers in Japan preferred not to challenge U.S. supremacy. They reasoned that Japan could never equal America's power, since the United States was the sole superpower in the free world, and that it would be in the national interest to maintain a subordinate role.[25]

In the 1990s, the United States further tried to make Japan engage in military cooperation with the United States in case of a military conflict in East Asia. Yet neither the Japanese constitution nor the U.S.-Japan Security Treaty allows the SDF's overseas military engagement. Pacifist sentiments are still deeply embedded in the Japanese mind. The sense of the total discrediting of the military derived from the experience of World War II, including Japan's defeat, the atomic bombings at Hiroshima and Nagasaki, as well as the peace constitution drafted by the U.S. occupation forces. U.S. defense secretaries, among them William Perry, have urged Japan to revise its defense policy so that the SDF can engage in overseas military cooperation with the United States in East Asia. In 1995, Japan finally revised its obsolete national defense program outline that had been enacted in 1976. Among other things, the new outline stipulates Japan's contribution to the maintenance of international peace and security, through its participation in international peacekeeping operations and in international emergency assistance activities (see Chapter 10).[26]

At the Clinton-Hashimoto summit meeting in April 1996, Japan agreed to start a review of military cooperation under the framework of the U.S.-Japan Security Treaty. This agreement resulted in the new U.S.-Japan guidelines for defense cooperation announced in September 1997. The new guidelines replaced the 1978 guidelines, which focused on military attacks on Japan. The new guidelines instead expanded the scope of Japan's defense cooperation to the areas surrounding Japan. They also stipulated that Japan offer the U.S. forces a wide range of logistical support, from supplying fuel and oil and transportation of personnel and materials, to use of facilities, including civilian airports and sea ports, and minesweeping operations. The new guidelines caused bitter controversies in the Japanese Parliament over the definition of the "area surrounding Japan"—whether it includes Taiwan—and over the constitutionality of the nature of the defense cooperation—whether it constitutes the "collective self-defense" (the government interprets that Japan cannot exercise the collective self-defense right under Article 9) (see Chapter 9).[27]

Although Japan's third *kaikoku* has assumed a new dimension of military opening in addition to the original economic opening, the current *kaikoku* faces a serious obstacle: weak leadership in the Japanese government. Just as Perry's warships and MacArthur's occupation forces catalyzed the earlier *kaikoku*, so have American trade representatives, such as Carla Hills and Mickey Kantor, tried to expedite the liberalization of Japanese markets. Nonetheless, the third *kaikoku* is faltering. In the case of the previous two, strong political leadership guided Japan to achieve the objectives of modernization and military build-up (for the first *kaikoku*) and demobilization and democratization (for the second *kaikoku*). The Meiji government advanced the national objectives of "rich nation, strong army" and "Westernization" in the first *kaikoku*. In the second *kaikoku*, the astute statesmanship of Prime Minister Yoshida and his successors prompted Japan to adopt democracy and achieve the economic miracle. In contrast, the current *kaikoku*, especially since the fall of the Hosokawa cabinet in April 1994, lacks strong leadership. Since the collapse of the 1955 system of the LDP monopoly of power in 1993, no single party has been able to form a cabinet. The continuing turmoil in Japan's party politics has further stalled Clinton's economic framework negotiations.[28]

Strong political leadership and modifications of Japan's business culture and pacifism are crucial prerequisites for the success of the third *kaikoku*. Should the new Japanese government or a successor regime somehow break the cultural and political deadlock and succeed in internationalization and liberalization, Japan could then become a major political power in the world. Just as the first *kaikoku* unexpectedly made Japan a military rival of the United States and the second *kaikoku* an economic rival, the third could make it a political rival in the Pacific Rim and the world. Should that happen, Japan would have to assume greater responsibility for global prosperity and security along with the United States. At present, however, Japan is incapable and unwilling to assume such responsibility.

Whereas Commodore Perry visited Naha, Okinawa's capital, on his way to Uraga, Kanagawa, in 1853, to demonstrate American military power, William Perry was stationed in Okinawa during the Allied occupation after the end of World War II to investigate Okinawa's geography. Then, while serving as defense secretary, Perry managed to gain Japanese concessions to strengthen Japan's role in the U.S.-Japan Security Treaty, in exchange for the symbolic return of the Futenma Marine Air Station on Okinawa (sese Chapter 7).[29] As long as Japan remains unwilling to implement economic and military open-door policies in earnest, the United States will continue to use its clout to pressure Japan into a true *kaikoku*. As of August 1997, it remains to be seen whether Japan can overcome its domestic political scandals and successfully carry out its third *kaikoku*.

CHAPTER TWO

The *Sakoku* Mentality and Japanese Perceptions of *Kokusaika*

J apan embarked on internationalization, or *kokusaika,* as a national objective more than a decade ago. This open-door policy *(kaikoku)* involves not only trade liberalization and market opening to foreign
goods and services but also a broader liberalization of Japanese systems in
general and the opening of Japanese society to foreigners. The Japanese government reluctantly embraced *kokusaika* under the pressure of foreign governments, especially those of the United States and Europe, which alleged
that Japanese systems were closed, exclusive, and discriminatory against foreign goods and services. Japan has made only modest progress at a superficial level, however, by allowing an increase in certain foreign goods in its
domestic markets and a limited relaxation of regulations on foreign trade
and investment.

A more fundamental *kokusaika* is difficult to achieve, for it requires not
only tangible changes in Japanese systems but also intangible changes in the
Japanese way of thinking. This chapter argues that the *sakoku* mentality
constitutes a cultural impediment to Japan's internationalization and that
government policies and business practices are direct byproducts of this
mentality. Since the *sakoku* mentality is deeply rooted in the Japanese psyche, it is extremely difficult to remove and hence is the most fundamental
barrier to Japan's overall *kokusaika.* Despite their modern outlook, most
Japanese retain the *sakoku* mentality, one of the most fundamental causes
for trade disputes between the United States and Japan.

Although Japan has substantially reduced its trade barriers, its markets
are not yet completely open to foreign goods and services. The Bush administration's Structural Impediments Initiative failed because the Japanese
way of conducting business is deeply rooted in traditional corporate culture. The Clinton administration's economic framework talks have not
been successful because setting numerical targets does not change Japanese

business customs, as was seen in the automobile negotiations. In fact, Glen Fukushima, a former USTR (U.S. Trade Representative) senior staff member, says that psychological barriers that cannot be measured in numbers impede U.S. corporations' access to Japanese markets.[1]

Chalmers Johnson calls such intangible barriers "cartels of the mind." Johnson argues that Japan is thoroughly cartellized, not only in business practices (cartels of production) but also in the manner in which the Japanese think, and that the latter insulates the Japanese from the outside world and helps to preserve the traditional attitudes and ways of thinking in modern Japan. An interesting point of his argument is that he does not think these cartels are the result of culture or history. Rather, he maintains that they are the direct result of restrictive rules of the Japanese government and that the government is using Japan's group-oriented culture as an excuse to justify these cartels. He further argues that they could be changed overnight if the government had any real interest in internationalization and that until Japan reforms these cartels of the mind, its process of *kokusaika* is "meaningless."[2]

It is difficult to determine whether these cartels of the mind were created by government rules or if they flow from Japanese culture or history. This book argues that both cartels of the mind and government rules are direct byproducts of the traditional Japanese *sakoku* mentality and that cultural and man-made mores constitute formidable barriers to Japan's *kokusaika*.

Origins of the Japanese *Sakoku* Mentality

As historians and sociologists such as Edwin O. Reischauer and Chie Nakane have pointed out, the *sakoku* mentality has roots in Japan's geography and history. Over the centuries, Japan's geographic isolation created a homogeneous culture and an island-nation mentality, or *shimaguni konjô*. The natural geographic isolation also forged a sense of strict distinction between *uchi* (inside) and *soto* (outside) among the Japanese. In addition to geography, the Tokugawa Shôgunate government's *sakoku* policy from 1639 to 1868 reinforced the *shimaguni konjô*. This combination of natural and artificial isolation forced the Japanese to live separately from the rest of the world and enabled them to develop a distinct culture and mentality. Although the original geographic and self-imposed isolation no longer exist, that legacy still lingers as the *sakoku* mentality, characterized by exclusiveness and parochialism, and it constitutes the cultural determinant of the Japanese mind-set and behavior.[3]

Japanese Xenophobia

The manner in which the Japanese treat foreigners most clearly illustrates the *sakoku* mentality. As of January 1995, about 1.6 million foreigners (slightly more than one percent of the total Japanese population) lived in Japan. Due to the largely homogeneous nature of their society, the Japanese consciously distinguish foreigners from themselves. They treat foreigners politely but always as outsiders. They call all foreigners *gaijin,* which literally means "people from outside." Yet most Japanese think of Caucasians when they refer to *gaijin* because of their encounters with the Americans and Europeans during the first *kaikoku* in the Meiji era. The Japanese treat Western *gaijin* with deference, an expression of their inferiority complex toward Western advanced technology and civilization. Nevertheless, although the term *gaijin* in itself has no derogatory connotation, it emphasizes the exclusiveness of the Japanese attitude and thus has taken on pejorative overtones that many Westerners resent.[4]

The picture suddenly changes when it comes to Asian *gaijin:* The politeness toward *gaijin* disappears. Due to their ethnic closeness, the Japanese do not consider Asians genuine *gaijin* and do not tolerate their assimilation into Japanese society. As a result, *gaijin* of Asian origin encounter numerous forms of discrimination in Japan. The worst case involves the so-called Korean residents in Japan. The Japanese treat Koreans who grow up in Japan and speak fluent Japanese as *gaijin.* Due to the history of Japan's annexation of Korea during 1910–1945, the Japanese still look down on the Koreans and treat them as second-class citizens. For instance, the Japanese call automatic-focus cameras *bakachon kamera. Baka* means fools in Japanese and *chon* is a derogatory term referring to Koreans. Thus, *bakachon kamera* means cameras that even fools and Koreans can operate.

There are countless situations in which individual Korean residents are discriminated against. A young Korean male recently observed that people cannot tell that he is a Korean resident from his appearance and the way he speaks Japanese, but once he filled out his name in job applications, his applications were rejected because he retains a Korean name. Some Koreans conceal their true identities by adopting Japanese names. But once a potential employer finds out that an applicant is a Korean resident, the applicant will not be hired. When a landlord finds out that a potential tenant is a Korean resident, that person will not get a lease. If parents find out that their daughter's fiancé or son's fiancée is a Korean resident, they will break the engagement. Worse yet, children of Korean residents are common targets of *ijime* (bullying) at school. In a notorious *ijime* incident, a Korean schoolboy in Saitama prefecture, adjacent to Tokyo, committed suicide after persistent bullying by his classmates and a teacher in charge of the class.[5]

Thus Korean residents, who are ethnically and culturally close to the Japanese, are discriminated against on a daily basis. This discriminatory attitude extends to other foreign residents in a varying degree. The *sakoku* mentality has not only fostered xenophobia but also is accountable for the Japanese reluctance to get involved in international affairs in general.

Japanese Perceptions of *Kokusaika*

A public opinion poll on diplomacy conducted by the Japanese Prime Minister's Office in October 1995 revealed that the Japanese public holds ambivalent views of Japan's *kokusaika* and that they are still wary of Japan's assumption of a greater security role in the global scene. Every October, the Prime Minister's Office conducts a public opinion survey on diplomacy involving 3,000 adults chosen nationwide. The poll asked prospective respondents to choose two answers out of eight choices concerning Japan's *kokusaika*. The choices included "promoting *kokusaika* is Japan's international responsibility as a great power;" "*kokusaika* is a necessary process for Japan to secure mid-term and long-term prosperity;" "*kokusaika* will spread Japanese culture to the outside world;" "*kokusaika* will further develop Japanese industries;" "*kokusaika* will have a grave impact on Japanese industries;" and "*kokusaika* will deprive Japan of its cultural and societal merits" (see Table 2.1).[6]

The most popular response was "promoting *kokusaika* is Japan's international responsibility as a great power." At first glance, 42.1 percent seems to be a high score; considering that respondents were able to choose two answers out of eight, however, this number is not as high as expected. Although the figure was slightly higher than that of the previous year, it was substantially lower than those of the past several years. This result indicates that the majority of Japanese do not think that *kokusaika* is an urgent issue; they do not fully realize Japan's responsibilities as the world's second-largest economy.[7]

The number two response was "*kokusaika* is a necessary process for Japan to secure mid-term and long-term prosperity" (41.3 percent). This ranking was similar to that recorded for the past several years. This answer considers *kokusaika* in terms of Japan's national economic interest and fails to see it from a global perspective. Although it is understandable for Japanese citizens to put Japan's national interest first, it is also important for them to think of Japan's global role commensurate with its economic power. The result indicates that many Japanese have a narrow-minded view of Japan's *kokusaika*.[8]

Table 2.1   Japanese Perceptions of *Kokusaika*

	1990	1991	1992	1993	1994	1995
Japan's international responsibility	46.6%	48.2%	44.1%	45.7%	41.6%	42.1%
Necessary to Japan's prosperity	42.4	40.9	41.6	40.9	41.2	41.3
Spread Japan's culture	19.8	19.6	21.3	18.2	18.2	19.4
Develop Japan's industries	18.1	17.0	17.8	14.8	15.8	14.7
Have grave impact on Japan's industries	9.8	11.0	12.0	13.4	10.3	11.6
Deprive cultural & social merits	8.3	9.6	8.8	8.4	6.4	9.4
Others	0.3	0.1	0.0	0.1	0.3	0.6
Not sure	17.5	16.0	15.0	16.4	17.3	16.1

(two choices out of eight)

Source: Public Information Division, Prime Minister's Office, ed., *Seron chôsa: gaikô* (Public opinion polls: diplomacy), Vol. 28, No. 4 (April 1996), pp. 3–4.

The third and fourth responses were "*kokusaika* will spread Japanese culture to outside world" (19.4 percent) and "*kokusaika* will further develop Japanese industries" (14.7 percent) respectively. These answers completely miss the essence of *kokusaika*. Japan's *kokusaika* was not designed to promote Japanese culture and industries. Instead, it attempts to open the Japanese mind to other cultures and values as well as transform Japanese systems to meet internationally accepted norms and standards. Further, 11.6 percent of respondents feared that "*kokusaika* will have a grave impact on Japanese industries" (a 1.3 percent increase) and 9.4 percent worried that "*kokusaika* will deprive Japan of its cultural and societal merits" (a 3.0 percent increase). Both consider *kokusaika* even harmful to Japanese culture and industries. It should be also noted that the percentages for both responses have increased over the previous year.[9] In conclusion, the results of this poll demonstrate that the majority of the Japanese are not as enthusiastic about promoting *kokusaika* as they should be. This lack of enthusiasm reflects the *sakoku* mentality.

Japanese Perceptions of *Kokusaikôken*

The Prime Minster's Office poll also questioned Japanese perceptions of *kokusaikôken*. The poll asked prospective respondents to choose, out of eight choices, two major roles they think Japan should play in international society. The possible answers included "contributions to solving global environmental problems and other global issues"; "contributions to the maintenance of international peace, including human contributions, such as efforts toward peaceful solution of regional conflicts"; "international efforts to protect freedom, democracy, human rights, and other universal values"; "contributions to the wholesome development of the world economy"; "cooperation for the development of developing countries"; and "contributions to international cultural exchanges such as cooperation for preservation of world cultural heritage" (see Table 2.2).[10]

The most frequent answer was "contributions to solving global environmental problems" (43.1 percent). The second choice was "contributions to the maintenance of international peace" (38.0 percent). The answers "international efforts to protect universal values" (25.0 percent) and "contributions to the wholesome development of the world economy" (23.7 percent) came in third and fourth respectively.[11]

That "contributions to solving global environmental issues" was the most popular answer (a 0.2 percent increase from the previous year) suggests that the majority of Japanese still think that Japan should contribute only to "low politics" and avoid getting involved in "high politics" and military/security

Table 2.2 Japanese Perceptions of *Kokusaikôken*

	1990	1991	1992	1993	1994	1995
Global environmental problems	43.2%	49.7%	49.7%	48.4%	42.9%	43.1%
Maintenance of international peace	34.7	37.5	31.4	28.8	35.2	38.0
Freedom, democracy, human rights	n/a	n/a	22.9	26.1	20.7	25.0
Wholesome development of world economy	38.1	34.4	28.9	28.9	25.9	23.7
Development of developing countries	30.7	29.2	27.5	21.0	23.5	22.1
International cultural exchanges	12.2	11.6	8.1	9.0	7.1	8.6
Others	0.2	0.2	0.0	n/a	n/a	0.3
Not sure	12.1	9.2	8.4	9.4	11.7	10.9

(two choices out of eight)

Source: Public Information Division, Prime Minister's Office, ed., *Seron chôsa: gaikô* (Public opinion polls: diplomacy), Vol. 28, No. 4 (April 1996), pp. 5–6.

issues. Also, although the "contributions to the maintenance of international peace" was the second choice (2.8 percent increase), in the opinion of this author, it was because the question in the poll carefully avoided mentioning any form of military contribution. The poll only mentioned nonmilitary contributions by saying "such as efforts toward peaceful solution of regional conflicts." Had it added the phrase "including the use of force," the number would have been lower.[12]

The results of the poll suggest that the majority of Japanese are hesitant to commit Japan to the maintenance of international peace and security. The reason the Japanese are reluctant to participate in military/security issues derives from their pacifism. As Ikutaro Shimizu, a prominent sociologist, once wrote, the Japanese take peace for granted and regard national security as being as free as air and water.[13] Traditionally, Japan did not perceive the need for national security, due to its geography and history. The oceans surrounding the Japanese archipelago provided a natural barrier against foreign intrusion. The Tokugawa Shôgunate's *sakoku* policy further secluded Japan. Externally, Japan remained a pacifist country, with the exception of a few attempts to invade Korea earlier in its history.

In turn, militarism replaced Japan's traditional pacifism when the Meiji leaders embarked on the first *kaikoku* in the late nineteenth century. This period of militarism was short-lived and ended with Japan's defeat in World War II. The whole war experience reimplanted pacifism into the Japanese psyche. As Chapter 1 mentioned, the major objectives of the Allied occupation forces were to put an end to Japan's militarism and to reinstate democracy in Japan (the second *kaikoku*).

Shimizu holds General MacArthur at least partly responsible for modern Japanese pacifism. When MacArthur called for Japan to be the "Switzerland of the Orient," the Japanese thought of Switzerland as an ideal pacifist country because of its neutrality, all the while ignoring the fact that the latter was a heavily armed nation. They mistook Switzerland's armed neutralism for utopian pacifism. The image of Switzerland as neutral and peaceful appealed to Japanese because of their defeat in the war and the tragedy of the two atomic bombings. Thus, the Japanese erroneously adopted the utopian notion of unarmed pacifism and regarded Article 9 of the constitution as sacrosanct. The Japanese considered peace a virtue, security a vice. They did not understand that peace and security were inseparable. Under these circumstances, the majority of Japanese abhorred military force and worshipped the peace constitution.[14]

The Japanese did not have to recognize the necessity of national security because U.S. forces provided it. After the United States demilitarized Japan, making any possession or use of force unconstitutional, the Cold War fundamentally changed the nature of U.S.-Japan relations. The outbreak of the

Korean War transformed Japan from a former enemy into an important ally. The conclusion of the San Francisco Peace Treaty in 1951 incorporated Japan into the U.S. global strategy against the Soviet Union. The United States could not rearm Japan, however. Although Japan created the Self-Defense Forces (SDF), their size was kept minimal because many Japanese (especially those on the left) considered it unconstitutional. Thus, the United States provided Japan's national security under the U.S.-Japan Security Treaty. As a result, the Japanese began to take U.S. protection for granted. They were immersed in pacifism to the extent of *heiwaboke* (dementia caused by peace). In this sense, the second *kaikoku,* although it transformed Japan through complete demilitarization and the reinstitution of democracy, ironically closed the Japanese mind to military and security issues.

It was another irony that Japan's postwar pacifism took the form of anti-Americanism. Although U.S. forces provided for Japan's national security under the U.S.-Japan Security Treaty, Japanese on the left opposed the treaty, arguing that it would involve Japan in the Cold War. The Japan Socialist Party (JSP), the largest opposition in the Japanese Diet advocated unarmed neutrality and staunchly defended the peace constitution. Paradoxically, socialists were promoting anti-U.S. platforms while defending the peace constitution "imposed" by the United States. They seemed oblivious to the fact that U.S. forces provided Japan's national security. The leftists' anti-U.S. movement culminated in *Ampo Tôsô* (protest against the U.S.-Japan Security Treaty) and died with its defeat in 1960.

The majority of Japanese continued to support the peace constitution after the collapse of the Soviet Union. Although the United States is no longer willing to provide free security to Japan in the post–Cold War era, the majority of Japanese remain utopian pacifists. As for Japanese socialists, they could have vindicated their platforms by saying that Japan neither needs the U.S.-Japan Security Treaty nor the SDF now that the Soviet threat is gone. Instead, the SDPJ has stunned the Japanese by changing its platform to accept the treaty and the SDF after its leader, Tomiichi Murayama, was coopted into the ruling coalition led by the LDP and became prime minister in 1994.

Japanese Perceptions of UNPKO Participation

The results of another poll on Japan's *kokusaikôken* taken in October 1995 also demonstrate how deeply rooted is the *sakoku* mentality. When the Prime Minister's Office asked about views on Japan's participation in UNPKO, only 23.5 percent of respondents answered that "Japan should participate in UNPKO more actively than in the past." Although the figure is 8 percent higher than the previous year, the number is still very low;

especially in the light of how the question was phrased. The poll reads "currently more than eighty countries in the world send personnel to UNPKO. Japan has also participated in international humanitarian aid activities based on the International Peace Cooperation Law. Do you think that Japan should participate in such PKO activities in the future?" Such a mildly phrased question seems to lead to a positive answer (see Table 2.3).[15]

In contrast, 46.4 percent said that "Japan should participate in the same degree as in the past," which was a 3 percent increase from the previous year. Almost half of the respondents prefer to remain hands-off and consider the current level of involvement satisfactory. The result indicates a lack of enthusiasm for Japan's participation in UNPKO. Further, 18.3 percent thought that "Japan should participate in UNPKO but must keep the level of participation minimal" (a 6.7 percent decrease), whereas 5.7 percent considered that "Japan should not participate in UNPKO" (a 2.9 percent decrease). Although these two negative views of Japan's participation in UNPKO have decreased from the previous year, these views represent almost a quarter of the respondents (18.3 percent plus 5.7 percent). As many as 24 percent are still skeptical about Japan's overseas engagement, even in UNPKO.[16]

The results of the poll confirm that the Japanese are still immersed in utopian pacifism and are highly sensitive to any involvement in security issues. For example, a Japanese male expressed his reservation about Japanese participation in UNDOF (Golan Heights) in a major Japanese newspaper:

> I am concerned with the plight of the SDF personnel who were on duty on the UNDOF. The SDF was sent to the Golan Heights because it was supposed to be a safe zone. However, the recent Israeli army's attack on southern Lebanon indicates that there is no guarantee of peace in the Middle East. The SDF personnel there are almost unarmed. Japan would lose face if it withdraws the mission, while Japan would violate the constitution if it sends weapons there. I urge members of the Japanese Diet to do something about the safety of the SDF personnel.[17]

Two Japanese casualties (a policeman and a young volunteer) in the UNTAC mission in Cambodia (1992) caused a fury in Japan. The majority do not realize how unrealistic it is to think that Japan should not participate in UNPKO because the Japanese constitution prohibits any use of force. They do not understand how selfish it is to think that Japan should not participate in UNPKO because the SDF personnel might get injured or killed.

Table 2.3   Japanese Perceptions of UNPKO Participation

	More active	Same as before	Limit to minimum	None	Others	Not sure
1994	15.5%	43.4%	25.0%	8.6%	0.9%	6.6%
1995	23.5	46.4	18.3	5.7	0.4	5.7

Source: Public Information Division, Prime Minister's Office, ed., *Seron chôsa: gaikô* (Public opinion polls: diplomacy), Vol. 28, No. 4 (April 1996), pp. 15–16.

They do not see how anachronistic it is not to participate in UNPKO because the *sakoku* mentality and the utopian pacifism are so deeply embedded in their psyche.

In conclusion, all three public opinion polls concerning Japan's *kokusaika* and *kokusaikôken* demonstrate that the *sakoku* mentality keeps the Japanese from assuming greater political and military roles in the global setting.

Japanese Policy Makers' *Sakoku* Mentality

The Japanese public is not the only group enmeshed in the *sakoku* mentality. As we have seen, Japanese policy makers are not free from it and have formulated *sakoku* policies in the postwar period. Postwar Japanese diplomacy is characterized by minimalism and reactiveness, which prevents *kokusaika* from progressing in earnest. *Kotonakareshugi,* or bureaucratic inertia, has further discouraged bureaucrats from drafting and implementing new policies supporting *kokusaika*. Even worse, Japanese bureaucrats have been caught up in unprecedented corruption scandals (notably at the Ministry of Finance). Meanwhile, Japanese politicians are preoccupied with forming new parties and with shifting alliances amid domestic political upheavals. Thus, policy decision makers are incapacitated by petty domestic affairs. Under these circumstances, the Japanese government has no zeal for its nation's *kokusaika* and is reluctantly taking it up only due to *gaiatsu* pressure.

The *sakoku* mentality still gravely affects the Japanese mind. The Japanese public is unwilling to integrate foreigners into Japanese society and is reluctant to assume a more active role in the international community. Japanese bureaucrats are preoccupied with unprecedented corruption scandals as well as with traditional bureaucratic inertia. Japanese politicians are struggling to survive successive cabinet turnovers and financial scandals. At the grass-roots and local government levels, however, there are some encouraging signs for *kokusaika*. For example, various nongovernmental organizations (NGOs) created by Japanese volunteers are helping refugees in Southeast Asia, Africa, and other parts of the world. Local governments, such as those in Hokkaido, Niigata-*ken,* and Oita-*ken* (Kyushu), are promoting *kokusaika* as a means of decentralizing Japan's highly centralized systems as well as stimulating local economies. The problem remains the central government. Unless drastic events awaken the Japanese and turn Japanese politics upside down, a genuine inward *kokusaika* or *kokoro no kokusaika* is unlikely to occur.

CHAPTER THREE

Japanese Perceptions of the United States

Japanese have had an inferiority complex toward Westerners and have treated them with deference since the first *kaikoku* during the Meiji era. However, as Japan caught up with the West in terms of technology and economic power, Japanese perceptions of the West seemed to change. It was in this context that this author found two recently coined words expressing Japanese feelings toward the Americans interesting and relevant to the analysis of the *sakoku* mentality.

The Sunday *Washington Post* of March 1, 1992, astonished Japanese as well as American readers. An unusual Japanese word, *bubei,* appeared in the middle of two front-page articles on U.S.-Japan relations. The size of the *kanji* (Chinese characters used in the Japanese language) for *bu* and *bei* was exceptionally large—about four square inches. What was unusual was not only the size of the characters but also the unfamiliarity and meaning of the word. It was "foreign," not to be found in any Japanese dictionary. It was also derogatory and provocative: *Bu* literally means "insult," and *bei* stands for "the United States." Since *kanji* are ideographic characters, they can be used in different combinations to create word images. In this case, *bu* combined with *bei* (*bubei*) means "contempt for the United States." Although the word may be new to the Japanese language, its use can easily and quickly convey negative images and derogatory feelings.

One of the two articles, entitled "Japanese View U.S. with New Negativity" (hereafter referred to as the "*Post* article"), gave an explanation of *bubei.* It was written by T. R. Reid and Paul Blustein. According to Reid, *bubei* is "a Japanese neologism coined to describe the feeling of superiority mixed with sympathy that *many* people in Japan now hold toward the United States. *Bubei* is *not* common parlance—most Japanese have probably *never* heard the word—but it is getting increasing use among scholars and opinion leaders . . . The word is gaining currency among *some* in Japan, reflecting new strains in relations."[1] Because of the unusual way the word was introduced in the *Post* article, it seized the attention of the Japanese mass media and was immediately carried as "news" in the *Yomiuri Shimbun,* the largest newspaper in Japan.[2]

In another article entitled "U.S.-Japan Relations Seen Suffering Worst Downturn in Decades," Don Oberdorfer attributed the downturn in relations to President Bush's ill-fated trip to Japan in January 1992. The Bush trip, he said, revealed a "crisis of leadership," an inability to control disputes and tensions: "To a greater degree than in earlier crises, the current disputes have spread beyond specific differences over economic and security politics to a broader collision of two dissimilar societies, their leaders and peoples."[3]

It was true that President Bush's mission to sell U.S. automobiles and his entourage of car manufacturing executives projected a negative image. His collapse at a state dinner further reduced his credibility as a world leader. The scene in which Prime Minister Kiichi Miyazawa held the stricken president (captured by a hidden camera) symbolized the two nations' changing relationship. Bush's visit to Japan also sent a message that the United States was no longer a competitor and signaled America's awareness of declining U.S. economic power. In essence, the two articles said that the Japanese regarded Americans with pity.

In addition to *bubei,* the *Post* article introduced another new word, *kenbei* ("disliking the United States"). Reid notes, "[A]cademics and journalists began using another word, formed from the characters for 'dislike' and 'America.' This word seemed to mean resentment of what was viewed here as a domineering attitude by Americans. The new noun, Bubei, is harsher in that it suggests America is now too weak to be domineering."[4]

The *Post* article introduced the kanji for *bubei* in an extraordinary size on the front page but it did not print out the kanji for *kenbei.* Tension between the United States and Japan is not "new news" these days. Few Japanese, however, have expressed their views of the United States in such a derogatory fashion as through the use of *bubei* or *kenbei.* Herein lies a serious information gap between the United States and Japan concerning each other's perceptions: Americans are interested in how the Japanese perceive the United States, whereas Japanese are obsessed with how Americans perceive Japan. In this particular case, the American press reported that many Japanese now had *bubei* and *kenbei* feelings, sentiments most Japanese had never even heard of. This in turn caught the attention of the Japanese press, which reported the alleged emergence of negative sentiments back to Japan. An irony is that the Japanese learned how *they* perceive the United States through the U.S. media, regardless of whether it was true or not. The problem with this information gap is that it widens perception gaps. Should Americans think that Japanese truly have *bubei* and *kenbei* feelings, their perceptions of Japan will worsen. In turn, when Japanese learn that American perceptions of Japan have worsened, their perceptions of the United States will deteriorate, starting a vicious circle. This perception gap could have a grave impact on U.S.-Japan relations.

Problems of the *Post* Article

There are three fundamental problems with the *Post* article concerning the neologism. First, it is doubtful that the sentiments expressed journalistically by such words as *bubei* and *kenbei* represent the perceptions of a majority of Japanese toward the United States. Indeed, Reid himself admits that *bubei* is *not* common parlance and that most Japanese have never heard the word. *Kenbei* is also a word that only some academics and journalists began to use.

Second, the reason the article introduced words that are unfamiliar even to most Japanese is questionable. Was the intent to provoke sensationalism? The problem with introducing words such as *bubei* and *kenbei* through the mass media is that once the words are reported, readers will not remember that they are used only by a fraction of Japanese intellectuals. Readers will think that most Japanese have feelings of *bubei* and *kenbei*. Should the majority of the Japanese not have these feelings, the responsibility of the *Post* article in having planted a misperception in the minds of American readers is not negligible.

The third problem is that the article does not identify who coined the words and who is using them. If the words are neologisms, their origin should have been explained. If the words are "getting increasing use among scholars and opinion leaders," these users should have been identified. In essence, the article fails to prove the authenticity of its arguments.

Japanese Perceptions of the United States: Do Japanese Like the United States?

Public opinion polls played a key role in testing the validity of the arguments in the *Post* article. The results of polls conducted by the Japanese Prime Minister's Office in October 1991 and released just after the *Post* article send a contradictory signal. It turned out that 78.1 percent of the respondents liked the United States: 37.7 percent felt friendly toward the United States, whereas 40.4 percent felt somewhat friendly. The combined number that liked the United States increased by 4.0 percent from the previous year (October 1990). Conversely, 17.6 percent of the respondents answered that they did not like the United States: 11.2 percent did not really feel friendly toward the United States, whereas 6.4 percent did not feel friendly at all toward the

United States. The total number that did not like the United States decreased by 3.6% from the previous year (see Figure 3.1).[5]

The polls published in April 1992 were actually taken in October 1991 and thus did not reflect what the Japanese thought of President Bush's visit in January 1992. The polls taken in October 1992 resulted in a 4.4 percent decrease in the number of the respondents who liked the United States (see Figure 3.1). Although it is difficult to pinpoint the exact causes for the decline in U.S. popularity, it is possible to regard President Bush's visit as one reason for the decline. Yet the result was surprising if one had only the *Post* article on which to base Japanese perceptions of the United States. The fact remains that the great majority of Japanese (73.7 percent) liked the United States in October 1992. As far as Japanese public opinion polls were concerned, there was no indication that *many* Japanese had *kenbei* and *bubei* sentiments, as the *Post* article argued in March 1992.

The numbers have not changed significantly since then. The latest poll, taken in October 1995 and published in April 1996, indicated that 71.2 percent of respondents liked the United States: 29.3 percent felt friendly toward the United States, whereas 41.9 percent felt somewhat friendly. The combined number that liked the United States decreased slightly, by 2.4 percent from the previous year. In contrast, 25.9 percent of respondents did not like the United States: 16.5 percent did not really feel friendly and 9.5 percent did not feel friendly at all. The total number that did not like the United States increased slightly, by 2.4 percent from the previous year (see Figure 3.1).[6] The rape of a 12-year-old-schoolgirl by three U.S. servicemen in Okinawa (in September 1995) and the subsequent Okinawa base issue may have contributed to the decline.

In conclusion, as far as the Japanese poll results were concerned, there was no indication that many Japanese have *kenbei* and *bubei* sentiments, as the *Post* article argued. About three quarters of Japanese have consistently liked the United States for the past few decades, whereas from one fifth to one quarter did not. It is important to note that a great majority of Japanese (74.1 percent) *did not* have *kenbei* and *bubei* feelings even in 1995, just after the rape of the girl in Okinawa. Polls demonstrated that *kenbei* and *bubei* sentiments do not represent the majority of Japanese perceptions of the United States (see Figure 3.1). In essence, polls showed that America is still by far the favorite foreign country for Japanese, despite growing criticism.[7]

A comparison of Japanese perceptions of Russia to those of the United States will make this clearer. According to the same poll (October 1995), only 9.9 percent of respondents liked Russia: 1.5 percent felt friendly toward Russia and 8.4 percent felt somewhat friendly. In contrast, 86.4 percent respondents did not like Russia: 36.6 percent did not really feel friendly, while

Figure 3.1 Do the Japanese Like the United States?

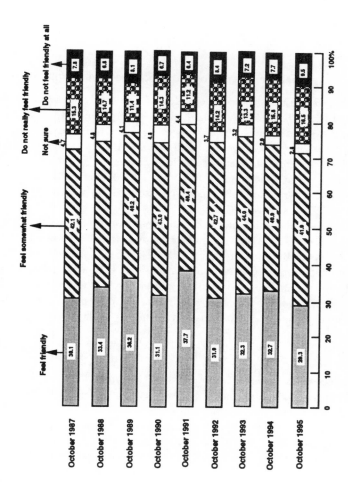

Source: Public Information Division, Prime Minister's Office, ed., *Seron Chōsa: Gaikō* (Public opinion polls: diplomacy), Vol. 28, No. 4 (April 1996), pp. 51-52.

49.8 percent did not feel friendly toward Russia at all. Russia has consistently been an unpopular country for the Japanese for the past few decades, and it has remained so even after the collapse of the Soviet Union. Russia's unpopularity was relatively lower only in 1990 (70.8 percent) and in 1991 (69.5 percent), when the Japanese had high expectations for the new Russia. The unpopularity rebounded in 1992 to 79.6 percent.[8]

The comparisons of Japanese perceptions of the United States to those of Russia show that the United States remains the favorite country of Japanese. Only a minority have *kenbei* or *bubei* feelings.

Japanese Perceptions of U.S.-Japan Relations

The second question in the same polls was concerned with what Japanese think of U.S.-Japan relations. The results were consistent with those for the first question. Although a majority of the Japanese (66.7 percent) thought that U.S.-Japan relations were good in October 1991, the number had declined by 4.1 percent in October 1992. The number that thought relations were good surged to 68.6 percent in October 1993 and then declined in the following two years (to 64.8 percent in October 1994 and to 62.7 percent October 1995) (see Figure 3.2).[9]

In essence, the polls indicated that the majority of Japanese regarded U.S.-Japan relations as basically good, even though they acknowledged there were problems. But there are no bilateral relations without problems. Moreover, a majority of the Japanese public considers U.S.-Japan relations good despite the chronic economic frictions concerning U.S. trade deficits and security issues involving U.S. forces in Japan. The polls demonstrated that a majority of Japanese had rational perceptions of U.S.-Japan relations.

Genesis of *Kenbei-ron* and *Bubei-ron*

Other questions remain concerning the *Post* article. First, where did the words *bubei* and *kenbei* come from, who created them, and who is using them? Unfortunately, the author was one of the majority of Japanese "who have never heard the word," as Reid and Blustein claimed.[10] Second, what is the significance of the words, and what do they really mean? How do they differ from the *hanbei* (anti-United States), which has traditionally been used to describe negative perceptions of the United States? Previously, the Japanese language had only two words to describe Japanese sentiment toward the United States: *shinbei* (pro-United States) and *hanbei* (anti-United States). Japanese politicians and political analysts have been labeled as either *shinbei* or *hanbei*. The debate over U.S.-Japan relations has split into two schools; either *shinbei-ron* (pro-U.S. arguments) or *hanbei-ron* (anti-U.S. arguments).

Figure 3.2 Do the Japanese Think U.S.–Japan Relations Are Good?

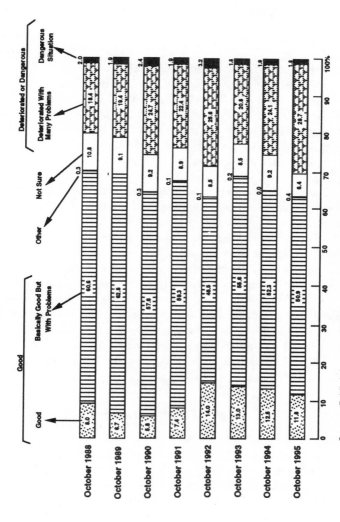

Source: Public Information Division, Prime Minister's Office, ed., *Seron Chōsa: Gaikō*
(Public opinion polls: diplomacy), Vol. 28, No. 4 (April 1996), pp. 53–54.

The problem with *bubei* and *kenbei* is that they have a more negative connotation than *hanbei*. *Hanbei* is a dry word, simply meaning anti-United States, whereas *bubei* and *kenbei* have a connotation of emotional aversion to the United States.

An extensive search for publications on U.S.-Japan relations published over the past three years prior to the *Post* article revealed that an article in *Bungei Shunjû* (June 1991 issue), a popular monthly magazine on political issues, used both *kenbei* and *bubei* for the first time in print. The article is based on a transcription of discussions by Jun Eto, a professor at Keio University, and Nagayo Homma, professor emeritus at the University of Tokyo. Both Eto and Homma are well-known *opinion rîdâ* (opinion leaders) or *bunkajin* (cultured people), as influential intellectuals are called in Japan. These *opinion rîdâ* frequently appear on TV talk shows and magazine interviews. Their influence on the formation of public opinion is considered to be enormous. The article in *Bungei Shunjû* was entitled *"'Shinbei' to 'hanbei' no aida": Nihonjin wa naze Amerika ga kiraika?"* ("In-between 'pro-U.S.' and 'anti-U.S.': Why do the Japanese dislike America?"). Eto used the word *kenbei,* whereas Homma referred to *bubei* in the *Bungei Shunjû* article. However, both Eto and Homma treated the words as though they were already established in the language.

A further search for the words in Japanese literature published prior to the *Bungei Shunjû* article continued in vain until the author found an article by Kenji Suzuki, editor of the *Mainichi Shimbun,* a major national newspaper in Japan.[11] Suzuki partly solved the mystery of the origin of *kenbei* and *bubeï* "The coinage of the word *kenbei* is attributed to Yasuo Tanaka. It is considered that Tanaka used the word for the first time in a magazine called *CREA* (May 1991 issue); although the real origin of words is hard to identify. Meanwhile, the word *bubei suddenly* appeared in the *Washington Post* and its origin is unknown."[12] Suzuki apparently did not have the *Bungei Shunjû* article in mind.

Origin of the Word *Kenbei*

The origin of the word *kenbei* then became clear. It first appeared in a short, three-page article in the May 1991 issue of *CREA,* a fairly new magazine for women begun in 1990. *CREA* is the Japanese counterpart of *Cosmopolitan* or *Vogue*. It was extremely difficult to locate the word's origin, since few expect the creation of political jargon in such a magazine. The article in which the word appeared was entitled *Yûkoku hôdan* ("Foolish Talks on the Nation"). The article is a transcription of talks by Yasuo Tanaka and Akira Asada. Tanaka is a young novelist, who, after having received an award for popular literature, has become a celebrity and appears on Japanese TV as a *bunkajin.* Asada was introduced as an assistant professor at the University of Kyoto; his specialization was not mentioned.[13]

The main subject of the Tanaka-Asada talks was the Gulf War, which they both opposed. They argued that the lesson of the Vietnam War was that a superpower cannot destroy Third World nations by force. To make matters worse, in their opinion, the "victory" in the Gulf War made the United States forget the valuable lessons of the Vietnam War. In this vein, Tanaka stated that the Gulf War marked the beginning of the U.S. "defeat." Tanaka said that during the Vietnam War, Japanese attitudes toward the United States were in general *shinbei-hansen* (pro-United States and anti-war), meaning that the Japanese were pro-United States but were against the Vietnam War. As a result of the Gulf War, however, a new mood that can be called *kenbei-ensen* ("disliking the United States and detesting the war") emerged in Japan.[14] This, according to Suzuki, the *Mainichi Shimbun* editor, is the origin of the word *kenbei.*

The *CREA* article suffers from problems similar to those of the *Post* article. First, the opinion polls did not support Tanaka's argument. As seen earlier, the Prime Minister's Office polls taken in October 1991 indicated that the great majority of Japanese (78.1 percent) liked the United States, which was a 4.0 percent increase from October 1990. Also, the number that did not like the United States decreased by 3.4 percent from 21.0 percent (October 1990) to 17.6 percent (October 1991) (see Figure 3.1). These statistics mean that U.S. popularity actually increased after the Gulf War.

Second, Tanaka did not define the word. In introducing the word *kenbei,* Tanaka mentioned that "only [the words] *shinbei* (pro-U.S.) and *hanbei* (anti-U.S.) used to exist in Japan."[15] But he neither explained how the word *kenbei* was different from *hanbei* nor why *hanbei* was unsuitable for expressing current Japanese sentiment toward the United States. Further, the reason Tanaka created such a provocative word is in question. To propagate a word like this would arouse sensationalism and hysteria not only among Japanese but also among Americans. One cannot help asking what motivations were behind the coinage of such a sensational word.

In the author's opinion, the origin of the word was unsound. The word was published in a new women's fashion magazine rather than in a journal of politics. It was coined by a young novelist rather than by a scholar in political science. It was created in an absurd article entitled, "Foolish Talks on the Nation." Why, then, did Jun Eto, a distinguished scholar in Japan, pick up Tanaka's coinage and use the word in the *Bungei Shunjû* article? In order to understand this, it is necessary to examine Eto's major arguments in the article.

Creation of the *Kenbei-ron*

In the *Bungei Shunjû* article published in June 1991, Jun Eto argues that the *hanbei-kenbei* (anti-United States and disliking the United States) sentiment seems to have spread rapidly not only among the younger generation but also among the public. In his opinion, this was caused by U.S. pressure on Japan concerning the Gulf War. According to Eto, U.S. foreign policy is characterized by westward expansion. While imposing isolationism vis-à-vis the Old World across the Atlantic Ocean, the United States pursued expansionism across the Pacific Ocean. The Black Ships led by Commodore Perry that forced Japan to end its isolation in 1853 is an example. The best embodiment of American expansionism, in Eto's view, is the Japanese constitution. U.S. occupation forces drafted and imposed the constitution on Japan after World War II. Eto considered the Gulf War an extension of U.S. westward expansionism. In Eto's opinion, this expansionism derives from the fact that the United States is devoid of history: the United States expands in space because it lacks history; it is an "ahistorical space." The United States believes that its mission is to assimilate the world into American space under the guise of democracy and freedom. This is generally referred to as American universalism. Therefore, Eto argued, Japan should keep its distance from the United States.[16]

Eto further stated that the problem with Japan is that both the *shinbei* group on the right and the *hanbei* group on the left wrongly believe in this American universalism. *Shinbei* Japanese are simplistic believers of American universalism. *Hanbei* Japanese at least de facto accept American universalism because they believe in the Japanese constitution.[17]

Eto is sarcastic about the Japanese left's position on the Japanese constitution. An irony is that the Japanese left, anti-United States by nature, staunchly supports the constitution drafted by the U.S. occupation forces. The Japanese left believes in pacifism; it advocates an unarmed neutrality defense policy. It therefore believes in a "peace constitution" by which Japan renounces war as a right of the nation and as a means of settling international disputes (under Article 9, known as the "war-renouncing article"). Herein lies the irony of the Japanese left: It is anti-United States but pro-constitution.

Overall, Eto's arguments are underlined with a sense of aversion to the United States. One should remember that Eto is a scholar of politics with nationalist convictions. Japanese on the right are resentful that the United States drafted the Japanese constitution and imposed it on Japan. They demand an amendment to Article 9, which denies a nation's inalienable right to defend itself. Eto represents the pro-amendment group on the constitution. Eto is also highly critical of the censorship policy enforced by the U.S. occupation forces after World War II.

In the article, Eto tried to make the point that *kenbei* sentiment has rapidly spread among the public, but he did not present any statistics to prove his point. In fact, statistics proved the contrary, as we have seen. As far as the polls were concerned, there was *no* indication that *kenbei* sentiment has rapidly spread among the public, as Eto argued (see Figure 3.1).

Origin of the Word *Bubei*

It is clear that the word *kenbei* was coined by Tanaka in the *CREA* article and was used by Eto in the *Bungei Shunjû* article. There was no publication earlier than the *Bungei Shunjû* article in which the word *bubei* was used, however. Two journalists who cover U.S.-Japan relations extensively—Richard B. Matthews, the *Atlanta Journal* editorial associate, and Motohiro Kondo, editorial adviser to *Gaikô Forum* (a monthly journal on diplomacy)—confirmed that the *Bungei Shunjû* article used the word *bubei* for the first time in print.[18] Nagayo Homma, who used the word *bubei* in the article, allegedly said that he did not coin the word but that he heard it from someone else.[19] Nevertheless, Homma used the word in print for the first time. It is therefore important to examine in what context Homma used the word in the *Bungei Shunjû* article.

Creation of the *Bubei-ron*

In reviewing the changes in postwar Japanese perceptions of the United States, Homma argues that those perceptions are categorized into two extremes: *shinbei* and *hanbei*. The former school holds *haibei* or *sûbei* (reverence for the United States) sentiment, whereas the latter holds *bubei* (contempt for the United States) sentiment. Both extreme perceptions are rigid. Homma argues that U.S. policies toward Europe and those toward Asia are fundamentally different. Policy toward Asia is based on the "American utopian geo-fantasy" (expansionism). He argues that U.S. policy toward Japan, based on this expansionism, was disguised by the jeeps and chocolates that the U.S. occupation forces brought to Japan. In Homma's opinion, President Reagan made this once-disguised American policy open up. The essence of the Reagan Doctrine is the imposition of "universal American justice." It holds that justice lies in the United States: whatever America considers to be moral is moral. It allows the violation of the sovereignty of other nations, justifying U.S. invasions into Grenada, Panama, and the Persian Gulf.[20]

Homma further states that the United States is descending from the throne of the hegemon and that treating Oliver North as a hero symbolized the fall of the United States. In Homma's opinion, President Bush's favorite phrase, "new world order," is a misnomer. What the Gulf War created was world disorder rather than a world order. Creation of a real world order, Homma argues, hinges on whether the United States and Japan can cooperate with each other. Now that the United States has become a debtor nation, it is temporarily looking inward and its frustration is targeted at Japan. Thus, it is dangerous for Japan to blindly follow the U.S. lead. Instead, Homma says, Japan should help the United States to "retire" from the throne with grace. Homma concludes that the best policy for Japan is neither blind *sûbei* nor rigid *bubei*, but *nonbei* ("saying no to the United States"): Japan should take a flexible stance and be able to say "no" to the United States in a normal fashion.[21]

Homma's views are not as extreme as Eto's in that Homma does not appear to hold *bubei* sentiment; he criticizes it as rigid and prefers the *nonbei* attitude. Homma tries to be somewhat amusing and plays with words because *nonbei* also means a "drinker" or "drunk" in Japanese slang. Homma is known as an authority on U.S. studies in Japan and has more objective views of the United States than Eto. Homma at least contributed to the creation of *bubei-ron,* however, by introducing the word for the first time in print. Further, Homma's arguments suffer from the same problem as Eto's in the same article: He does not provide any statistical data to show to what extent *bubei* sentiment has permeated the Japanese.

Problems of the *Bungei Shunjû* Article

Since both *kenbei,* as used by Eto, and *bubei,* as used by Homma, appear in the *Bungei Shunjû* article, it may be assumed that the *Post* was referring to this article when it stated that scholars and opinion leaders had begun using these words. The problem with the *Bungei Shunjû* article is that it became the vehicle for "propagating" the words *kenbei* and *bubei.* The *Bungei Shunjû* is one of several popular monthly magazines on politics in Japan that thrive on sensationalism. It is widely read by Japanese. Herein lies the problem of the sensationalism that the mass media foists on the public. In spite of the statistical data presented above, the article seemed to have established *kenbei* and *bubei* as accepted words used to express Japanese feelings toward the United States. By so doing, it also seemed to have legitimized the *kenbei-ron* (arguments for disliking the United States) and the *bubei-ron* (arguments for contempt for the United States) as proper positions in debating U.S.-Japan relations. The potential impact of the article on U.S.-Japan relations is grave.

Assessments: Causes of *Kenbei-ron* and *Bubei-ron*

Opinion polls have demonstrated that *kenbei* and *bubei* feelings do not represent the majority of Japanese perceptions of the United States. This finding should not be surprising, since most Japanese do not know the words *kenbei* and *bubei*. Even the *Post* article acknowledges this fact. It is unwise to dismiss *kenbei-ron* and *bubei-ron,* however, because approximately one fifth of the Japanese people have not liked the Unites States for one reason or another. Thus, it is useful to analyze the reasons for dislike of the United States. Some of the major reasons for the evolution of *kenbei-ron* and *bubei-ron* might include the perceived shifting power balance between the two countries, bilateral trade disputes, and the sensationalism of the mass media.

Perceived Shifting Power Balance

A primary reason for the emergence of *kenbei-ron* and *bubei-ron* can be attributed to growing perceptions of the shifting power balance between the United States and Japan. Since the end of World War II until the early 1970s, the U.S.-Japan power relationship was that of dominant-subordinate, reflecting the enormous power gap between the two nations. The relationship was unequal, with Japan being a dependent of the United States. Japan had no say over the United States. In essence, during this period, the Americans took care of this former enemy as if it were a little brother. The Japanese regarded General MacArthur, as a benevolent dictator and looked up to the United States as a big brother. The Japanese generally held *shinbei* sentiments, taken in by American "jeeps and chocolates."[22]

In the early postwar period, opposition parties on the left, such as the Japan Socialist Party and the Japan Communist Party, and the extreme right wingers were major advocates for *hanbei-ron* (anti-U.S. arguments). The former were anti-United States because they supported unarmed neutrality and were opposed to the U.S.-Japan Security Treaty. The latter was anti-United States because they were opposed to the constitution imposed by the United States and wanted an autonomous constitution. Nakasone Yasuhiro, an influential LDP politician on the right, had also advocated an autonomous constitution for nationalistic reasons, yet he was not anti-United States: When he became prime minister in 1982, he called for a constitutional revision for the sake of consolidating the U.S.-Japan alliance. At any rate, the political influence of anti-U.S. groups was contained, as the right-of-center conservative LDP group remained the mainstream in Japanese politics.

The left launched a massive *hanbei-ron* in 1960, revolving around the renewal of the U.S.-Japan Security Treaty. However, after the defeat of the *Ampo Tôsô* of 1960 (see Chapter 2), the main advocates for *hanbei-ron* were reduced to the extreme left. The Japanese geared themselves toward national economic growth. The United States has remained the most favored nation of the Japanese, and *shinbei-ron* became the mainstream school of thought.

The Japanese strove to achieve an economic miracle during the 1970s and achieved the status of the world's second-largest economy in the early 1980s. By the mid-1980s, the changing U.S.-Japan power relationship loomed larger. *The Rise and Fall of the Great Powers,* the best-seller written by the Yale University historian Paul Kennedy in 1987, accelerated the awareness of the decline of U.S. power. The more the Americans became conscious of the power shift, the more their frustration increased. Even worse, with the fall of the Soviet Union, Japan was perceived as the major adversary by some Americans. "Japan bashing" intensified.[23]

As Japanese realized the power shift, they became more self-confident and even arrogant. Public opinion polls conducted by a Japanese public broadcasting station, Nippon Hôsô Kyôkai (NHK) indicate the change. On the question of who the Japanese thought superior, Westerners or Japanese, in 1951, 47 percent answered Westerners, whereas only 28 percent answered Japanese. Although the poll changed the wording of the question, 95 percent of respondents said they were pleased to have been born Japanese in 1988. As Masaru Tamamoto at American University in Washington, D.C., notes, the increase in Japanese confidence reflects the Japanese economic recovery and prosperity. In this author's opinion, growing self-confidence on the part of the Japanese constitutes the backbone of the *kenbei-ron* and *bubei-ron.* This time, though, those on the right expressed anti-U.S. sentiments, since they were no longer willing to be "yes-men" for the United States. A prime example was Shintaro Ishihara, a best-selling novelist who became an LDP member of the Japanese parliament. He coauthored a controversial book, *"Nô" To Ieru Nihon* (The Japan that can say "no") in 1989 with Akio Morita, then-president of Sony corporation. At the time of the publication, he was a member of the House of Representatives (HR), the powerhouse of the Japanese Diet—equivalent to the House of Commons of the English Parliament.[24]

The book was originally published in Japanese. It caused a sensation across the Pacific when the U.S. Department of Defense (DOD) circulated an unofficial English translation without obtaining copyright permission. Ishihara protested that the Pentagon version was full of mistranslations and distortions. After Morita dropped out of the controversy (due to his business responsibilities), Ishihara published his English translation with Simon and Schuster in 1989. As a best-selling novelist and a vocal member of the LDP, Ishihara was popular among both young and female constituents and ranked high in opinion polls as a desirable prime minister for Japan. Yet he resigned from the HR in 1995 as his disappointment with Japanese domestic politics deepened.[25]

In the book, Ishihara argued that the United States exploited Japan's subordinate position to its advantage and that Japan should be able to say "no" to the United States in order to defend its own national interests. Ishihara's views attracted broad attention in Japan because of growing perceptions of the decline of U.S. power and the rising power of Japan. His views appealed to the Japanese ego and helped to enhance a sense of superiority over the United States. In this regard, the highly publicized remarks by some Japanese politicians on the American work ethic reflect self-confidence on the part of the Japanese. It will suffice to cite one remark by former prime minister Kiichi Miyazawa: "America has reached a point that the mindset to produce things and create values has loosened sharply . . . many people getting out of college have gone to Wall Street for very high salaries . . . the work ethic is lacking as far as the United States is concerned."[26]

Some Japanese felt as if there were nothing more to learn from the Americans and thus looked down on the United States. It was therefore at least theoretically viable that Japanese perceptions of the United States could go through a diametrically opposite shift from "unquestioned reverence" to "sheer contempt," as Homma argued. The polls, however, did not support this argument. Only a minority of the Japanese have such an arrogant attitude as *bubei.* The sense of superiority is also superficial and shallow. It is merely a symptom of the inferiority complex that the Japanese have had toward the West in general and toward the United States in particular.

Japan's Inferiority Complex Toward the West

Japanese developed an inferiority complex toward the West when they encountered advanced Western technology in the late nineteenth century. As seen in Chapter 1, this inferiority drove the Japanese into the *Fukoku Kyôhei* (rich nation, strong army) campaigns in the first *kaikoku.* The Japanese succeeded in catching up with the West militarily in the first *kaikoku* and economically in the second *kaikoku.* Yet the Japanese have not fully overcome their inferiority complex toward the West (especially toward the United States). The plethora of American culture and the abuse of the English language demonstrate this. The Japanese excessively use *gairaigo* (words of foreign origin adopted into the Japanese language) or *yokomoji* (horizontally-written letters) because they think that Western languages sound more fashionable. For example, instead of using the word *kissaten,* the Japanese word for a coffee shop, the Japanese prefer to say *kôhî shoppu.* Ishiwata Toshio, a leading scholar of *gairaigo,* considers that the foremost reason for the excessive Japanese use of *gairaigo* is a lack of confidence in their own culture.[27]

The excessive imports of American culture (words) and the excessive exports of Japanese goods to the United States epitomize the ambivalence of the Japanese inferiority complex and the superiority complex toward that country.

Bilateral Trade Dispute

Another reason for the evolution of the *kenbei-ron* and *bubei-ron* is the ongoing trade dispute between the two countries. The Prime Minister's Office polls indicated that an increasing number of Japanese considered U.S. responses to the bilateral trade issue "emotional" rather than "reasonable." According to the polls taken in October 1992, after the publication of the *Post* article, 42.4 percent of respondents thought that the U.S. responses were emotional, whereas 30.5 percent thought that they were reasonable. The "emotional" answer increased by 2.9 percent; the "reasonable" answer decreased by 2.3 percent from October 1991. Also, a more recent poll (in October 1995) showed a further increase in the "emotional" answer (44 percent) as well as a further decrease in the "reasonable" answer (29.9 percent) (see Figure 3.3).[28] These results indicated that an increasing number of Japanese were exasperated by escalating U.S. demands for Japanese trade concessions.

Trade frictions became visible, and the "free-ride" accusation against Japan was launched by the United States in the 1970s as Japan succeeded with its economic miracle. Given the increasing trade deficit, the United States demanded that Japan enter a new relationship based on equal partnership. This trend intensified further in the 1980s. Japan grudgingly succumbed to U.S. pressure without making the substantial changes that the United States wanted. Thus, U.S. demands for Japanese trade concessions culminated in the Structural Impediments Initiative (SII) in the late 1980s under the Bush administration. Despite Japanese concessions to U.S. pressure, U.S. trade deficits with Japan have hovered around $50–60 billion. These economic factors—chronic U.S. trade deficits, Japanese frustration over incessant U.S. demands to open Japanese markets, and the nouveau riche attitude the Japanese have recently acquired—account for the evolution of the *kenbei-ron* and *bubei-ron*.

Yet the question remains as to why intellectuals like Eto and Homma developed *kenbei-ron* and *bubei-ron* if the majority of Japanese still like the United States. It seems that other reasons motivated these intellectuals into campaigning for *kenbei-ron* and *bubei-ron*, one of them being the sensationalism of the mass media.

Sensationalism of the Mass Media

The Japanese public is influenced by opinion leaders. There are at least three conceivable reasons why Japanese opinion leaders create sensational jargon and develop extreme arguments through the mass media. First, scholars might introduce new jargon purely for academic and intellectual reasons. They are quicker to perceive a new direction in U.S.-Japan relations than is

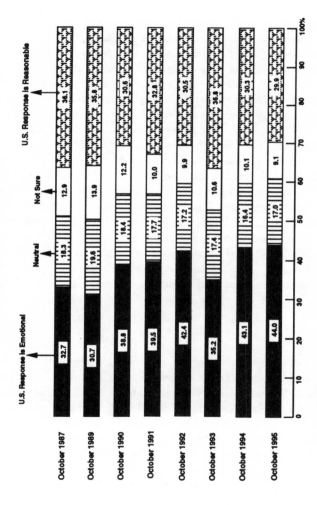

Figure 3.3 Is U.S. Response to U.S.- Japan
Trade Frictions Emotional or Reasonable?

U.S. Response is Emotional   Neutral   Not Sure   U.S. Response is Reasonable

October 1987   32.7   18.3   12.9   36.1
October 1989   30.7   19.6   13.9   35.8
October 1990   38.8   18.4   12.2   30.6
October 1991   39.5   17.7   10.0   32.8
October 1992   42.4   17.2   9.9   30.5
October 1993   35.2   17.4   10.6   36.8
October 1994   43.1   16.4   10.1   30.3
October 1995   44.0   17.0   9.1   29.9

0   10   20   30   40   50   60   70   80   90   100%

* Date for October 1988 is not available.

Source: Public Information Division, Prime Minister's Office, ed., *Seron Chōsa: Gaikō*
(Public opinon polls: diplomacy), Vol. 28, No. 4 (April 1996), pp. 55–56.

the public, and they create new words to describe the change. Thus, they play the role of foretelling a new trend to the general public by creating new jargon. Second, some opinion leaders might deliberately try to change the perceptions held by the general public for political reasons. Most opinion leaders have a certain political agenda in mind; they want to mold the perceptions of the public to their own. Some try to arouse anti-U.S. sentiment among the Japanese. They do not like the way Japanese governing circles handle relations with the United States. They especially do not like the obsequious attitudes of the Ministry of Foreign Affairs, which is allegedly the champion of the "yes" school vis-à-vis the United States. They might also try to change the public's perceptions of the United States by infusing *kenbei* and *bubei* sentiments into the public mentality. Third, there are practical and economic reasons. Opinion leaders must be popular in order to survive and thrive. To be popular, they must think of something new and striking. The nature of the mass media then comes into play. The mass media must appeal to the public to stay on the competitive edge and thus often resort to sensationalism.

The *CREA* and *Bungei Shunjû* articles seem to do exactly this. Instead of using the existing word *hanbei* to express anti-U.S. sentiment, these articles either created or propagated the sensational and derogatory words *kenbei* and *bubei*. After all, opinion leaders are the product of the mass media. They create and use catchy and sometimes sensational words to appeal to the masses. The coinage of the word *kenbei* by the novelist Tanaka, who has little expertise on U.S.-Japan relations or political science, is a prime example. In this manner, the mass media propagate sensational words and opinions and thrive on such sensationalism.

Bridging Perception Gaps

Neither the evolution of *kenbei-ron* nor of *bubei-ron* prove that the majority of Japanese have *kenbei* and *bubei* sentiments. Public opinion polls demonstrated that these sentiments were only shared by a minority of the Japanese. *Kenbei-ron* and *bubei-ron* were advocated by a fraction of opinion leaders who had nationalistic orientations and were exasperated by U.S. pressure.

In the final analysis, the United States is *the* essential country necessary for the survival of Japan. The United States and Japan need each other for their survival, and their interdependence goes beyond the economic prosperity of the two nations. Under these circumstances, the two nations must find ways to solve their differences and accommodate each other. They cannot afford the time to engage in "verbal wars" launched by the mass media across the Pacific. It is a waste of time, serving a fraction of groups who benefit from the sensationalism. It eventually will jeopardize the national interests of the two countries.

In conclusion, it is necessary to monitor the mixed signals that the Japanese opinion poll results have sent. The polls indicated that the United States has remained the most engaging nation to the Japanese, but they showed signs of a slight decline in popularity. People in both nations should not be swayed by the sensationalism of the mass media. Instead of agitating with *kenbei-ron* and *bubei-ron,* opinion leaders should try to bridge the perception gaps between the two nations and reestablish a credible and wholesome relationship. Former U.S. ambassadors to Japan have expressed their caution and hopes for maintaining stable U.S.-Japan relations. For example, Mike Mansfield said, "We had better face up to realities, and become *less emotional,* but more practical and realistic."[29] His successor, Michael Armacost, stated, "It is high time we cease hurling accusations and recriminations back and forth across the Pacific, roll up our sleeves, and get back to work. That is the best way of assuring that long-standing allies remain firm friends and that commercial competition does not breed geopolitical rivalry."[30] It is hoped that *kenbei-ron* and *bubei-ron* will remain with only a vocal minority and that these emotional arguments will die out, as did the *hanbei* movements in the early 1960s, so that reason will prevail in U.S.-Japan relations in the next century.

CHAPTER FOUR

Japanese Perceptions of Asia

The Japanese have looked down on Asians and have discriminated against them since the first *kaikoku* in the Meiji period. This prejudice, a clear reflection of the *sakoku* mentality, is still evident in Japanese foreign policy toward Asian countries. Shin Sakurai, Japan's Minister of the Environment in the Murayama coalition cabinet, said in a political meeting in August 1994 that the Pacific War (World War II) was not a war of aggression. The Japanese press picked up this statement and published it in the major newspapers in Japan. The publication of his comments caught the attention of South Korea's (Republic of Korea) embassy in Japan. The South Korean government protested Sakurai's statement and demanded his resignation. As a result, Sakurai resigned the ministerial post. Yet he remained in the House of Representatives.[1]

It was not the first time that incumbent Japanese ministers have denied Japan's wartime responsibilities toward Asia. In each case in which a minister stated a distorted view of history, the statements were published in major newspapers or in popular magazines in Japan. In response, Asian governments protested the statements and demanded the resignation of the minister. As a result, the minister either resigned or was forced to resign the post. Although they lost their ministerial positions, these conservative Japanese politicians retained their seats in the Japanese Parliament, remained influential members of the ruling Liberal Democratic Party (LDP), and have continued to express these views at political gatherings. Their Japanese constituents supported them and reelected them. Given these attitudes, it is not surprising that Japan has yet to settle war compensation issues with Asia, and Asians still distrust Japan fifty years after the end of the war.

The question arises as to why Japanese politicians deny history. Why does the same pattern of behavior—of making arrogant statements, provoking protests from the Asian countries, and resigning from ministerial posts—recur? What is the source of their perceptions, or what Michael Brecher et al. called the "attitudinal prism?"[2]

Japanese Politicians' "Attitudinal Prism" toward Asia

The attitudinal prism, or the psychological predispositions of policy makers, constitute the screen through which policy makers' perceptions of the operational environment are filtered.[3] In the case of Japanese foreign policy toward Asia, the feeling of racial superiority toward Asia makes up the backbone of Japanese foreign policy makers' attitudinal prism toward the region. The Japanese formed such views of Asia as a backlash to their inferiority complex toward the West. This attitudinal prism has distorted their views of Asia and resulted in unsuccessful foreign policy toward the region. The arrogance of postwar Japanese politicians angered Asians and strained Japan's relations with its neighbors. Faced with Asian governments' demands for apologies for Japanese acts of aggression, Japan was obliged to conduct so-called *zange gaikô* (redemptive diplomacy) toward Asian countries, providing generous economic aid and financial assistance. Yet recurrent offensive remarks by Japanese political leaders indicated that Japanese apologies were superficial rather than sincere. The vicious cycle of Japanese leaders' arrogant attitude toward Asia, Asian governments' angry protests, and the resultant worsened relations between Japan and Asian countries was repeated in the 1980s and 1990s. It was most evident in 1995, the fifty-year anniversary of the end of World War II.

Roots of the Japanese Attitudinal Prism toward Asia

Japanese politicians' attitudinal prism toward Asia derives from history. The sense of racial superiority toward Asia reflected their inferiority complex toward the West during the late nineteenth and the early twentieth century. As seen in Chapter 1, Commodore Perry's visit to Japan in 1853 catalyzed Japan's drive for Westernization. The Meiji leaders set the national goals of modernizing industry and gaining economic and military parity with the West. They also promoted *Bunmei Kaika* (civilization, enlightenment) to infuse the Japanese people with Western ideas and ways of living. As a result, Japanese developed a deep inferiority complex toward the West and began to emulate Westerners, wearing Western clothes and eating beef.[4]

At the same time, aware of China's backwardness, the Meiji elites began to hold China and other Asian countries in contempt. As a result, Japan chose to become an imperial power at the expense of Asia under the *Datsua Nyûô* slogan. Noted experts on Asian studies have argued that Japanese formed a sense of racial superiority over Asia in the late nineteenth century. For example, Toru Yano holds *Datsuaron* ("Discourse on exiting Asia") envisaged by Yukichi Fukuzawa, a philosopher and ideologue in the Meiji era, accountable for this Japanese attitude toward Asia. The Meiji government adopted this ideology to infuse Japanese with Western ideas. In Yano's words, this "*datsua* consciousness" was institutionalized in Japanese society and made into policies. Thus, Japan separated itself from the tributary system centering on China and attempted to accommodate itself to the European balance-of-power system under the slogan of *Datsua Nyûô*. This new view of Asia forged a sentiment of contempt toward Asians and even the depersonalization of Asians. Japanese have had a preconceived notion of Asia as being backward and inferior to this day.[5]

In a similar vein, Yasuaki Onuma points out that as a result of the Japanese assimilation into modern European civilization since the Meiji era, the Japanese formed feelings of contempt and prejudice against non-Caucasians. This is the other side of the coin of their reverence toward Europeans and Americans. These newly formed feelings toward Asians had a decisive impact: Through the process of modernization, the Japanese learned an ugly aspect of their teachers' culture and emulated European imperialism. Thus, Japan colonized Taiwan and Korea and invaded China.[6]

Frank Gibney says that in the course of the Sino-Japanese War of 1894, suddenly the great respect Japan had had for China's age-old culture just dissolved and Japan began to look at China with contempt. He further states:

> The victories over China and Russia established Japan as the leading military power in Asia—and for the first time in Japan's history a force to be reckoned with in the Western world as well. For the Meiji people this sudden rise to prominence was exhilarating and rather unsettling—like the "bends" of deep-sea divers too quickly pulled to the surface. It produced a curious ambivalence of attitude, which remains to this day. Something happened to the Japanese mind as people read the newspaper accounts of victories over the Chinese. For centuries Japan had looked up to China as the mother civilization. Yet here they fought the Chinese—and found them weak. They began to look on the Chinese with contempt. *Changoro* or *chang-chang* they would call them in the writings and popular caricatures of the day—the equivalent of the American deprecatory word "*Chinks.*"[7]

It is not difficult to imagine how the Japanese thought of the rest of Asia if they looked down on China, which Japan had revered so much and for so long. This attitude helped to rationalize Japan's expansionism to create the "Great East Asia Coprosperity Sphere" during World War II. To quote Chalmers Johnson, "Japan was then confronted with a choice as to whether it was to lead an Asian renaissance against Western colonialism or should join the colonialist club." Japan chose the latter and invaded its neighbors under the slogan of *Datsua Nyûô*.[8]

Japan's victories over China, Korea, and Southeast Asia strengthened the Japanese superiority complex toward Asia. Indeed, Japanese felt that they were so superior to other Asians that they did not even regard Japan as part of Asia. This sentiment carried over to the postwar Showa period and was reinforced by the miraculous economic success Japan achieved in the 1960s. The Japanese look down on Asia because Asia is still developing, whereas Japan has become the world's second-largest economic power. In a sense, the Showa leaders have inherited and realized the Meiji leaders' dream of *Datsua Nyûô.*

Statistically, however, it is difficult to prove this point, because few Japanese would willingly admit that they think they are superior to other Asians, even if they feel that way. The Japanese talk about what they think of the Chinese and the Koreans in private but do not express it in public. For instance, parents express their negative views about Koreans at home to their children, and thus the sense of superiority is passed on to younger generations. This feeling does not manifest itself in public, however, but is hidden in the minds of the Japanese. This is because Japanese culture distinguishes what people really think *(honne)* from what they say in public *(tatemae)*, especially true if the views are negative. People are reluctant to express negative views in public and prefer to use ambiguous and euphemistic expressions. Thus, even if the Japanese think that they are superior to other Asians, they do not say so in public. For this reason, the sense of superiority over the Asians does not often manifest itself in Japanese popular culture.

Another reason for the lack of manifestation is that Japanese take their *besshi* (contempt) feeling toward Asians for granted. For example, Onuma assumed such sentiment as a given condition when he stated that the tendency that foreign laborers (mostly from Asia) were increasingly replacing Japanese workers in menial labor markets in Japan would deepen the Japanese *besshi* feelings toward Asians.[9]

That Japanese ruling LDP politicians have denied Japan's war responsibilities toward Asia, despite this culture of euphemism and understatement, is surprising. The recurrence of such comments is astonishing, since high-ranking politicians must be prudent about what they say publicly. The undiplomatic statements have recurred because conservative politicians truly believed what they said, and they really felt superior to Asians. Their statements are a strong manifestation of the arrogance and the sense of superiority toward Asians on the part of Japanese.

The Japanese Emperor's Apology

As part of postwar *zange gaikô* toward Asia and in response to Asian protest against the historic amnesia of its conservative politicians, Japan's emperors had expressed regret over Japan's wartime acts of aggression on several occasions. When Chinese premier Li Peng visited Japan in April 1989, Emperor Akihito, who just succeeded to the throne in January, apologized for Japan's wartime role in China. Also, during South Korean president Roh Tae Woo's state visit to Japan in May 1990, the emperor expressed his "deepest regret" over Japan's colonial rule in Korea. Akihito's apology was more explicit than the one made by his father, the late Showa emperor. When South Korean president Chun Doo Hwan visited Japan in September 1984, Hirohito said that it was regrettable that there was an unfortunate past between the two countries in this century. The South Korean government criticized Hirohito's statement as insufficient and demanded a real apology. Thus, Akihito's apology was a step beyond his father's.[10]

Akihito's apology was not well received by Japanese conservative politicians and rekindled controversies as to whether the emperor should be held responsible for the acts of the nation, as the symbol of the state, and whether public statements by the emperor should be construed as the acts in matters of state. As a result, the emperor stopped short of making unequivocal apologies when he visited Thailand, Malaysia, and Indonesia in October 1991 and China in October 1992. In Beijing, Akihito only said that it was "my deep sorrow" that in the long history of Japan-China relations, there was an unfortunate period in which Japan caused the Chinese people much suffering. Thus, the ruling LDP failed to use the first imperial trips to Asia to liquidate bitter wartime memories between Japan and Asia and end the redemptive diplomacy toward Asia. The failure enabled Asian countries to continue to demand a sincere apology from Japan and use this as leverage vis-à-vis Japan.[11]

Fusen Ketsugi

A controversy over the Japanese Parliament's *fusen ketsugi* (no-war resolution) to renounce war on the fiftieth anniversary of World War II is further evidence of Japanese historical amnesia. The resolution was stalled over whether the wording should include the phrases "act of aggression" and "colonial rule." Conservatives were reluctant to admit Japan's wrongdoing. They justified the past by saying that Japan's Imperial Army had been forced to compete with Western colonial powers and fought for the liberation of the region. Thus, even the coalition cabinet, led by socialist prime minister Tomiichi Murayama, who was more willing to admit Japan's war responsibilities than LDP politicians, had been unable to pass the resolution. In June 1995, coalition leaders reached a compromise draft that includes the two controversial terms without making it clear which countries committed these acts. The resolution also avoided the term *apology* and instead used the ambiguous term *reflection* to express Japan's remorse for causing pain to people in Asia. In addition, the term *fusen ketsugi*, the original name of the resolution, disappeared. It was simply referred to as the "postwar fifty years resolution."[12]

Japanese Politicians' Perceptions of China

Postwar conservative Japanese politicians have also looked down on China and denied Japan's acts of aggression toward China before and during World War II. They even tried to justify the Nanjing Massacre. When Japan's Imperial Army seized Nanjing in 1937, it massacred countless Chinese civilians. The Far East International Military Tribunal that tried Japanese war criminals in 1946 determined that 155,000 Chinese were murdered. The diaries of Reverend John Maggie, an American missionary, describe brutal scenes, including one depicting scores of Chinese being buried alive in a ditch. China claims that 300,000 people were massacred and calls the event the "Rape of Nanjing."[13]

Some conservative Japanese politicians refused to acknowledge this historical fact. In September 1986, Masayuki Fujio, minister of education in the Nakasone cabinet, said in an interview article in *Bungei Shunjû* that the truth about the Nanjing incident is not known. Fujio, an LDP member, said in the article that killing in war is not a crime according to international law and that it is meaningless to exaggerate the number of victims or to discuss it. When the Chinese embassy in Tokyo read the article, the Chinese government in Beijing protested Fujio's statement and demanded his resignation. Since Fujio refused to resign, Prime Minister Yasuhiro Nakasone dismissed him from his ministerial post, but he remained in the House of Representatives.[14]

Yet Japanese politicians did not seem to be affected. In April 1988, Seisuke Okuno, director-general of the National Land Agency in the Takeshita cabinet, asked in a political meeting how China dare call Japan an aggressor. Okuno, another LDP member, argued that Japan was forced by Caucasian aggressors to open itself and compete with them militarily. China protested Okuno's comments. Okuno resigned the post three weeks later but remained in the House of Representatives (see Table 4.1).[15] In November 1990, Shintaro Ishihara, another LDP member and a former minister of transportation, said in an interview with *Playboy* magazine that the "rape of Nanjing" was a fabrication by China. Ishihara stated that he does not believe the massacre happened and that it is a lie to say something happened when it did not. Ishihara added that most of the LDP politicians do not believe that it happened, either. China

Table 4.1   Japanese Politicians' Denial of Japan's Acts of Aggression in Asia

Year	Name	Ministerial position (held then)	Statements' major points
1986	Masayuki Fujio	Minister of Education	Denial of Nanjing Massacre. Japan was not to blame for the annexation of Korea.
1988	Seisuke Okuno	Director-General, National Land Agency	Japan was not an aggressor toward China.
1990	Shintaro Ishihara	Former Minister of Transportation	Denial of Nanjing Massacre.
1994	Shigeto Nagano	Minister of Justice	Denial of Nanjing Massacre. Pacific War was not a war of aggression.
1994	Shin Sakurai	Minister of the Environment	Pacific War was not a war of aggression.
1995	Michio Watanabe	Former Minister of Foreign Affairs, Former Deputy Prime Minister	Japan's annexation of Korea was made in an amicable fashion. Japan's rule of Korea was not colonial rule.
1995	Takami Eto	Director-General, Management and Coordination Agency	Japan's rule of Korea was not colonial rule.

Sources: *"Sensô sekinin o meguru saikin no kakuryô no hatsugen"* (Recent ministers' comments on war responsibilities), *Yomiuri Shimbun*, August 14, 1994, and *"Eto sômuchô chôkan ofureko hatsugen"* (Management and Coordination Agency director-general Eto's off-the-record remarks), *Yomiuri Shimbun*, November 10, 1995.

protested Ishihara's comments, but it did not cost Ishihara his political life because he did not hold any ministerial post at that time and remained in the House of Representatives.[16]

To endorse Ishihara's belief, Shigeto Nagano, minister of justice in the Hata coalition cabinet, also said in May 1994 that the Nanjing Massacre was a fiction. Nagano, a 71-year-old graduate of the now-defunct Japanese Imperial Military Academy, stated in a political meeting that he was in Nanjing just after the incident and that Japan had not intended to occupy or annex Nanjing. His statement provoked a strong protest from the Beijing government. Nagano immediately retracted his remarks but was obliged to resign his ministerial post. Yet he remained in the House of Councillors. A former LDP member, he switched to the Renewal Party when that splinter of the LDP was formed in 1992.[17]

It should be noted that all the denials of history came from (present and former) LDP politicians. This conservative party, whose members include nationalists, has ruled postwar Japan's politics for nearly five decades.

Japanese Public's Perceptions of China

The majority of the Japanese public shares the same views of China with their leaders and does not have a favorable view of that nation. According to the public opinion poll conducted by the Prime Minister's Office in October 1995, only 9.6 percent of respondents said they "feel friendly" toward China, whereas 17.4 percent said they "do not feel friendly at all." The former was the lowest since the poll began, and the latter was the highest (see Figure 4.1). Also, only 3.3 percent of the Japanese thought that Sino-Japanese relations were "good," whereas 10.1 percent thought that relations were "not good." Again, the former was the lowest since the poll began, and the latter was the highest (see Figure 4.2).[18]

In comparison, Japanese perceptions of the United States have been consistently much more favorable than those toward China. According to the same poll, 29.3 percent of the respondents said they "feel friendly" toward the United States, whereas only 9.6 percent felt so toward China. Also, 11.8 percent thought that U.S.-Japan relations were "good," whereas only 3.3 percent thought that Sino-Japan relations were "good."[19]

Given the chronic and incessant trade disputes that have strained U.S.-Japan relations for years, it is surprising that the Japanese still have a much more favorable view of the United States than of China. It is even more surprising when one considers that Japan had looked up to China as a mentor for centuries. Though the Prime Minister's Office's poll did not provide the reasons for the unfavorable views of the Japanese public toward China, it is possible to cite certain reasons for the negative views. They include China's communist ideology and human rights violations. More important, however, the lack of respect and the sense of racial superiority toward China on the part of the Japanese also account for the negative views. This sense of superiority, coupled with the Japanese insular and provincial character, has enabled postwar Japanese policy makers to ignore Japan's war responsibilities toward China. This attitude angered China, which in turn worsened Japanese perceptions of China—a vicious cycle. It was most evident in 1995, the fifty-year anniversary of the end of World War II. Several unsettled disputes between the two countries that originated in Japan's wartime conduct still irritate their bilateral relations.

Figure 4.1 Do the Japanese Like China?

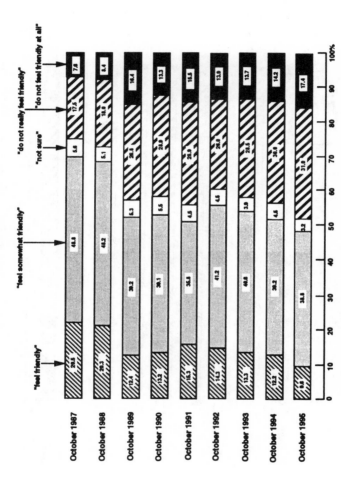

Source: Public Information Division, Prime Minister's Office, ed., Seron Chôsa: Gaikô (Public opinon polls: diplomacy), Vol. 28, No. 4 (April 1996), pp. 61-62.

Figure 4.2 Do the Japanese Think Sino–Japan Relations Are Good?

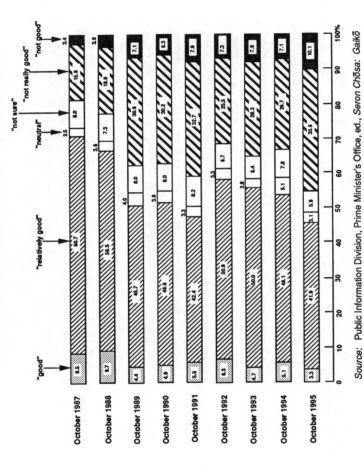

Source: Public Information Division, Prime Minister's Office, ed., *Seron Chōsa: Gaikō* (Public opinon polls: diplomacy), Vol. 28, No. 4 (April 1996), pp. 63-64.

Legacy of Japanese Aggression in China:
Ienaga Textbook Trials

It has been the conventional wisdom that Japanese history textbooks skip World War II and that Japanese schoolchildren learn sugar-coated versions of Japan's role in the war. This is so because the LDP-ruled government fears that children might become unpatriotic and anti-LDP if they learn what Japan actually did during the war. To prevent this, the Ministry of Education has censored history textbooks by employing the *kentei seido* (certification system). In order to pass the ministry's advance screening, textbook authors have been obliged to use ambiguous language and euphemisms in describing World War II. For instance, instead of saying Japan's Imperial Army "invaded" China, a textbook has to say it "advanced to" China. Political parties on the left, such as the Japan Socialist Party (JSP) and the Japan Communist Party (JCP), have opposed the war and criticized *kentei* as censorship. Yet the ministry asserted that textbooks were overly tilted to the "left" and tightened the screening.[20]

Under these political circumstances Saburo Ienaga at Tokyo University of Education sued the government over *kentei* of his high-school textbook in 1965. In his first lawsuit, Ienaga argued that enforcement of revisions in his textbook is unconstitutional (a violation of academic freedom). All three court rulings—by the Tokyo District Court (1974), the Tokyo High Court (1986), and the Supreme Court (1989)—judged that *kentei* is constitutional. In his second lawsuit, Ienaga demanded the removal of the administrative order (to revise his textbook). The Tokyo District Court in 1970 ruled that *kentei* itself is not unconstitutional, but if the screening goes beyond the bounds of checking whether textbooks meet the guidelines set by the Ministry of Education, it is considered censorship and therefore unconstitutional. Yet the Supreme Court repealed the district court ruling in 1982. The "Ienaga Textbook Trials" became the focal point of the *kentei* controversy. After Ienaga's defeat in the two lawsuits, China and South Korea have launched protests against the *kentei* system since 1982.[21]

When the Ministry of Education ordered Ienaga to revise his new high-school textbooks for fiscal 1980 and 1983, Ienaga again sued the government (the third Ienaga lawsuit). Among other things, the ministry ordered Ienaga to insert the words "amid confusion" into his description of the Japanese Army's conduct in the Nanjing Massacre. The added phrase would have the effect of diminishing the army's responsibility for the incident. The ministry also told him to delete the account of Japanese soldiers' atrocities against Chinese women in Nanjing. In 1989, the Tokyo District Court ruled *kentei* constitutional and rejected Ienaga's claim. In October 1993, the Tokyo High Court rejected the district court ruling, saying that the ministry's *kentei* of the description of the Nanjing Massacre was beyond its discretion, and *was* illegal. Yet the court ruled that *kentei* on other accounts in question (three out of five) were legal and also ruled that *kentei* itself is not censorship and, therefore, constitutional. It was a partial victory to Ienaga.[22]

Ienaga once again appealed to the Supreme Court. In August 1997, the Supreme Court overturned the Tokyo High Court ruling that endorsed the *kentei* on the description of the Japanese Imperial Army's Unit 731 (discussed below in this chapter), and ordered the government to pay a ¥400,000 (about $3,000) compensation to Ienaga. Nevertheless, the Supreme Court ruled the *kentei* system constitutional and endorsed the High Court's rulings on the *kentei* on other accounts. This Supreme Court's decision concluded the third Ienaga lawsuit. Eighty-three-year old Ienaga's battle with the *kentei* system is over after 32 years since his first lawsuit in 1965. *The Pacific War,* one of more than 50 books Ienaga wrote, is used in American universities. Meanwhile, owing to pressure from China and South Korea, Japanese public schools began to use textbooks with more accurate descriptions of Japan's wartime conduct. A *Washington Post* survey of the twelve textbooks used in Japanese schools in 1994 indicated that the textbooks have considerably increased their coverage of Japan's role in the war.[23]

Japanese Orphans Left in China

The so-called *Chûgoku zanryû koji* (orphans left in China) became a focal point of postwar settlements between Japan and China. During World War II, a number of Japanese settled in Manchuria as part of *Manmô kaitakudan* (immigration mission to develop Manchuria and Mongolia). When the former Soviet Union declared war against Japan in 1945, in the final stage of World War II, it sent troops to Manchuria. Many Japanese immigrants left behind their infants as they fled the chaos. They thought that their children would be killed during the retreat and asked Chinese to adopt them. It is estimated that there are about 2,000 Japanese orphans in China.[24]

The issue emerged when Japan concluded a peace treaty with the People's Republic of China (PRC) in 1978. After the resumption of Sino-Japan relations, the orphans wished to meet their biological parents in Japan. Most of them even do not know their Japanese family names. The only indication of their identity was a name tag (first name and age) attached to the clothes they were wearing when their parents left China. Japan agreed to receive identification missions from China. A total of 1,242 orphans visited Japan from the first mission in 1981 to the eleventh mission in 1986. Among them, 416 found their identities. As missions have continued, however, the identification rate has dropped to less than 10 percent. A number of parents did not want to reveal their identities, since they have hidden the fact that they had left their infants in China. Also, many orphans' biological parents have already died. Orphans now are lucky if they can find any relatives at all. Thus, when 36 orphans, ranging between 50 and 55 years old, visited Japan in November 1994 for two weeks, only two found their identities.[25]

In addition to the emotional reasons, economic factors seem to account for their desire to find their identities. They would like to live in Japan because of the huge gap in living standards between China and Japan. If they can prove their Japanese identity, then they and their families are entitled to live in Japan. As identification has become more difficult, Japan has allowed even those who could not prove Japanese identity to settle in Japan since 1985. Yet even if they are allowed to live in Japan, their life in Japan is difficult. Japan's Department of Health and Welfare estimates that at least 14,420 orphans, including their immediate families, have immigrated to Japan through governmental financial aid. (The number of those who did so at their own expense is not available.) A third of them are second and third generation. Few of these immigrants speak Japanese, and they encounter discrimination in many forms. In addition, to solve a new issue regarding how the returnees who have settled in Japan would take care of their aging foster parents left in China, Japan agreed to pay a lump sum that covered fifteen years' worth of monthly allowances of 60 yuan (about $25) to their foster parents. This orphan issue is a unfortunate byproduct of the legacy of the Japanese occupation of Manchuria.[26]

Bacteriological Experiments in Manchuria

Another unresolved issue haunts Japan concerning its occupation of Manchuria. Japan's Imperial Army allegedly conducted bacteriological experiments on about 3,000 prisoners, mainly Chinese, in northeast China before and during World War II. The army's Unit 731, a germ warfare laboratory in Manchuria, is said to have sent human specimens to a military institute in Shinjuku, Tokyo. This action is well documented in a three-volume book, *Akuma no Hôshoku* (Insatiable appetite of a devil), by Seiichi Morimura, a popular nonfiction writer in Japan.[27]

In July 1989, the issue reemerged when the remains of more than 100 people of Asian origin were found at the new construction site of the National Institute of Health in Shinjuku, which used to be the site of a military institute that had close relations with Unit 731. Some of the skulls had scars, apparently from surgery. When Shinjuku Ward announced a plan to cremate the remains, 109 Shinjuku residents filed a lawsuit against the plan. They argued that it is necessary to investigate the remains to identify potential war victims and determine the cause of death. They protested that the planned cremation is a violation of international law. The Tokyo District Court rejected the demand in December 1994, saying that the residents' lawsuit should only aim at preventing unlawful use of public money and that the expense of the planned burial, 4.5 million yen (about $35,000), is not a large amount. Thus, the court sided with the authority's intention to "bury" the evidence of Japanese atrocities in China.[28]

Poisonous Gas Bombs Left in Manchuria

Japan's Imperial Army installed two million poisonous gas weapons in three dozen locations in northeast China during World War II. In response to China's request in 1990 to dispose of these poisonous gas bombs, Japan sent four fact-finding missions and admitted that the bombs had been installed by Japan's army. The two million bombs contain one million tons of a poisonous chemical substance. The bombs are similar to the mustard gas bombs used in the Iran-Iraq War during 1980s, which cause abrasions to the skin and respiratory organs. So far, 2,000 local Chinese residents have been affected by liquid leaking from the weapons.[29]

In December 1994, Bu Ping, vice president of the Academy of Social Sciences in the northeastern Chinese province of Heilongjiang, visited the site of a now-defunct factory on Okuno Island, Hiroshima, where poisonous gas containers were produced. He urged that Japan swiftly dispose of the gas bombs in China. Also, the Chemical Weapon Ban Treaty, which obliges nations to dispose of chemical weapons they left behind in other nation's territories, came into effect in 1995. Under these circumstances, the Murayama cabinet planned to send SDF missions in 1996. Yet execution of the plan stumbled over technical details. A cautious group argued that it required a revision of the SDF law because it did not provide for the SDF's overseas engagement for such a task. Another group believed that it was possible to send a small SDF contingent by putting the Ministry of Foreign Affairs (MFA) in charge of such a mission. In the end, the government sent a small emergency mission made up of SDF and MFA personnel to remove the most hazardous weapons in February 1995 and, later, a regular SDF mission in 1996.[30]

Outstanding War Compensation with Taiwan

Following President Nixon's historic visit to Beijing in 1972, Japanese prime minister Tanaka visited the Chinese capital to sign the Japan-PRC Joint Communiqué and normalize relations. In the communiqué, Japan expressed its deep regret for the damage it had inflicted on China during World War II and acknowledged the PRC as the sole legitimate government of China. In return, the PRC relinquished its claims to war compensation. The two also agreed to begin peace treaty negotiations to legally end their state of war. After six years of stormy negotiations, involving the "hegemonic clause" against the Soviet Union, the two signed the Japan-PRC Peace Treaty in 1978.[31]

Although war compensation with the PRC has been settled, that is not the case with the Republic of China (ROC) in Taiwan. When Japan signed the joint communiqué with the PRC in 1972, Japan repealed the peace treaty with the ROC that it had signed in 1952. In response, the ROC suspended diplomatic relations with Japan. The Taipei government requested compensation from Japan for unpaid postal saving accounts of the Taiwanese during the Japanese control of Taiwan from 1895 to 1945. It also requested compensation for unpaid salaries of Taiwanese soldiers who were conscripted into the Imperial Army. Japan has maintained that the Taiwanese were not eligible for these payments, however, because they had lost their Japanese citizenship at the end of the war (through the so-called nationality clause). Although Japanese war veterans and their survivors have been handsomely paid, the Taiwanese who fought for Japan's Army have been neglected. To date, the number of the Taiwanese claims has reached 2.5 million. Japan decided to pay 120 times the principal amount for all the claims. The process stalled, however, because some Taiwanese were not satisfied with the amount.[32]

Japanese Politicians' Perceptions of Korea

LDP politicians have even deeper contempt toward Korea than toward China and deny Japan's war responsibility toward Korea altogether. In September 1986, Education Minister Masayuki Fujio said in a *Bungei Shunjû* article that Japan was not to blame for the annexation of Korea and that Korea was partly responsible for it. The South Korean government protested his statement. Fujio, who also denied the Nanjing Massacre, was dismissed from the ministerial post. But in 1994, both Justice Minister Shigeto Nagano and Environment Minister Shin Sakurai stated at political meetings that the Pacific War was not an act of aggression committed by Japan. Sakurai also said that Japan is not solely responsible for the war and that as a result of the war, Asian nations gained independence from European colonizers and achieved economic recovery. The Seoul government protested these comments, which resulted in their resignations from the ministerial posts, but they remained in Parliament (see Table 4.1).[33]

Even after this sequence of political gaffes involving Korea, former deputy prime minister Michio Watanabe said in June 1995 that Japan and

Korea concluded a treaty annexing Korea to Japan in a way acceptable to both sides in 1910 and that Japan's rule of the Korean Peninsula from 1910 to 1945 was thus not colonial rule. The South Korean government's stand is that the treaty was null and void because it was concluded in the midst of a threat of military force. The South Korean Foreign Ministry denounced Watanabe's remarks as "anachronistic and paranoiac" and said that the South Korean people could not contain their resentment and indignation (see Table 4.1). Watanabe was an influential LDP leader and also served as foreign minister. He died in September 1995 without achieving his dream of becoming prime minister.[34]

Japanese politicians never seem to learn. In November 1995, yet another incumbent minister denied Japanese colonial rule over Korea in a political seminar. Takami Eto, director-general of the Management and Coordination Agency of the Murayama coalition cabinet, was obliged to resign.[35]

Japanese Public's Perceptions of South Korea

The Japanese public shares its elites' views of South Korea and has more negative perceptions of that nation than toward China. According to the October 1995 opinion poll conducted by the Prime Minister's Office, only 7.6 percent of respondents said they "feel friendly" toward South Korea, whereas as many as 20.8 percent said they "do not feel friendly at all." The number who "feel friendly" decreased slightly, by 0.3 percent from the previous year, whereas the number who "do not feel friendly at all" increased by 2.8 percent from the previous year. In fact, the number that "feel friendly" toward South Korea was the lowest since the poll began, along with that of October 1989 (see Figure 4.3). Similarly, only 3.9 percent of respondents thought that Japan-ROK relations were "good," whereas as many as 10.6 percent thought that Japan-ROK relations were "not good." The former decreased by 2.6 percent from the previous year and was the lowest since the poll began. Conversely, the latter increased by 2.0 percent from the previous year and was the highest (see Figure 4.4).[36]

In comparison, more Japanese definitely felt friendly toward China (9.6 percent) than toward South Korea (7.6 percent). The primary reason for the less favorable view of South Korea is the legacy of Japan's occupation of Korea. Japanese look down on Koreans much more than they do on Chinese because Japan ruled Korea from 1910 to 1945, whereas it never ruled all of China. Also, as mentioned earlier, Japan had looked up to China, whereas Japan and Korea were both tributary nations to China in their early history.

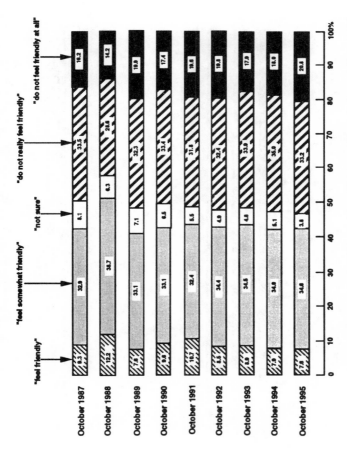

Figure 4.3 Do the Japanese Like South Korea?

"feel friendly" "feel somewhat friendly" "not sure" "do not really feel friendly" "do not feel friendly at all"

	"feel friendly"	"feel somewhat friendly"	"not sure"	"do not really feel friendly"	"do not feel friendly at all"
October 1987	6.3	32.9	6.1	33.5	16.2
October 1988	12.2	38.7	6.3	28.4	14.2
October 1989	7.6	33.1	7.1	32.3	19.9
October 1990	9.3	33.1	6.6	33.1	17.4
October 1991	10.7	32.4	6.6	31.3	18.0
October 1992	8.5	34.4	4.9	32.4	18.3
October 1993	8.0	34.6	4.9	33.3	17.8
October 1994	7.3	34.0	5.1	35.0	18.0
October 1995	7.8	34.8	3.6	33.2	20.8

0 10 20 30 40 50 60 70 80 90 100%

Source: Public Information Division, Prime Minister's Office, ed., *Seron Chōsa: Gaikō*
(Public opinon polls: diplomacy), Vol. 28, No. 4 (April 1996), pp. 65-66.

Figure 4.4 Do the Japanese Think Japan-ROK Relations Are Good?

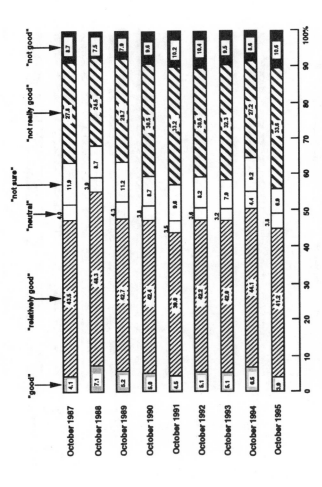

Source: Public Information Division, Prime Minister's Office, ed., *Seron Chōsa: Gaikō* (Public opinon polls: diplomacy), Vol. 28, No. 4 (April 1996), pp. 67-68.

Legacy of the Japanese Occupation of Korea: Korean Residents in Japan

After Japan annexed Korea in 1910, the Imperial Army brought thousands of Koreans to Japan. They were engaged in forced labor and suffered tangible and intangible forms of discrimination in Japan. When the Great *Kantō Daishinsai,* a record earthquake in the area surrounding Tokyo, claimed 140,000 lives and destroyed 570,000 houses in 1923, countless Koreans were massacred in the turmoil. They were falsely accused of arson, as the calamity worsened due to fire following the earthquake. Similarly, Korean residents in Japan were also falsely accused of arson in the 1995 *Hanshin Daishinsai,* the earthquake that shook Kobe, near Osaka, which took more than 6,400 lives. Eiichi Nakamura, a member of *Heiseikai,* an LDP splinter group in the House of Councillors, stated that there were rumors of Koreans setting fires in Kobe after the earthquake. The rumors proved false. Nakamura apologized.[37]

There are currently about 700,000 Korean residents in Japan who have settled in Japan with children who were born in there. When Japan concluded the Basic Relations Treaty with the ROK in 1965 and normalized relations, Japan agreed to give permanent residency to the first and second generations of Korean residents in Japan. But as resident aliens, they were required to submit to fingerprinting when they registered for residency. When Prime Minister Kaifu visited Seoul in 1991, he apologized for Japan's colonial rule and agreed to remove the fingerprint requirement. However, Japan still does not grant Korean residents automatic citizenship. If they wish to become Japanese citizens, they must submit their curriculum vitae and adopt Japanese names. Those who retain their Korean identity may not vote and are disqualified from public service. As an exception, a few local governments (the Kanawaga and Kochi prefectures and Yokohama city) decided to remove the nationality clause and make non-Japanese eligible for employment in 1997. (Foreign labor policies are examined in Chapter 6.) Under these circumstances, Korean residents in Japan still suffer from political, economic, and social discrimination.[38]

Outstanding War Compensation with Korea

With the conclusion of the Japan-ROK Basic Relations Treaty in 1965, which nullified the Japan-Korea Annexation Treaty of 1911, Japan agreed to provide $300 million in war reparations, $200 million in governmental loans, and more than $300 million in commercial credits to South Korea. When Japan began negotiations to normalize relations with North Korea (Democratic People's Republic of Korea) in 1990, North Korea decided to claim compensation from Japan, both for losses incurred under Japan's colonial rule and for "losses" during the forty-five years after World War II.[39]

In addition, Korean war victims now demand individual compensation. They assert that individual compensation is separate from war reparations at the governmental level. Japan maintains that all war reparations had already been settled by the Japan-ROK Basic Treaty of 1965. The former so-called comfort women epitomize the individual compensation issue with Korea. During the war, Japan's army ordered Korean businessmen to operate "comfort houses" so that Japanese soldiers would not commit atrocities against local women. They were run by Koreans to deflect Japan's responsibility. The former *jûgun ianfu* (comfort women) had not sued in the past to avoid embarrassment of disclosing such experiences. As they aged, however, they began to demand individual compensation from Japan. This issue spilled over to comfort women of other nationalities, notably, the Dutch in Indonesia, Filipinos, and even Japanese.[40]

In December 1994, the Murayama coalition cabinet's "Army's Comfort Women Issue Subcommittee" of the "Project Team for Postwar Fifty Years Issues" announced a plan to establish a private fund at the Japan Red Cross to raise *mimaikin* (consolation money). By creating the private fund, the government intended to evade formal compensation as well as responsibility toward individual victims. It was another indication of arrogance on the part of the Japanese government. The committee merely recommended that the government should contribute as much as possible to the fund and that the amount range from $20,000 to $40,000 per victim.[41]

As noted earlier, despite strong recommendations by the International Commission of Jurists (ICJ) and the UN Commission on Human Rights, the Japanese government refused to pay state compensation to the former comfort women. The Asia Peace and Friendship Fund for Women, a private fund established by Japanese volunteers, failed to pay temporary compensation to former victims by the end of 1995, as it had promised. In April 1996, with international criticism and exposure of the issue, Prime Minister Hashimoto decided to pay *mimaikin* (approximately $20,000 through the private fund) to about 300 former victims. Nevertheless, he insisted that the issue of state compensation had already been legally settled. Under these circumstances, the majority of the victims refused to accept the payment. As of July 1997, only 25 former victims had received the compensation.[42]

The above discussion demonstrates that the Japanese attitudinal prism toward Asia is grossly distorted and that this attitudinal prism has made Japanese policy makers ignore and delay postwar settlements with Asian countries. The majority of Japanese support their leaders' views on Asia and have unfavorable perceptions of their neighbors. This attitudinal prism derives from

Japan's drive for Westernization since the Meiji period and the Japanese victories in Asia during the late nineteenth and the early twentieth centuries. The deeper the Japanese inferiority complex grew toward the West, the stronger the superiority complex grew toward Asia. This sense of racial superiority enabled Japan to rationalize its invasion of Asia during the war and ignore individual war compensation for Asians in the postwar period. Faced with Asian demands for sincere apologies for Japan's wartime acts of aggression, Japan has conducted *zange gaikô* in the postwar era. Nonetheless, the recurrent offensive remarks by Japanese ministers indicate that Japan's apologies were superficial. This superficial "apology diplomacy" toward Asia has prevented Japan from establishing credible relations with its neighbors.

Kenzaburo Oe, the Japanese recipient of the Nobel Literature Prize for 1994, made an acceptance speech entitled "Ambiguous Japan and I" in Stockholm in December 1994. In the lecture, Oe said that ambiguity exists in Japan in many forms: Modernization of Japan meant Westernization, yet Japan preserved its traditional Asian culture. In other words, while opening itself to the West, Japan kept its dark aspects. In Oe's opinion, this ambiguous progress drove Japan to invade Asia, and as a result, Japan became isolated from Asia politically, socially, and culturally.[43]

Oe's word, "ambiguity," can be rephrased as "paradox." This paradox is the source of the ambivalence of the inferiority complex toward the West and the superiority complex toward Asia in the Japanese mind. The gaffes by Fujio, Okuno, Ishihara, Nagano, Sakurai, Watanabe, and Eto reflect what ruling conservative politicians really believe. The majority of the Japanese have supported these policy makers. The arrogance of Japanese elites has infuriated Asians, reminded them of bitter memories of war, and compelled them to demand sincere apologies and individual compensation from Japan. At least until the generation that survived the war passes away, Japan will continue to face individual compensation claims. Yet the heaviest "debt" of Japan's wartime acts of aggression is not individual compensation but the redemptive diplomacy Japan was obliged to conduct for the past fifty years. This superficial apology diplomacy has prevented Japan from formulating more constructive foreign policy toward Asia.

World leaders and intellectuals expressed ambivalent views of the settlement of Japanese responsibilities during World War II. According to a poll conducted by the *Yomiuri Shimbun* in late 1994, only 10 percent of respondents thought that "Japan has already solved the wartime settlement issue," whereas 37 percent answered that "Japan has almost solved the wartime settlement issue." In contrast, 22 percent still considered that "Japan has hardly solved the matter," and 16 percent said that "Japan has not solved the matter at all."[44]

In conclusion, Japan cannot achieve a new goal of "re-Asianization" or *Datsuô Nyûa* ("exit West, enter Asia") unless it fully admits its wrongdoing, settles individual compensation issues expeditiously, and thereby clears up all the misgivings held by people in Asia. That seven Japanese politicians' (including five incumbent ministers) remarks denying Japan's acts of aggression toward Asia became public from 1986 to 1995, and all these ministers were obliged to resign the posts, suggests that the Japanese have yet to learn a lesson from their history. They should embrace the axiom that those who do not learn from the past are condemned to repeat it.

CHAPTER FIVE

Japanese Perceptions of ASEAN and Japan's Economic Diplomacy

This chapter focuses on Southeast Asia (Indonesia, Malaysia, Singapore, the Philippines, and Thailand) and examines how the *sakoku* mentality affects Japanese perceptions and Japan's diplomatic relations with Southeast Asia. Since these five nations are the original members of ASEAN (the Association of Southeast Asian Nations) and data for new members are not available, these countries are referred to as ASEAN nations. The chapter also examines correlations among perceptions, national interest, and foreign policy.[1]

The case of Japan and ASEAN countries is an interesting one. First, there is a gap between Japanese perceptions of ASEAN states (contemptuous feelings) and Japan's foreign policy toward these nations (active economic diplomacy, as part of Japan's outward economic *kokusaika*). Second, there is also a contradiction between ASEAN elites' perceptions of Japan (deep-rooted animosity) and their foreign policy toward Japan (active economic diplomacy). Given these apparent gaps between perceptions and foreign policy in Japan-ASEAN relations, this chapter addresses the following questions:

- Has Japan formulated its foreign policy toward ASEAN states objectively, despite its contempt toward these nations?
- Why has Japan pursued active economic diplomacy toward ASEAN countries (enormous economic aid) despite its disliking of the latter?
- Why has Japan refused to admit its acts of aggression toward ASEAN countries during World War II if it wants to maximize its economic and other interests in these states?
- Have ASEAN nations formulated their foreign policy toward Japan objectively, despite lingering resentment against Japan's wartime conduct?

- Have ASEAN states pursued active economic diplomacy toward Japan and obtained maximum economic assistance from Japan despite their deep-rooted animosity toward Japan?
- Or have ASEAN countries been unable to overcome their animosity toward Japan and thus have failed to gain maximum economic and other benefits from Japan?

This chapter primarily employs Brecher's model to answer these questions. This model postulates that the attitudinal prism distorts the way foreign policy elites see the operational environment, which results in unsuccessful foreign policy.[2] For instance, if Japanese foreign policy elites do not like ASEAN nations for one reason or another, they might decide not to give these countries as much economic aid as they would if they liked these states, even though giving more aid would better serve Japan's national interest.

To supplement Brecher's model, this chapter uses the complex interdependence hypotheses envisaged by Robert Keohane and Joseph Nye, Jr. The significance of Keohane and Nye's thesis, as an alternative paradigm to political realism, is the emphasis on the importance of economic policy in a complex, interdependent world, as opposed to the emphasis on the preeminence of military power in the realist's paradigm. Keohane and Nye assumed that interstate relationships in a complex, interdependent world consist of "multiple issues," where military security does not consistently dominate the policy agenda and there is no clear hierarchy of priority among issues.[3]

Their assumptions are applicable to postwar Japan's foreign policy in that Japan has not pursued any military diplomacy and instead has focused on economic diplomacy. It is important to bear in mind, however, that Japan has pursued economic diplomacy because it was deprived of its military power and had little choice but to formulate nonmilitary policy. The realist assumption of the preeminence of military power might be still tenable here in the sense that U.S. guarantees of Japan's security dictated Japan's foreign policy options. As Keohane and Nye themselves acknowledged, the reality is somewhere between the realist and the complex interdependence assumptions.[4]

Keohane and Nye's perspective has become more applicable to international relations in the post–Cold War era, in which the preeminence of military power has, at least on the surface, given way to economic power in an interdependent world. For example, Japan's economic need of ASEAN nations, as a market for its manufactured products and as a cheaper site of production, has never been stronger in the context of the escalating trade disputes with the United States. In turn, ASEAN states need Japan as a primary provider of financial and technological assistance and as an investor in infrastructure construction and in manufacturing industries.

The end of the Cold War changed Japan-Southeast Asian relations. The United States' lessened need of Japan as an "unsinkable aircraft carrier" for its global military strategy undermined the basic underpinning of Japan's postwar foreign policy. Japan can no longer formulate solely economic diplomacy. In trying to redefine its basic foreign policy, Japanese foreign policy decision makers must choose to continue to depend on the United States or to develop an independent defense. ASEAN states also have encountered an agenda-setting problem. ASEAN leaders are trying to reassess Japan's role in the region—whether it is desirable for Japan to play political and military roles in addition to an economic one. Some leaders, such as Malaysian prime minister Mahathir bin Mohamad, argue that Japan should play a military role in the region to fill a power vacuum in the aftermath of further U.S. military withdrawals and thus become a counterweight to the Chinese military build-up. Other leaders, notably the former Singaporean prime minister Lee Kuan Yew, are still wary of a possible resurgence of Japanese militarism and are opposed to such an idea. In this case, Keohane and Nye's multiple issues hypothesis, which would make policy decision-making options more complex, is more applicable than the realist approach.

Based on the theoretical frameworks on foreign policy behavior examined above, this chapter sets up the following hypotheses on correlations among perceptions, national interest, and foreign policy: Foreign policy decision makers do not always see a situation or the operational environment objectively because subjective factors in the psychological environment, such as their perceptions of another country, prevent them from seeing the operational environment correctly. Objective foreign policy decision making is further impeded by the multiple issues that confront decision makers in a complex, interdependent world. As a result, a nation could fail to formulate foreign policy objectively and to maximize its national interest vis-à-vis other nations. This chapter tests the proposed hypotheses with the cases of Japan and ASEAN countries.

Japanese Perceptions of ASEAN States

The Japanese do not have favorable views of ASEAN states. According to the October 1994 public opinion poll conducted by the Prime Minister's Office, only 6.1 percent of the respondents said they "feel friendly" toward ASEAN and 27.7 percent said they "feel somewhat friendly." In contrast, 35.5 percent said they "do not really feel friendly" toward ASEAN and 19.2 percent said they "do not feel friendly at all." Japanese perceptions of ASEAN nations have not changed over the years. Polls taken in previous years indicate that the Japanese have consistently held relatively unfavorable views of these countries (see Figure 5.1).[5] In comparison, the Japanese have held much

Figure 5.1 Do the Japanese Like ASEAN Countries?

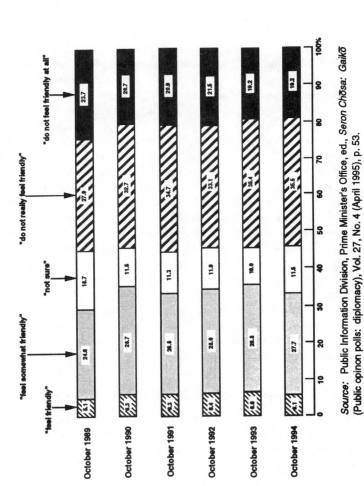

Source: Public Information Division, Prime Minister's Office, ed., *Seron Chōsa: Gaikō* (Public opinon polls: diplomacy), Vol. 27, No. 4 (April 1995), p. 53.

more favorable views of China. Even Japanese perceptions of South Korea have been more favorable than those toward ASEAN, despite the bitter history between Japan and Korea.[6]

In a similar vein, Japanese have negative views of their country's bilateral relations with ASEAN states. The prime minister's poll showed that 46.0 percent of the respondents thought that Japan-ASEAN relations were good (4.8 percent "good" and 41.2 percent "relatively good"). In comparison, 53.3 percent thought that Sino-Japanese relations were good (5.1 percent "good" and 48.1 percent "relatively good"), whereas 50.6 percent thought that Japan-South Korean relations were good (6.5 percent "good" and 44.1 percent "relatively good"). Also, 64.8 percent thought that U.S.-Japan relations were good (12.5 percent "very good" and 52.3 percent "basically good although there are problems"). These results illustrate a clear correlation between Japanese perceptions of ASEAN states and their views of Japan-ASEAN relations (see Figure 5.2).[7]

Sources of Japanese Perceptions of ASEAN States

Though the Prime Minister's Office poll did not provide explanations for the unfavorable views of the Japanese toward ASEAN countries, it is possible to attribute certain reasons for that. This chapter postulates that a sense of superiority over their Asian neighbors on the part of the Japanese is a major source of the unfavorable views. As was examined in Chapter 4, the Japanese forged a sense of superiority over Asia during the Meiji era. Having realized the backwardness of China, Japan followed the path of the Western imperialism and invaded China in 1894. It is not difficult, then, to imagine what the Japanese thought of the rest of Asia if they had begun to look down on China, which Japan had revered so much and for so long. As Akira Iriye points out, the Japanese had revered China as the Rome and Greece of the Orient because Chinese elites had defined their country as a civilization, rather than as a military power or economic system, and had not conquered its tributary nations.[8]

In contrast, Japanese ignored the rest of the Asian nations because they did not flourish as a great civilization. The Japanese were not interested in Asian states because they thought that their ethnic cultures were primitive. This attitude helped to rationalize Japan's expansionism to create the "Great East Asia Co-prosperity Sphere" during World War II, while its ally, Nazi Germany, was pursuing racist expansionism in Europe. The sense of superiority carried over to the postwar Showa period and was reinforced by the miraculous economic success that Japan achieved. As a result, the Japanese do not even regard Japan as part of Asia. They do not have an affinity for Asians, although they are geographically and ethnically

Figure 5.2 Do the Japanese Think Japan-ASEAN Relations Are Good?

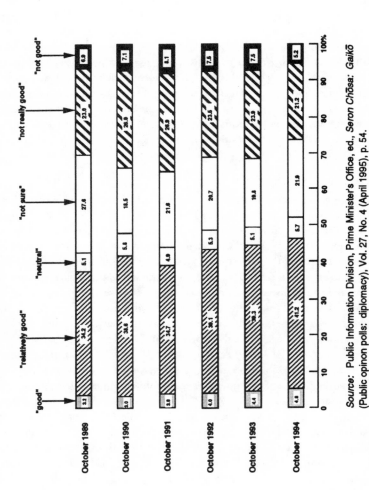

"good" "relatively good" "neutral" "not sure" "not really good" "not good"

October 1989	3.2	34.2	6.1	27.6	23.0	6.9
October 1990	3.0	36.6	6.8	18.5	26.9	7.1
October 1991	3.6	34.7	4.9	21.6	26.9	8.1
October 1992	4.0	36.1	6.3	26.7	23.5	7.5
October 1993	4.6	38.3	6.1	19.6	23.5	7.5
October 1994	4.8	41.2	6.7	21.9	21.2	5.2

Source: Public Information Division, Prime Minister's Office, ed.,, *Seron Chōsa: Gaikō* (Public opinon polls: diplomacy), Vol. 27, No. 4 (April 1995), p. 54.

close. Japan has little interest in Asia apart from economics. These perceptions of Japanese toward Asia in general constitute the underpinnings of
the unfavorable views of ASEAN countries.

Japan's Foreign Policy toward ASEAN States

Japan's foreign policy toward ASEAN states reflects Japanese disrespect and
indifference toward these nations. The U.S.-Japan Security Treaty of 1951
prescribed the basic course for Japan's postwar foreign policy. Japan renounced war as the right of the nation in its constitution revised during the
U.S. occupation. Consequently, the United States has assumed the role of
defending Japan under the Security Treaty framework. Japan has fully taken
advantage of the security arrangement and has pursued a so-called traders'
diplomacy (a diplomacy of the economy, by the economy and for the economy) in the postwar era. As a result of the aggressive economic diplomacy,
the image of Japan as an "economic animal" that only tries to maximize its
economic interest has spread all over the world.

Japan's pragmatism is evident in its policy toward ASEAN states. Japan
has actively pursued its economic interest in Southeast Asia, a convenient
supplier of raw materials and a potentially large market for its products. As
Thai scholar Chaiwat Khamchoo notes, the reparations and subsequent economic aid gave Japan access to ASEAN markets, which led to Japan's economic expansion in the region. By the late 1960s, Japan had become a
primary trading partner of ASEAN, replacing the former colonial powers of
Europe and surpassing the United States. Japan also has become a primary
provider of overseas development aid (ODA), investment, and technology to
the region. It has done so despite political and economic instability and the
postwar remnants of anti-Japanese sentiment in the region.[9]

The Fukuda Doctrine marked a shift in Japan's policy toward ASEAN
countries. In 1977, Prime Minister Takeo Fukuda enunciated the three
diplomatic principles toward Southeast Asia. The doctrine was designed to
depart from a solely economic diplomacy and formulate a comprehensive
diplomacy encompassing political, economic, and cultural policies toward
the region. The doctrine committed Japan (1) to reject the role of a military
power; (2) to build a relationship of mutual confidence based on "heart-to-
heart" understanding; and (3) to be an equal partner of ASEAN. The
Fukuda Doctrine was instrumental in strengthening Japan's ties with
ASEAN. For example, Japan created SEAPCENTRE (Southeast Asia Promotion Centre for Trade, Investment, and Tourism), an intergovernmental
organization between ASEAN and Japan. Japan has also enhanced cultural
exchanges with ASEAN through the establishment of the ASEAN Cultural
Fund. Japan's political engagement in the region has been unsuccessful,

however, with few tangible results. As Sueo Sudo notes, there was a gap between "the dramatic declaration of the Doctrine and its little substantive impact on international relations in Southeast Asia." In essence, the area in which Japan has successfully promoted its national interest in the region has remained largely economic.[10]

Japan's Trade and Investment toward ASEAN States

Statistics illustrate clearly the economic interdependence between Japan and ASEAN states. As for ASEAN's imports from Japan in 1991, Japan was the largest exporter to Indonesia (24.5 percent share), Malaysia (26.1 percent), and Singapore (21.3 percent), whereas it was the second-largest exporter to the Philippines (19.7 percent). As for ASEAN's exports to Japan in the same year, Japan was the largest importer of goods from Indonesia (36.8 percent share), whereas it was the second-largest importer from the Philippines (20.2 percent), and the third-largest importer from Malaysia (15.9 percent) and Singapore (8.7 percent).[11]

At the same time, ASEAN nations have become one of Japan's leading trade partners. In 1993, Singapore was Japan's seventh-largest trade partner; followed by Thailand, the ninth; Indonesia, the tenth; Malaysia, the eleventh; and the Philippines, the eighteenth. The combined trade volume of the five ASEAN nations with Japan reached almost $82 billion, or 14 percent of Japan's world trade. Among the ASEAN nations, Indonesia, an oil exporter, was the only country with which Japan incurred a deficit ($6.5 billion) (see Table 5.1).[12]

Japan's investment in ASEAN nations has increased as well. As for Japan's direct overseas investment in 1993, Indonesia was Japan's ninth-largest investment recipient; followed by Malaysia, the tenth largest; Singapore, the twelfth; Thailand, the thirteenth; and the Philippines, the twenty-first. The combined volume of the five ASEAN states exceeded $3 billion, or 8.4 percent of Japan's total overseas direct investment in that year. As for the cumulative amount for the fiscal years 1951–1993, Japan's direct overseas investment in ASEAN states was $38 billion (9 percent share) (see Table 5.2).[13]

These statistics indicate that Japan has achieved its economic interest in ASEAN nations. But its economic success has created negative by-products as well. As mentioned earlier, Japan has been perceived as an economic animal. The indifference to the diverse cultures and traditions in developing countries on the part of Japanese "corporate warriors" caused friction with local people. Southeast Asia was no exception to this. *Business Week* reports that "having long looked down on Asia, the Japanese are finding that they

Table 5.1 Japan's Top Twenty Trading Partners, 1993

1	United States	160,641	11	Malaysia	17,291
2	China	37,838	12	United Kingdom	16,998
3	Taiwan	31,759	13	Canada	14,393
4	Republic of Korea	30,379	14	Saudi Arabia	12,974
5	Germany	27,807	15	United Arab Emirates	11,482
6	Hong Kong	24,675	16	France	10,576
7	Singapore	20,203	17	Netherlands	8,762
8	Australia	19,912	18	Phillippines	7,194
9	Thailand	18,763	19	Italy	7,039
10	Indonesia	18,500	20	Mexico	5,035

(unit: million dollars)

Source: Keizai Kôhô Center, ed., *Japan 1995: An International Comparison* (Tokyo: Keizai Kôhô Center, 1995), pp. 38–39.

Table 5.2 Top Twenty-One Recipients of Japan's Direct Overseas Investment, 1993

1	United States	14,725	11	Germany	760
2	United Kingdom	2,527	12	Singapore	644
3	The Netherlands	2,175	13	Thailand	578
4	Australia	1,904	14	Canada	562
5	China	1,691	15	France	545
6	Panama	1,390	16	Liberia	502
7	Hong Kong	1,238	17	Switzerland	426
8	Cayman Islands	841	18	Brazil	419
9	Indonesia	813	19	Taiwan	292
10	Malaysia	800	20	Republic of Korea	245
			21	Philippines	207

(unit: million dollars)

Source: Keizai Kôhô Center, ed., *Japan 1995: An International Comparison* (Tokyo: Keizai Kôhô Center, 1995), p. 55.

are out of touch with their neighbors' cultures." For instance, Indonesian employees of Sanyo, a Japanese electronic manufacturer, went on strike after the management refused to allow its female assembly-line workers to wear traditional Muslim dress. The company insisted that they wear designated uniforms for safety reasons. This is an example of the lack of understanding of Southeast Asian cultures and traditions that has adversely affected Japanese business dealings with ASEAN countries.[14]

Japan's ODA toward ASEAN States

Japan has provided sizable ODA to ASEAN states. In 1993, Indonesia was the second-largest recipient of Japan's ODA of $1,149 million (total disbursement of grant aid, technical cooperation, and loan aid); the Philippines was third ($758 million); and Thailand was fourth ($350 million). Singapore received $18 million. Malaysia, however, incurred a debt of $22 million because Japan took out its yen-denominated loans after Malaysia had refused to pay these loans back. (The amount Malaysia owed to Japan had increased substantially with the sharp appreciation of yen.) The combined volume of Japan's ODA to the five ASEAN nations in 1993 was $2.3 billion, or 28 percent of Japan's total ODA for that year (see Table 5.3).[15]

Japanese Foreign Policy toward ASEAN States: Testing the Hypotheses

The above discussion demonstrates the gap between the Japanese perceptions of ASEAN states and Japan's economic interest in these nations. It allows two possible interpretations on the hypotheses proposed earlier in this chapter. The first interpretation disproves the hypothesis: Despite the low number of Japanese who like ASEAN states (6.1 percent) and of those who think that Japan's relations with ASEAN nations are good (4.8 percent), Japan deployed active economic diplomacy toward ASEAN states and has succeeded in establishing strong economic relations with them. To quote Khamchoo, "Few nations have been fortunate enough to be able to acquire by peaceful means what they failed to get militarily." ASEAN nations shared 14 percent of Japan's world trade, 9 percent of its cumulative overseas direct investment, and 28 percent of its total ODA in 1993. These facts seem to render an interpretation that Japan has formulated its foreign policy toward

Table 5.3 Top Ten Recipients of Japan's Bilateral ODA, 1993

1	China	1,351	6	Egypt	275
2	Indonesia	1,149	7	Pakistan	188
3	Philippines	758	8	Bangladesh	185
4	Thailand	350	9	Sri Lanka	147
5	India	296	10	Kenya	142

(unit: million dollars)

Source: Economic Cooperation Bureau, Ministry of Foreign Affairs, ed., *Japan's ODA: Annual Report 1994* (Tokyo: Association for Promotion of International Cooperation), 1995, p. 110.

ASEAN states objectively and has achieved its national interest in these countries.[16]

Nonetheless, the question remains as to why Japan is reluctant to fully acknowledge its responsibilities for wartime acts of aggression toward Asia. Had Japan realized the vital importance of the region to its economy, for instance, it could have admitted its guilt in order to eliminate the deep-rooted animosity in the region. If Japanese leaders would like to promote Japan's national interest, they could have apologized even if they were not really sorry. The Japanese reluctance, as evidenced by the LDP politicians' repeated denials of the Japanese army's acts of aggression and the controversy on the non-war resolution, seem to indicate that Japanese policy makers have not always acted objectively toward Asia in terms of maximizing Japan's national interest.

It is difficult, however, to give a definitive answer as to whether LDP politicians have acted objectively or subjectively: They might think that Japan's relations with ASEAN countries would not deteriorate seriously even if they did not admit Japan's responsibilities for the wartime acts. They might think that they do not have to admit guilt because ASEAN states need Japan as much as Japan needs them.

In summary, Japan's foreign policy toward ASEAN nations suggests two interpretations. The first interpretation disproves the chapter's hypothesis in that Japan has separated its economic interest in ASEAN states from its views of these countries. Japanese foreign policy decision makers think that their ASEAN counterparts distinguish their economic interest in Japan from their views of Japan. They think that ASEAN countries desperately need Japan's economic assistance and that the anti-Japanese sentiments expressed by certain ASEAN leaders are, to a large extent, rhetorical and thus negligible.

The second interpretation, however, supports the chapter's hypotheses in that Japanese arrogance toward ASEAN nations has resulted in the failure to admit responsibility for acts of aggression during World War II, to remove Southeast Asia's deep-rooted resentment against Japan, and to understand the region's native cultures. These failures have prevented Japan from assuming a greater role in ASEAN nations beyond the economic one. In the author's opinion, Japanese foreign policy toward ASEAN states has been characterized by ambivalence, and both interpretations provide a useful insight into Japan's foreign policy toward ASEAN nations.

ASEAN Leaders' Perceptions of Japan

The *Chûnichi Shimbun* conducted an opinion poll in 1994 with 380 young leaders in ASEAN nations, who play leading roles in both the public and private sectors. One hundred responded, out of which 42 were Thai, 25 Indonesian, 17 Malaysian, 9 Singaporean, and 7 Filipino. Fifty-two were male and 46 female; the average age was 36.8. The *Chûnichi* poll presented young elites' ambivalent views of Japan. First, the result showed certain positive perceptions. Out of the 100 respondents, 82 said they liked Japan, whereas only three said they disliked Japan. Also, 72 respondents said they supported Japan's bid for a permanent UN Security Council seat, whereas 16 said that they were opposed to it (see Figure 5.3).[17]

The poll also revealed negative perceptions. For example, 35 respondents thought that "Japan had not regretted enough its conduct during World War II," whereas 32 respondents thought that Japan had regretted enough. In breakdown by nationality, Singapore was most negative on this issue (66.7 percent), followed by the Philippines (42.9 percent), Indonesia (36.0 percent), Malaysia (29.4 percent), and Thailand (28.6 percent). In addition, 51 respondents said that they were wary of Japan becoming a military giant, whereas 35 respondents said that they were not. Wariness was highest in Singapore (67 percent), followed by the Philippines (57 percent), Indonesia (56 percent), Malaysia (53 percent), and Thailand (43 percent). The result is consistent with that of the question on Japan's regret of its wartime conduct (see Figures 5.4 and 5.5).[18]

Further, only 23 respondents said they would support the Japanese Self-Defense Forces' participation in UN peacekeeping operations (UNPKO), whereas 55 said they would support such engagement provided that it is limited to nonmilitary engagement; 5 said they were opposed to any participation in UNPKO. The combined number of those who were opposed to such engagement and those who supported it conditionally (60) outnumbered those who supported it (23). By nationality, the opposition rate was highest in Malaysia (65 percent), followed by Indonesia (64 percent), Thailand (60 percent), the Philippines (57 percent), and Singapore (44 percent). In an open-ended question as to what they expect from Japan in the future, about 60 percent of the respondents said they expect Japan to play a key role in economic development in Southeast Asia. A number of Malaysian respondents even said that Japan should grow out of its "dependent diplomacy on the U.S." and play a leadership role in East Asia (see Figures 5.3 and 5.5).[19]

Sources of ASEAN States' Perceptions of Japan

The ambivalent views of Japan revealed in the *Chûnichi* poll reflect ASEAN leaders' deep resentment against Japan's acts of aggression during World War II. This resentment has lingered even though Japan settled war reparations with ASEAN nations by providing massive economic, financial, and technological assistance and several Japanese prime ministers have expressed

Figure 5.3 ASEAN Elites' Perceptions of Japan
(out of 100 respondents)

Q1: Do you think that Japan has regretted enough its conduct during World War II?

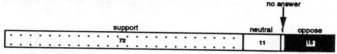

regretted enough	neutral	not regretted enough
32	33	35

Q2: What do you think of Japan's bid for a permanent UN Security Council seat?

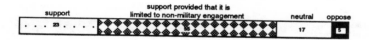

no answer

support	neutral	oppose
72	11	16

Q3: What do you think of the Japanese SDF's overseas engagement in UNPKO?

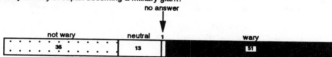

support	support provided that it is limited to non-military engagement	neutral	oppose
23	55	17	5

Q4: Are you wary of Japan becoming a military giant?

no answer

not wary	neutral	wary
35	13	51

Q5: Do you like or dislike Japan?

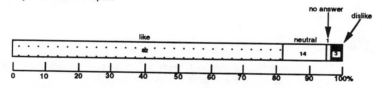

no answer   dislike

like	neutral	
82	14	3

0   10   20   30   40   50   60   70   80   90   100%

Source: "Tonan Aija no Tainichikan" (Southeast Asian perceptions
of Japan), *Chūnichi Shimbun*, January 1, 1995.

mild regret concerning Japan's wartime conduct. For instance, the poll
showed that the majority (60 percent) were still cautious of Japan's military
engagement even in UNPKO, even though the great majority (72 percent)
supported Japan's bid for a permanent UN Security Council seat. The older
generation that experienced the war feels much stronger resentment and
wariness toward Japan.[20]

Figure 5.4 ASEAN Elites' Perceptions of Japan: Japan's Regret for Its Conduct During World War II (comparisons among five nations)

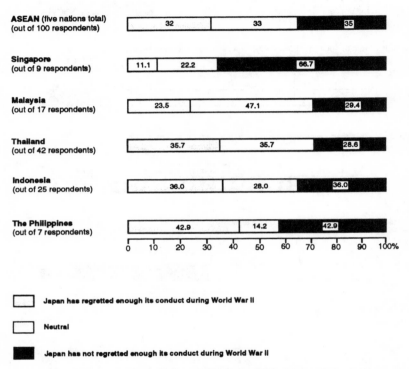

Japan has regretted enough its conduct during World War II

Neutral

Japan has not regretted enough its conduct during World War II

Source: "Tonan Aija no Tainichikan" (Southeast Asian perceptions of Japan), Chūnichi Shimbun, January 1, 1995.

It should also be noted that the ASEAN elites' views as to whether Japan had adequately regretted its acts of aggression correspond to the degree of the atrocities committed by Japan against an individual nation. Singapore and the Philippines, where the acts of aggression against local residents by the Japanese army were grave, showed higher numbers of elites who thought Japan had not regretted enough. (For Singapore, the figure was 66.7 percent, and for the Philippines, 42.9 percent, whereas the overall average for ASEAN was 35 percent). In comparison, the numbers were lower in

Figure 5.5 ASEAN Elites' Perceptions of Japan: Wariness toward Japan (comparisons among five nations)

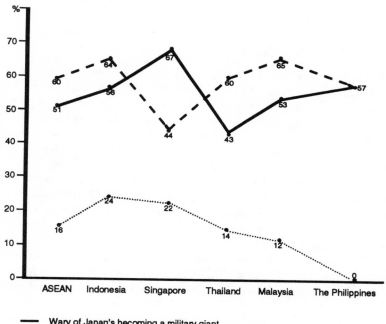

——— Wary of Japan's becoming a military giant

- - - either "opposed the Japanese SDF's overseas engagement in UNPKO" or "support it provided that it is limited to non-military engagement"

······ opposed Japan's bid for a permanent UN Security Council seat

ASEAN (five nations total) (out of 100 respondents)
Indonesia (out of 25 respondents)
Singapore (out of 9 respondents)
Thailand (out of 42 respondents)
Malaysia (out of 17 respondents)
The Philippines (out of 7 respondents)

Source: "*Tonan Aija no Tainichikan*" (Southeast Asian perceptions of Japan), *Chūnichi Shimbun*, January 1, 1995.

Malaysia (29.4 percent) and Thailand (28.6 percent), where people are less wary of Japan's military power and more willing to forget the past. In fact, Malaysian prime minister Mahathir told Prime Minister Murayama during his visit to Southeast Asia in August 1994 that Japan should drop its apology diplomacy and play a leadership role to promote peace and prosperity in Asia.[21]

ASEAN States' Foreign Policy toward Japan

ASEAN states' foreign policy toward Japan reflects the ambivalent perceptions of the elites toward Japan. ASEAN leaders have actively sought Japanese cooperation in the region's economic development in the form of financial aid, direct investment, and technological assistance. Yet simultaneously, they have strongly objected to any indication of a Japanese military build-up both at home and abroad. They expressed fear when Japan's defense budget exceeded the 1 percent of the GNP ceiling, even if Japan did so because of U.S. pressure. As the *Chûnichi* poll indicated, they are even wary of the SDF's engagement in UNPKO, although these missions are strictly for peacekeeping. In essence, ASEAN elites are still haunted by the past experiences with Japan's army and have yet to forgive Japan completely.

A new international environment poses another dilemma to ASEAN leaders. In the wake of a diminished Russian threat and U.S. plans to reduce its military presence in the region, some ASEAN decision makers expect Japan to fill the power vacuum and play a greater security role in the region. This awareness is heightened by the increasing threat posed by China, with its continued military budget increases, underground nuclear testing, and the dispute over the Spratly and Paracel Islands. Prime Minster Mahathir is in favor of Japan playing an increased security role in the region as a counterweight against China. He is also in favor of a greater Japanese role because he would like the East Asian Economic Caucus (EAEC) to serve as an alternative economic institution to the Asia-Pacific Economic Cooperation forum (APEC). EAEC consists of solely East Asian nations, whereas APEC includes "non-Asian" Pacific nations, such as Australia, Canada, New Zealand, and the United States. Other ASEAN decision makers are concerned that Japan might assume a political and military role in the region and fear that Japan might take advantage of the power vacuum. Former Singaporean prime minister Lee Kuan Yew supports a continued U.S. military presence in Asia as a means to restrain Japanese as well as Chinese power. Lee's views still represent the majority sentiment in the region. Most ASEAN leaders will feel uneasy about Japan's increased military role, unless it is sanctioned by the United States.[22]

ASEAN States' Foreign Policy toward Japan:
Testing the Hypotheses

ASEAN states' foreign policy toward Japan suggests two possible interpretations. The first interpretation disproves the chapter's hypotheses in that ASEAN nations have achieved their national interest vis-à-vis Japan. They have received massive ODA and direct investment from Japan and have greatly promoted their economic interest with Japan. Among others, Malaysia and Thailand are less wary of Japan's military policy and are more willing to set aside the emotional issues with Japan.[23]

In contrast, Singapore and the Philippines seem to support the hypotheses in that their perceptions of Japan prevent them from accepting Japan's greater political and security role in the region, even if such a role would enhance ASEAN's regional security and welfare. They are still distrustful of Japan, and former Singaporean prime minister Lee has frequently expressed concern over Japan's defense policy. The Philippines also decided to demand individual compensation fifty years after World War II.[24]

The question remains, however, as to whether some ASEAN decision makers have failed to formulate their policies toward Japan objectively because of their wariness of Japanese defense policy. It is possible that these ASEAN elites are merely acting as if they were still angry in order to arouse a sense of remorse among Japanese. They might be using the Japanese sense of guilt as a bargaining chip to coax greater concessions from Japan. Or they might be pretending that they are wary of Japanese defense policy even if they know that Japan has no intention to revert to militarism. If this is the case, ASEAN leaders are objectively formulating their policies toward Japan. This conjecture is hard to prove, however, because once these leaders admit to it, they can no longer use it as leverage.

The preceding analysis presented ambivalent results on the hypotheses on perceptions and foreign policy proposed in this chapter. Japan has succeeded in promoting its national interest, specifically its economic interest, with ASEAN nations thus far; it remains to be seen, however, whether Japan can continue to do so in the future. In the author's opinion, Japan cannot achieve its new goal of re-Asianization or *Datsuô Nyûa* unless it fully admits its responsibilities for wartime acts of aggression in Southeast Asia, settles wartime victims' individual compensations expeditiously, and thereby clears all the misgivings held by people in the region. In essence, the Japanese have to overcome their *sakoku* mentality and discard their contemptuous feelings toward ASEAN. Although Japan may have succeeded in the outward economic *kokusaika*—toward ASEAN and other parts of the world—it has yet to achieve the inward *kokusaika*—of the mind. It remains to be seen whether

Japanese policy makers will guide the nation to become more understanding of the different local cultures of Southeast Asia, remove the image of an economic animal, and make Japan a true leader in the region. It also remains to be seen whether ASEAN leaders will be able to overcome lingering resentment against Japan and help to establish a regional organization that would encompass both security and economic collaboration with Japan.

PART TWO

Japan's Sakoku *Policy: Case Studies*

CHAPTER 6

Japan's Immigration and Foreign Labor Policies

The way the Japanese treat foreigners most clearly illustrates the *sakoku* mentality. Japanese legislation embodies this attitude and treats *gaijin* as second-class citizens. No other legislation more vividly embodies the *sakoku* mentality than the immigration and labor laws. These laws are important gauges for measuring the progress of Japan's *kokusaika* because they are directly concerned with how Japanese society receives *gaijin*. This chapter focuses on Japan's immigration and labor policies and assesses the progress Japan has made in these areas as an integral part of its *kokusaika*.

Nationality *Sakoku*

Japanese nationality law is, first and foremost, a by-product of the *sakoku* mentality. Japan follows the "blood principle" for acquiring Japanese nationality as opposed to the "birthplace principle." Previous Japanese nationality law stipulated that only newborns whose fathers were Japanese could acquire Japanese nationality. Thus, children whose mothers were Japanese but whose fathers were foreigners could not obtain Japanese nationality. With pressure from foreign male residents who married Japanese women and their lawyers, the Ministry of Justice revised the law in 1989. Under the new version, newborns with Japanese fathers or mothers can assume Japanese nationality. The law provides, as an exception, the birthplace principle for newborns who are born in Japan but whose parents are unknown, to prevent abandoned newborns from becoming "non-nationalities." The increase in the number of Southeast Asian females engaged in prostitution in Japan has increased the number of such abandoned babies. According to 1994 statistics from the Ministry of Justice, out of about 1.3 million foreigners who registered as residents in Japan, 1,500 were without nationality. Among these, 138 were infants under age four, whereas there were only 74 such infants in 1992. The ministry estimates a considerably higher actual number, because foreign females working illegally in Japan do not report the birth of their newborns, fearing that the authorities might deport them.[1]

A recent Tokyo High Court ruling involving a non-nationality infant symbolized the Japanese legal system's *sakoku*. In 1991, a Southeast Asian woman, apparently a Filipino, bore a boy in Komoro city. Before she disappeared, she left the boy with an American missionary, who went to the Filipino embassy in Tokyo and applied for Filipino nationality for the boy. The application was rejected because the boy's mother was not proven to be a Filipino. When the missionary went to the Tokyo local government, the government registered the boy as a non-nationality foreigner. The minister filed suit, alleging that the government should give the boy Japanese nationality because his mother is unknown, not to mention his father (presumably Japanese). But the Tokyo High Court ruled in 1995 that the boy could not obtain Japanese nationality unless the plaintiff proved that the boy's mother was unknown. The plaintiff deplored the court's ruling, observing that while the Japanese government's words called for internationalization, its attitudes were exactly the opposite.[2]

The most notorious nationality issue, however, involves Korean residents in Japan. Even with the revised nationality law, children of Korean residents cannot naturally acquire Japanese nationality because both parents are resident aliens. If they want to obtain Japanese nationality, they have to undertake naturalization procedures, as do other foreigners. Thus, the Japanese nationality law still embodies the *sakoku* mentality.

Refugee *Sakoku*

The Japanese government had traditionally employed a highly restrictive policy toward the immigration of political refugees. It was not until 1982, under international pressure, that Japan enacted the Law Concerning Refugees to accept Indochinese refugees. The government increased the maximum number of Indochinese refugees who can live in Japan from 5,000 to 10,000 in 1985. Yet these refugees did not want to stay in Japan because of the stringent settlement procedures and the discriminatory atmosphere. They preferred instead to leave Japan and emigrate to other countries, such as Canada and the United States. Also, on many occasions, the Ministry of Justice deported Chinese refugees who sought asylum in Japan. As of May 31, 1995, only 10,015 refugees, 9,807 from Indochina (Cambodia, Laos, and Vietnam) and 208 from other countries, live in Japan. These statistics reflect Japan's unpopularity as a country to live in and the *sakoku* mentality.[3]

Labor *Sakoku:* Unskilled Labor

The Japanese employment system also adopts the *sakoku* mentality. For example, to protect Japanese job market, the Japanese immigration law totally bans foreigners from engaging in unskilled labor. According to statistics of the Ministry of Labor in May 1993, 87,996 foreigners had legal work permits, whereas 298,646 foreigners worked illegally in Japan. Along with the internationalization of economic activities, the number of illegal foreign workers from Third World countries entering Japan with tourist visas has increased. Japanese businesses, especially middle-sized companies, employ these illegal workers because they are willing to perform menial labor, which most Japanese are no longer willing to do, for lower wages. The Japanese call these undesirable jobs 3K—*kiken, kitsui, kitanai—rôdô* (dangerous, hard, and dirty labor).[4]

With the influx of illegal foreign workers, the Ministry of Justice revised the immigration law in 1989, renamed it the Law Concerning Immigration and Refugees, and tightened regulations on illegal unskilled labor. For instance, the revised law punishes those who employed foreigners for illegal work and those who acted as agents for such work, as committing the crime of aiding illegal employment. Nonetheless, during the early 1990s, the number of illegal foreign workers has risen sharply in the aftermath of the unprecedented boom of the "bubble economy" of the late 1980s.[5]

According to Ministry of Justice statistics, the number of illegal foreign workers almost tripled from 1990 to 1993. In July 1990, 106,497 foreigners worked illegally in Japan. The number rose to 298,646 in May 1993. By nationality, the number of illegal foreign workers in 1993 was highest from Thailand (18.1 percent), followed by South Korea (13.8 percent), China (12.2 percent), and the Philippines (12.2 percent). The four nations alone shared 56.4 percent of the illegal foreign worker population. By gender, 70.2 percent were male, whereas 29.8 percent were female. By work category, most males worked in construction (39.7 percent) and factories (31.6 percent). Among female workers, 36.5 percent were bar hostesses, and 18.1 percent were factory workers.[6]

The number of illegal foreign workers declined in 1994, reflecting the collapse of the bubble economy and Japan's subsequent economic recession. But the Ministry of Justice reported that there were as many as 294,000 illegal foreign workers in May 1994. Although the number was less than in 1993, problems involving illegal foreign workers have become more serious. For example, out of all the foreigners in Japan, including Chinese and Koreans, the percentage of illegal foreign workers who committed serious crimes rose from 39 percent in 1991 to 53 percent in 1993. As for drug-related crimes, the number doubled. Also, the number of AIDS patients has surged, because prostitutes from Southeast Asia have spread AIDS and borne children with the disease. Furthermore, the period that illegal foreign workers stay in Japan has lengthened. Indeed, the number of illegal foreign workers who have remained in Japan for more than three years increased from 21 percent in 1990 to 32 percent in 1994. The prolongation of their stay posed broader social problems, and some local governments were compelled to adopt welfare measures to improve the illegal foreign workers' housing, medical and employment benefits, and education.[7]

Despite the adverse impact of illegal foreign workers upon Japanese society, an increasing number of Japanese favor accepting and legalizing unskilled foreign labor. Shimada Haruo, a professor at Keio University, argues that foreign workers are playing important roles in the Japanese economy and society and that the government should give them equal rights. In fact, a public opinion poll conducted by the Ministry of Foreign Affairs revealed a surprisingly wide acceptance of foreign workers by the Japanese public.[8]

According to that poll, conducted in late 1990, 71.4 percent of respondents favored allowing the employment of unskilled foreign laborers, who are currently barred by law from taking jobs in Japan. They considered such legalization necessary because these foreigners provide cheap labor and do the "3K labor" spurned by the Japanese. Most respondents (56.5 percent), however, said that they would allow such employment only under certain conditions. In contrast, only 14.1 percent of respondents favored continuing the current policy of not allowing admission. The reasons for the opposition included "public order and morality may deteriorate," and "unemployment among Japanese may increase in times of economic slowdown."[9]

In addition, a majority of respondents (55 percent) considered illegal employment, while bad, as inevitable. Some explanations were because of "the domestic shortage of labor," and because it was "natural for people from less developed countries to come to Japan in search of higher wages." Many thought these workers would come to Japan anyway, regardless of tightening restrictions on immigration policy, and that it was a responsibility Japan had to assume as the most industrialized nation in Asia. Finally, 41 percent of the respondents favored cracking down only in cases involving organized crime, prostitution, and other serious crimes, whereas 34 percent favored deporting all violators in strict accordance with the law. Only 11 percent were opposed to any crackdown in business sectors where labor shortages exist, preferring to leave the situation as it is.[10]

The Japanese public's wide acceptance of foreign workers, although the poll was taken at the height of the economic boom, indicates the gap between their views of foreign labor and those of the government, which still practices *sakoku* toward unskilled labor. The government should respond to the public calls for labor *kaikoku* (opening a country), an integral part of Japan's *kokusaika*. Yet in reality, labor *sakoku* exists not only in unskilled labor but in professional work as well.

Professional Labor *Sakoku:*
The "Nationality Clause" in Public Services

The Japanese Ministry of Home Affairs oversees matters concerning local governments, called *ken* (prefecture), and its equivalents, *to, dô,* and *fu*. All the 47 local governments have the so-called nationality clause in their laws concerning the employment of public servants. The clause precludes those who do not possess Japanese nationality from taking examinations for entering public service. The Tokyo metropolitan government, or Tokyo-*to,* repealed the clause only in the case of specialist class public service in 1986, as an exceptional measure. However, no government has ever repealed the clause for generalist class public service until 1997, because the Ministry of Home Affairs advised local governments to strictly adhere to the nationality clause for generalist category public service.[11]

With the rising tide of *kokusaika,* however, an increasing number of local governments are considering repealing the nationality clause for the generalist class employment. A *Yomiuri Shimbun* poll in 1996 revealed that as many as 19 local governments—about 40 percent of the total of 47 governments—said that they were either considering or would like to consider a revision of the nationality clause in the direction of repealing it for general public service. Yet Kochi-*ken,* the first local government to have announced a plan to repeal the clause in 1995, ended up postponing the plan in 1996. It was not until 1997 that the Kochi-*ken* personnel committee finally decided to repeal the nationality clause. Although the committee said that it still adhered to the principle that the formation of the public will and the exercise of public power require Japanese nationality, it left the judgement of the principle to the discretion of the governor. Kanagawa-*ken* and Yokohama city also announced that they would repeal the nationality clause, with the exception of specific job categories in 1997. Other local governments are still reluctant to actually repeal the clause and are hoping that the Ministry of Home Affairs will give them new guidelines.[12]

Furthermore, even if some local governments repealed the nationality clause for specialist class employment in the late 1980s, they do not allow foreigners to assume managerial positions in public service. A case in point is the practice of the Tokyo metropolitan government. Tokyo-*to* hired a second generation South Korean national, Chong Hyang Kyun, in 1988 as the first non-Japanese public health nurse in the government after it had repealed the nationality clause for specialist class public services in 1986. She was promoted to a junior managerial *shunin* position in 1993. But the Tokyo-*to* rejected her application when she applied to take an examination for a managerial position in technological medical science in 1994. The Tokyo-*to*'s rejection is based on the Ministry of Home Affairs' view that the exercise of public power requires Japanese nationality. Fighting this unwritten rule, Chong filed suit against Tokyo-*to* in September 1994, alleging that no law actually mandates such a policy and that she was illegally disqualified from taking the examination.[13]

In May 1996, the Tokyo District Court rejected her suit, saying that the constitution does not guarantee foreign nationals to assume managerial positions in local governments. Chong appealed the case to the Tokyo High Court. In November 1997, the Tokyo High Court ruled unconstitutional the Tokyo-*to*'s refusal to let a foreign national take a test for a managerial position in the government. The presiding judge, however, rejected Chong's appeal that the court recognize she was qualified to take the test, saying the issue was irrelevant as the test has already been administered.[14]

Academic *Sakoku*

The Japanese government still enforces *sakoku* in academic institutions as well. In response to foreign pressure to internationalize Japanese academic institutions, the government enacted the Law Concerning Employing Foreign Instructors in 1982. The law stipulated the employment of *gaikokujin kyôshi* (foreign instructors) at Japanese national and public universities on terms identical to those for Japanese *kyôshi*. Nonetheless, it left the period of service of *gaikokujin kyôshi* to the discretion of each university. In response, most national institutions have opted for short-term contracts, which average about three years. As of 1994, twelve years after the enactment of the law, only four *gaikokujin kyôshi* have received non-term-limited contracts identical to those held by Japanese *kyôshi*. Although *gaikokujin kyôshi* now enjoy academic titles and the privilege of attending faculty meetings, they have little clout in academic management because they are dependent on the goodwill of Japanese colleagues for their contract renewals.[15]

As of December 21, 1992, 2,575 *gaikokujin kyôshi*, or 2 percent of the total full-time staffers, taught at Japanese universities. Yet the Monbushô (Ministry of Education) is trying to fire senior *gaikokujin kyôshi* because they are costly. The Monbushô's memorandum regarding the employment of *gaikokujin kyôshi*, dated December 21, 1992, indicates that it had requested universities to employ younger *gaikokujin kyôshi* in order to cut the budget, and that it was considering cutting the number of *gaikokujin kyôshi* altogether. Ivan Hall, who taught at Gakushûin University in Tokyo, argued that the Japanese universities' restrictions of *gaikokujin kyôshi* were system-wide and deliberate, and that an attempt to genuinely integrate foreign scholars with regular Japanese staff under the 1982 law had failed. After Hall and six *gaikokujin kyôshi* met with Walter Mondale, the U.S. ambassador to Japan, the U.S. embassy issued a press release, expressing its concerns about the *Monbushô's* protectionism.[16]

As a result of this exclusive employment system for instructors, Japanese students were not learning to overcome the *sakoku* mentality. Masao Kunihiro, a member of the House of Councillors from the Socialist Party (he had lost in the 1995 election for a second term), stated that despite the call for internationalization, the Japanese educational system had failed to bring greater diversity and pluralism to the country because educational institutions were insulated from the larger society. It had failed to encourage students "to go beyond the parochial and often exclusionistic barriers of sovereign nation states in their perception[s.]"[17] Instead of learning how to think, students engaged in rote memorization for the cut-throat competition to get into prestigious schools and then into the governing circles, and thus they become integrated into the closed system.

Legal *Sakoku*

In addition to the education system, the Japanese legal system also practices the *sakoku* approach. Until 1987, no foreign lawyers could practice in Japan, and only those Japanese who passed the national bar examinations were qualified to register in the Japan Bar Association. The examination is much more difficult than U.S. bar examinations. With pressure from the Reagan administration and other foreign governments, the Japanese parliament enacted the Law Concerning Special Measures on the Handling of Legal Business by Foreigners in 1987. This law did not change the status quo significantly; however; it only licensed foreign lawyers to offer counsel about the laws of their home countries while prohibiting them from advising on Japanese laws. These foreign lawyers are called *gaikokuhô jimu bengoshi* (legal clerk authorized to practice the laws of a foreign jurisdiction). For example, an American lawyer who was a licensed *gaikokuhô jimu bengoshi* and had worked at a Japanese international business law firm in Tokyo for six years, from 1989 to 1995, was only allowed to provide advice regarding the effect of U.S. laws on Japanese clients' transactions and on activities of clients' U.S. subsidiaries and branch offices. Indeed, as of August 23, 1995, only 76 foreign lawyers, or 0.6 percent of the Japanese lawyers, practiced in Japan. As a result, the entrenched Japanese legal system is faced with increasing demands for reciprocity from law practitioners abroad.[18]

Press *Sakoku*

Even the Japanese press system is not free from the *sakoku* mentality. Japanese news sources are controlled by about 400 *kisha kurabu* (press clubs) at governmental agencies, political parties, or big business groups. As of December 31, 1992, there were 762 *gaijin kisha* (foreign journalists), 612 male and 150 female. These *gaijin kisha* cannot get information about stories of direct interest to their countries until a member of a *kisha kurabu* gives it to them. Even when *gaijin kisha* are admitted to press conferences or briefings, they cannot ask questions or report actual stories about institutions that provide information. Japanese *kisha kurabu* also exert implicit pressure on journalists (both Japanese and foreign) by monopolizing information sources. In return for acquiring information, *kisha* feel obliged to report favorable news about the institutions that do provide information. This practice is known as *goshûgi genkô* (obligatory articles) in Japanese press circles. Once they write negative stories, their access to the news sources is often cut. Thus, *gaijin kisha* have to follow suit and ingratiate themselves with the Fourth Estate.[19] The Japanese media's practice of *sakoku* indicates that not only the public sector but also the private sector employs the *sakoku* approach.

Baseball *Sakoku*

The *sakoku* mentality even extends to sports. For instance, there are only three professional *gaijin sumô* wrestlers currently active and registered at the Japan Sumô Association. This is still understandable, however, since *sumô* is a traditional Japanese sport, or *kokugi*. But the Japanese professional baseball association applies a quota to *gaijin* players on Japanese baseball teams, even though Japan "imported" baseball from the United States in 1874. The current professional baseball agreement provides that there can be only three registered *gaijin* players on each team. Worse yet, the number of active registered *gaijin* players who can participate in a game is limited to only two. Although each team is free to rotate the *gaijin* players on their rosters, only two of the three registered *gaijin* players are eligible to play at any given time. The third player must remain on the bench (see Table 6.1).[20]

Despite the abundance of talented ballplayers in North America, the *sakoku* policies of Japanese baseball interests restrict these players from entering the leagues and raising the quality of play. Those who are recruited from abroad face difficulties as minorities in each team. Language and cultural barriers as well as the discriminatory atmosphere prevent them from assimilating with their teammates. For instance, Troy Neel, a former Oakland Athletics' designated hitter, took an offer from the Orix Blue Wave, the winner of the Pacific League in 1995, with a $1 million annual contract, a salary

Table 6.1   *Gaijin* Baseball Players in Japan's Major Leagues

Pacific League	No. of Players	Central League	No. of Players
Orix Blue Wave	2	Yakult Swallows	3
Lotte Orions	3	Hiroshima Toyo Carp	2
Seibu Lions	3	Yomiuri Giants	3
Nippon Ham Fighters	3	Yokohama Taiyo Whales	3
Daiei Hawks	3	Hanshin Tigers	2
Kintetsu Buffaloes	2	Chûnichi Dragons	3

Sources: "Central League Club Rosters for 1995" and "Pacific League Club Rosters for 1995," *Japan Times,* March 20, 1995.

he could never have earned in the United States. Yet Neel says, "I'm going nuts," because he is having difficulty assimilating to a different culture. He also realizes that the Japanese do not play the game the way he does; they do not play aggressively. Even Julio Franco, another transplant to Japan at the Orix, who is making close to $4 million a year, is unhappy. Franco complains that "it's a different style of baseball. It's a different country. It's really frustrating how many things you have to get used to. But I have to remember the amount of money I'm being paid and suck it up."[21]

In addition, there is a horse race *sakoku,* in which no foreign-bred horses are allowed to compete. These practices of Japan's professional sports associations indicate that the private sector employs the *sakoku* approach. The widespread use of such exclusionist measures illustrates how deeply rooted is the *sakoku* mentality.

As we have seen, the Japanese *sakoku* mentality is widespread and entrenched deeply in Japanese immigration and labor policies. Immigration *sakoku* discourages foreigners from assimilating into Japanese society by applying stringent measures that restrict their ability to acquire Japanese citizenship. Labor *sakoku* not only bans foreigners from engaging in unskilled labor but also limits them from engaging in professional labor, such as public service, college education, legal service, journalism, and even sports.

The Japanese decision-making structure, especially the bureaucracy, is entrenched not only with the *sakoku* mentality but also with the *kotonakare shugi.* This mentality discourages decision makers from initiating innovative legislation for immigration and labor policies. This invisible structure helps sustain immigration and labor *sakoku.*

CHAPTER SEVEN

Okinawa and the *Sakoku* Mentality

The *sakoku* mentality defines a cultural framework for Japanese policy making, and as Chapter 6 showed, Japanese policy toward foreign labor is another expression of it. This chapter examines the extent to which Japanese policy toward Okinawa and the manner in which the Japanese treat Okinawans reflect this mentality.

The Japanese have long discriminated against their minority groups. Aside from the "genuine" Japanese, there are two ethnic minority groups in Japan: the Ainu in Hokkaido, the northernmost part of Japan, with a population of 24,000; and the Ryukyuans in Okinawa, with a population of 1.28 million, or roughly one percent of the total Japanese population. Although the Ryukyuans are ethnically close to the Japanese, they have developed a distinct ethnicity and culture, owing to the subtropical climate and stronger influence from China. Ryukyuans tend to have darker skin and rounder eyes than the Japanese. To most Japanese, they look exotic.[1]

Because of the differences in ethnicity, language, culture, and lifestyle, Japanese have looked down on Ryukyuans and discriminated against them. This was the mind-set within which the Meiji government imposed an assimilation policy on the Ryukyuans, forcing them to adopt the Japanese language and lifestyle. This book defines the policy as *sakoku* policy in that it reflects the discriminatory aspect of the *sakoku* mentality. This chapter examines to what extent Japanese policy toward Okinawa constitutes *sakoku* policy.

History of Okinawa

The most southwestern prefecture of Japan and the only subtropical area in Japan, Okinawa lies in the southern half of the Ryukyu Archipelago, between Kyushu (the southernmost mainland of Japan) and Taiwan. Okinawa consists of 160 large and small islands, stretching 250 miles from north to south, and 625 miles from east to west. In its earlier history, the Ryukyu Kingdom was closer to China than to Japan. In the fourteenth century, the Ryukyu Kingdom established tributary relations with China. The Chinese imperial rulers allowed tributary nations to maintain their autonomy and did not interfere in their internal matters. Under such control, Ryukyu absorbed Chinese culture and benefited from trade with China.[2]

The picture changed in the fifteenth century, when the Ashikaga Shôgunate unilaterally declared the Ryukyu Kingdom a tributary of Japan in 1415. Subsequently, during the Korean expedition of 1592–1596, Hideyoshi Toyotomi demanded that Ryukyu ship supplies to Korea. The final blow came in the seventeenth century, when Ieyasu Tokugawa, who unified Japan in 1603, declared Ryukyu a domain of Iehisa Shimazu, the lord of Satsuma-*han* (province) in southern Kyushu, and gave him the title "Lord of the Southern Islands." Shimazu sent troops to Ryukyu to assert his control over the islands in 1609. Yet he allowed the Ryukyu Kingdom to maintain the appearance of independence and its tributary relationship with China. Thus, the Tokugawa Shôgunate ruled Ryukyu as a semi-colony for more than 250 years. George H. Kerr well documented the history of subjugation of Okinawa in his book *Okinawa: The History of an Island People.*[3]

Forced Assimilation Policy of the Meiji Government

Steve Rabson, associate professor of East Asian Studies at Brown University, indicates that the Meiji government's forced assimilation of Okinawa was a blatant case of *sakoku* policy. Following the *Haihan Chiken* (abolish *han*, place *ken*), which abolished the *han* (province) system of the shôgunate and replaced it with the *ken* (prefecture) system, the Meiji government abolished the Ryukyu Kingdom and designated it as Okinawa-*ken* in 1879, despite protests from the kingdom and from China. Security concerns over Okinawa, because of its vulnerable geographical location, prompted the Meiji government to pursue a rigorous assimilation policy. Commodore Perry's port call at Naha, Okinawa's capital, in 1853 on his way to Edo (Tokyo) was fresh in the minds of the Meiji leaders.[4]

With the implementation of the assimilation policy, Japanese prejudice against Okinawans grew. Public officials who were sent to Okinawa reported on the bizarre habits and traditions of Okinawa, which were unfamiliar to mainland Japanese. The Japanese ridiculed the indistinguishable accents of the Okinawan dialect. Although the government asserted that Okinawa was an integral part of the Japanese empire, "the strange ways and speech of the Okinawans set them apart as rustic, second-class cousins within the Japanese nation-family." The mainland treated Okinawa as its internal colony, thus establishing the minority status of the Okinawans.[5]

The most blatant forms of the forced assimilation were in the realm of language and education. The Meiji government imposed on Okinawans a language standardization program. Although the Ryukyu language is structurally similar to the Japanese, it is vastly different phonetically. The government also discouraged local traditions and launched a campaign to eradicate these "bad habits." Moreover, whereas the government imposed higher taxes on Okinawa than on mainland Japan, it prohibited Okinawa from sending representatives to the Imperial Diet for 22 years, until 1912. After the Japanese victory in the Sino-Japanese War of 1894, some Okinawans began to take up the Japanese language voluntarily. Yet the Japanese continued to treat them with prejudice and discrimination. Okinawans who moved to the mainland were denied employment and housing, which forced them to emigrate to Hawaii and other parts of North and South America.[6]

Prejudice in Japan's Imperial Army

As part of their voluntary assimilation efforts, Okinawans began to serve in the Imperial Army after the Sino-Japanese War of 1894. Conscripted Okinawans were not immune from Japanese prejudice, however. The Imperial Army mistook Okinawan soldiers who spoke their language for the enemy and accused them of being spies. Fifty years later, the Battle of Okinawa, the worst battle of the Pacific War, took the lives of more than 200,000 Okinawans. Teenage boys in the *bôeitai* (defense corps) fought tenaciously against the advancing U.S. forces, while high school girls in the *Himeyuri gakutotai* (student corps) became dedicated combat nurses.[7]

The Japanese army also told civilians that the Americans would kill them and ordered them to choose honorable deaths. Okinawans threw themselves from cliffs, thus committing mass suicide. The Japanese army shot those who did not do so, accusing them of being spies. Survivors of this tragedy testified that they were hiding in caves, suffering from thirst and hunger, but the army told them not to leave the caves because the American soldiers would kill them. A female survivor, now in her sixties, said that "my baby brother kept crying because my mother had no milk. So, my mother gave him her saliva and even urine. He got sick."[8] One cannot help questioning whether the Japanese army would have treated mainland Japanese like they did the Okinawans.

Post–World War II

After Japan regained independence in 1952, the United States continued to occupy Okinawa until 1972, when Okinawa reverted to Japan. Nevertheless, the plight of Okinawa did not change, for the Japanese government allowed the continued stationing of U.S. military forces in Okinawa, based on the U.S.-Japan Security Treaty; the reversion was, in essence, in name only. Okinawa's strategically important location for U.S. global strategy was a major factor for a continued U.S. presence in Okinawa. As a result, Okinawan residents were subjected to forcible land seizures, the denial of legal rights, and crimes committed by U.S. military personnel.

To improve the adverse situation, Okinawa governors, from Chobyo Yara, the first governor after the reversion (who passed away in February 1997 at age 94), to Masahide Ota, the incumbent, have repeatedly requested that the Japanese government treat Okinawa as *hondo nami* (equal to the mainland). Nonetheless, Tokyo used Okinawa's remoteness from the mainland as a pretext and neglected these pleas. Here the term *hondo nami* symbolizes the unequal relationship between mainland Japan and Okinawa. The core *(hondo)* sacrificed the periphery (Okinawa) for the sake of the defense of the former. Okinawa was considered expendable.

With the continued stationing of U.S. troops, the quality of life in Okinawa has deteriorated. For example, the U.S.-Japan Status of Forces Agreement (SOFA) allows American military pilots to fly lower than the legal lowest range in densely populated residential districts. The deafening noise of bombers flying over school districts disrupts children's learning and damages their health. Toxic wastes from U.S. bases seep into the soil and run off into the sea. Accidents in the air and on the roads caused by U.S. military personnel, both on duty and off duty, are innumerable. Until the rape of the 12-year-old schoolgirl in September 1995, few people on mainland Japan and the rest of the world had paid attention to these problems in Okinawa.[9]

Okinawa-*ken* is not the only prefecture where U.S. forces are stationed in Japan. Thirteen local governments on the mainland, including Tokyo-*to,* Hokkaido, and Kanagawa-*ken,* also have U.S. military bases. Yet two thirds of 47,000 U.S. military personnel stationed in Japan and three fourths of the total U.S. military facilities based in Japan are in Okinawa-*ken,* indicating an uneven distribution of American military bases in Japan. The unevenness becomes more evident when one considers that Okinawa prefecture comprises only 0.6 percent of Japan's entire territory.[10]

The ratio of 75 percent bases to 0.6 percent land illustrates that Okinawa-*ken* has carried a disproportionate burden of maintaining the U.S.-Japan military alliance. Within Okinawa prefecture, U.S. military bases occupy 11 percent of the entire prefectural land and as much as 20 percent of Okinawa Island, the prefecture's largest island. In addition, U.S. military authorities control 29 sea zones and 15 airspace areas around the prefecture. These facilities have occupied the prime location of the prefectural land and have restricted the residents' daily life, economic activities, and city planning.[11]

Post–Cold War Era

Even after the end of the Cold War, Okinawa's situation has basically remained the same. Whereas U.S. military forces completely withdrew from Subic Bay and Clark Air Force Base in the Philippines, U.S. bases in Okinawa underwent only a 15.6 percent reduction in land space during the 25 years since the reversion. Today, U.S. facilities occupy about 23,500 hectares (comprising 37 facilities) of Okinawa's land, or 75 percent of all U.S. bases in Japan. Accidents and crimes committed by U.S. military personnel have risen. From 1972 to 1996, 4,823 crimes were committed by U.S. military personnel in Okinawa. Although the number of crimes per year has been declining, with 342 instances in 1977 as the highest, grave crimes, such as the rape of a 12-year-old schoolgirl, still occur.[12]

Accidents emanating from the U.S. military bases also involved major tragedies for local residents. A U.S. military airplane crash into an elementary school, which killed 17 schoolchildren and injured an additional 121 people in 1959, has been the most tragic one so far in terms of the number of victims. Even after the 1995 rape incident, military-related accidents and crimes have continued to occur. Yet the Japanese government has ignored Okinawa's repeated requests to revise the SOFA in order to prevent base-related incidents and to reduce and realign the military installations.[13]

One cannot help questioning whether some of the tragic accidents and crimes could have been prevented had the Japanese government listened to the pleas of Okinawa. Instead, Tokyo acted in unison with the U.S. government and treated Okinawa as expendable. A recent series of events involving Okinawa demonstrate that Tokyo's perceptions of Okinawa are unchanged.

Delayed Notification of Firing
Depleted Uranium Bullets

In December 1996, a U.S. military plane jettisoned a bomb into the waters off Naha City, Okinawa's capital. After the incident, the U.S. and Japanese governments agreed to review the notification system of accidents caused by the U.S. military in Japan and release reports of these accidents. In preparing the reports, U.S. authorities found that U.S. Marine jets had fired 1,520 depleted uranium bullets at Torishima Range, 62.5 miles off Okinawa Island, from December 1995 to January 1996. Firing depleted uranium bullets is prohibited in Japan. The U.S. government informed the Japanese government of the incident on January 16, 1997, more than a year later. Then, Tokyo informed Okinawa on February 10, 1997—25 days after the former received the report. Although Prime Minister Hashimoto expressed strong displeasure at the U.S. government's delayed notification, Governor Ota expressed distrust toward the Japanese government of its delayed notification. Ota said, "We had repeatedly requested the Japanese government to improve the notification system in vain. I wonder if Tokyo is really serious about it."[14]

Had the Hashimoto cabinet been more sensitive to Okinawa's problems, it would have notified Governor Ota immediately. Since Prime Minister Hashimoto himself got angry at the U.S. government's delayed notification, he could have called Governor Ota immediately. Questioned about the delay, Administrative Vice-Foreign Minister Hayashi replied, "We wanted to notify Okinawa, after fully understanding and evaluating the significance of the accident."[15] Obviously, the Hashimoto cabinet was evaluating the accident's adverse effect on the renewal of the land expropriation law (examined later) rather than on the environment.[16] This case indicates that Tokyo still subordinates Okinawa to its relationship with Washington.

After the delayed notification, Governor Ota requested Prime Minster Hashimoto to release the "May 15 Memorandum," which stipulated the conditions for the use of U.S. bases on Okinawa, and he also requested a reduction in the U.S. military forces in Japan (which indicates that the Okinawan people are not trying to impose their problems on the mainland). The memorandum was written at the time of the reversion of Okinawa and has been kept secret. The Okinawan people do not know how the U.S. bases are being used in Okinawa. Hashimoto promised Ota that he would consider the release of the memorandum. Yet he said it is difficult to consult with the U.S. government on the reduction of forces because both the U.S. secretary of state and the secretary of defense are new and the ambassador to Japan has not been appointed.[17]

Revision of the Land Expropriation Law

The Japanese Diet passed a bill to revise the existing Law Concerning Special Measures on the Land Expropriation by the U.S. Military in April 1997. The law has allowed compulsory land expropriation for the 12 U.S. military facilities in Okinawa but the leases of the 3,000 privately owned plots of land were to expire on May 14, 1997. Thus, the Japanese government proposed a bill to revise the law to allow the continued use after the expiration. In February 1997, Governor Ota officially asked Prime Minister Hashimoto not to revise the law. But both houses of the Japanese Parliament passed the bill with a overwhelming majority, including opposition parties, such as the New Frontier Party and the Democratic Party of Japan. The Social Democratic Party of Japan, part of the ruling coalition, voted against the bill.[18]

During the deliberation, Prime Minster Hashimoto only said repeatedly that fulfilling Japan's responsibility for the U.S.-Japan Security Treaty is essential for Japan's national security. He did not explain why it is necessary for U.S. troops to be stationed in Okinawa. Some lawmakers criticized the revised law as being discriminatory against Okinawa and sarcastically called it the law concerning special measures "on Okinawa" (instead of "on land expropriation by the U.S. military"). Shigeru Itoh of the SPDJ questioned the rationale for revising the law at this time, given that the law has not been applied to the mainland since 1965.[19]

After the passage of the bill, Hashimoto said that the revision was a "minimally necessary measure" to fulfill Japan's responsibility for the U.S.-Japan Security Treaty and asked for the support for the revision. Thus, Hashimoto secured the gift of a trip to the United States in late April and saved face vis-à-vis President Clinton. In contrast, Governor Ota said, "I am speechless. What is Okinawa to Japan? I wanted to hear real discussions. It is unbearable for Okinawa. I had repeatedly requested the Japanese government not to enact a law that would be applied only to Okinawa and therefore discriminatory." Deputy Governor Masanori Yoshimoto said that "Okinawa administratively lost its leverage against Tokyo 100 percent. Okinawa people are concerned that the mainland will forget Okinawa problems again as it did after the reversion of 1972."[20]

Referring to the arrest of 21 people in observer seats at the Diet for making noise during deliberations on the bill, an Okinawa resident said, "The arrest symbolizes the attitude of the Japanese legislature toward Okinawa. The sense of discrimination has not disappeared." Another resident said, "Why cannot the Japanese understand our feeling? Why do the bases have to remain concentrated on Okinawa?"[21] Again, Okinawa's voice was not heard. The revision of the law was another example of *sakoku* policy toward Okinawa.

"Return" of U.S. Facilities in Okinawa

Subsequent to the 85,000 local residents' protest against U.S. military bases on Okinawa and more than half a million petitions demanding changes in the U.S.-Japan security arrangement in the first referendum in Okinawa in October 1995, President Clinton agreed to reduce U.S. military activities in Okinawa at the U.S.-Japan Summit in Tokyo in April 1996. The agreement included a 21 percent reduction in U.S. military facilities (5,002 hectares out of 23,500 hectares), the complete return of Marine Corps Air Station Futenma within five to seven years, and termination of live artillery exercises over Prefectural Highway 104. In return, Prime Minister Hashimoto consented to assist both financially and substantively with the reduction and realignment of the U.S. bases in Okinawa. Japanese concessions included the construction of a new heliport at an existing U.S. facility in Okinawa as a replacement of a runaway in Air Station Futenma, the relocation of artillery live-fire training to mainland Japan, and the transfer of KC-130 refueling aircraft to Marine Corps Air Station Iwakuni (Yamaguchi-*ken*).[22]

Yet the more important bargain the United States obtained from the summit was Japan's consent to strengthen bilateral defense cooperation in the Asia-Pacific region. The return of U.S. facilities are only symbolic, because they will be relocated either to other parts of Okinawa or to mainland Japan. Without losing anything in substance, the United States gained substantially. Yoshito Sengoku of the Democratic Party of Japan commented that the April 1996 Joint Declaration transformed, in the absence of the Japanese people's debate, the nature of the U.S.-Japan military alliance from Japan's defense to a stabilizing mechanism of the area surrounding Japan. These American concessions were, according to Mike Mochizuki, "part of a tacit bargain both to revitalize Japanese domestic support for the alliance and to redefine the relationship to cope better with regional security challenges."[23]

Relocation of Bases

Relocation of U.S. military bases in Okinawa caused serious internal political dissent in Okinawa. For example, Camp Schwab (Nago City) was designated as a possible site for an offshore heliport to replace a runway at Air Station Futenma. Residents of Nago City bitterly debated the pros and cons of accepting environmental impact studies for the construction of an offshore U.S. marine heliport. Those who opposed the research argued that permitting such research means acceptance of the construction. In contrast, those who are in favor argued that a U.S. base is a big corporation and will bring benefits to them. In turn, those who are opposed said, "We do not want development in exchange for the heliport. We should get out of the dependence on U.S. bases."[24] In the end, Nago City accepted the environmental studies.

The relocation of U.S. facilities to the mainland has also created political controversies in Japan. For instance, all relocation sites of the live artillery exercises over Prefectural Highway 104 encountered strong opposition from respective local residents. Even if the mainland's local governments understand the need to transfer U.S. camps to the mainland, they are reluctant to accept them in their backyards. In the end, Tokyo managed to make all five local governments accept the relocation, including Hijudai (Oita-*ken*) and Higashifuji (Shizuoka-*ken*). In addition, Iwakuni City (Yamaguchi-*ken*) agreed to the transfer of KC-130 refueling aircraft to the Marine Corps Air Station Iwakuni.[25]

Although the Japanese government has settled each case so far, relocation poses the basic question of whether it is a real solution to Okinawa's problems. Jun Shimokobe, the former vice-administrative minister of the National Land Agency, who acted as an intermediary between Prime Minister Hashimoto and Governor Ota, opposes the relocation to the mainland. He says that relocation is not a real solution and that the Okinawan people do not support the transfer of U.S. bases to the mainland.[26] This leads to the more fundamental question of whether it is necessary to maintain 100,000 troops in East Asia in the post–Cold War era.

Obsolescence of the "100,000 Troops in East Asia?"

In 1995, Joseph Nye, Jr., then the Clinton administration's assistant secretary of defense, put forth a U.S. strategy for East Asia of maintaining 100,000 forward-based troops for deterrence in the region. As Tsuneo Akaha points out, Northeast Asia remains a potentially dangerous region, given the political uncertainty in nuclear China and Russia and the tension on the Korean Peninsula. Nevertheless, several dramatic developments in the region challenge the rationale for the Pentagon's strategy in the post–Cold War era. Eight years after the collapse of the Soviet Union, Russia officially joined the Advanced Countries' Summit ("Group of Eight") in June 1997 in Denver, where President Boris Yeltsin said that the time had come to confirm whether Russia had stopped targeting nuclear missiles at Japan. As for China, its military threat is vastly exaggerated. The growth in China's defense spending in the 1990s corresponds to its economic growth. China's primary goal remains economic growth, and with the reversion of Hong Kong in July 1997, China will further strive to expand its free-market economy. Both Russia and China will have to restrain themselves militarily in order to join the World Trade Organization (WTO) and other international economic institutions. Meanwhile, North Korea is moribund, suffering from its worst food shortage ever and defections of high-ranking officials.[27]

Against this geopolitical background several Asian experts have pointed out the obsolescence of the Pentagon's strategy. Chalmers Johnson and E. B. Keehn question the continued U.S. commitment to maintain 100,000 troops in the East Asia-Pacific region years after the end of the Cold War both in terms of military and financial necessities. They argue that such a presence is militarily unnecessary, because the tension surrounding the Korean Peninsula has vastly diminished with the recognition of South Korea by

Russia and China. Financially, economic growth of the countries in the region does not justify the more than $35 billion annual expense on the part of the United States. These Asian countries now have economic resources enough to build and maintain their own defense forces. In particular, they contend that continued U.S. commitment to Japan's defense will prolong Japan's dependence on the United States and prevent it from becoming an ordinary country. For Japan, "contributing $5 billion to the upkeep of U.S. troops in Japan is a budgetary windfall," because financing its own defense would be far more costly. An important point to bear in mind here, according to Johnson, is that security and stability in East Asia owe much more to accelerated economic growth than to the presence of foreign troops.[28]

Mike Mochizuki and Michael O'Hanlon argue that the United States should withdraw the Marines stationed on Okinawa. They think that policy makers in the U.S. and Japanese governments underestimate Okinawa's protest against U.S. military bases in the wake of the rape of the 12-year-old schoolgirl and argue that this incident should be a wake-up call for rethinking the U.S.-Japan security alliance before even more serious damage is done. In their opinion, moving the Marines away from Okinawa, either to Hawaii or to the U.S. mainland, would not jeopardize the U.S. military presence in East Asia: 20,000 Marines on Okinawa are poorly suited to make rapid deployments to a disputed area such as the Korean Peninsula. The four U.S. amphibious ships at Sasebo Base (in Kyushu) can carry only 3,000 Marines. The rest of the Marines on Okinawa have to wait for ships from the U.S. coast.[29]

They also think that if U.S. strategy targets China, the Navy and Air Force are better equipped to provide high-performance bombers and submarines. Thus, they contend that the absence of the Marines in Okinawa would be adequately compensated by the continued presence of Army, Navy, and Air Force personnel in other parts of Japan and in South Korea. They conclude that the U.S. commitment to maintain 100,000 personnel in East Asia is wrong and that U.S. strategy should be more flexible, based on the quality rather than the quantity of its military capabilities and duties.[30]

In a similar vein, James E. Auer, who served as special assistant for Japan in the Office of the Secretary of Defense, says that what is important is not the maintenance of U.S. military power but the maintenance of defense capabilities; thus, it is possible to reduce and realign U.S. military bases in Japan insofar as U.S. defense capabilities are maintained. In essence, according to Tsuneo Akaha, "neither Washington nor Tokyo has been able to articulate a compelling post–Cold War strategic vision on the bilateral security relations."[31] The Pentagon should reexamine the rationale for its strategy in East Asia and whether it is truly necessary to station 47,000 troops in Japan (and 31,000 in Okinawa) for deterrence purposes.

Consensus for Reducing the Burden on Okinawa

Belatedly, a quarter century after the reversion of Okinawa, there is a solid consensus among Japanese military experts on the need to reduce the disproportionate burden the Okinawan people have carried for more than half a century. The schoolgirl rape incident and the first referendum on U.S. bases in 1995 triggered the awareness of such a need among Japanese military experts. Even pro-U.S.-Japan Security Treaty specialists argue for the need to reduce the burden on Okinawa.

Masamichi Inoki, the former president of Japan's Defense Academy and a strong supporter of the U.S.-Japan military alliance, says that the Japanese government has ignored the plight of Okinawa and has not shown any sincerity for the integration and reduction of U.S. forces in Okinawa. Inoki says that Governor Ota realizes that an alliance with the United States is the only way for Japan's survival, and he has no intention of jeopardizing the alliance: Ota courageously and rightfully represented the Okinawan people and protested the insincerity of the mainland government and its people. In short, the governor's defiance against Tokyo was directed more at Tokyo's inability to equalize the burden of the security treaty in terms of base siting than at the bilateral security treaty per se.[32]

Yukio Okamoto, a former diplomat-turned-consultant, says that given the present situation in East Asia, to call for the reduction of U.S. military forces in Japan is irresponsible. Nonetheless, Okamoto, who was appointed as adviser to Prime Minister Hashimoto in charge of Okinawa, sees the need for reducing the burden on Okinawa and thinks that the only way to solve the Okinawa base problem is to relocate bases to the mainland. In his opinion, relocation stirred protest by local residents because the Japanese have little awareness of the need for national defense. The government has not concerned itself with teaching the Japanese a sense of national defense. Okamoto concludes that the Japanese government has to take up the relocation to mainland seriously in order to pay the *tsuke* (debt) of 25 years.[33]

Development of Perpetual Dependence

The revision of the Law Concerning Special Measures on the Land Expropriation of the U.S. Bases Stationed in Japan permitted the continual stationing of the U.S. military on Okinawa. This perpetuates the dependency of Okinawa's economy on the U.S. bases, creating a vicious cycle. The U.S. military's occupation of the prime land areas of Okinawa has prevented Okinawa from developing a self-sustainable economy. Because of the unique condition in which Okinawa was forced to accommodate the U.S. military, the Japanese government appropriated substantial subsidies for Okinawa's economic development. For 25 years since the reversion, Tokyo has spent a total of ¥4.96 trillion (about $43 billion) for Okinawa, on public projects such as road construction, sewerage, and port facilities. The Japanese government also pays ¥170 billion (about $1.5 billion) rent to Okinawan landlords annually, as part of its *omoiyari yosan* (host-nation budget) for the U.S. military in Japan.[34]

As a result, Okinawa's revenue has largely depended on the 3K—*kôkyô jigyô, kankô,* and *kichi kanren-shûnyû* (public projects, tourism, and base-related revenues). Ironically, the government's generous economic aid deepened the dependency of Okinawa on its fiscal policy and further prevented Okinawa's self-sufficiency. At present, Okinawa's per capita income is ¥2.12 million ($18,400), or 71.2 percent of that of the average Japanese. This is the lowest among the 47 local governments in Japan. Okinawa's unemployment rate is 6.5 percent—twice as high as the national average.[35]

Toward the Wholesome Development of Okinawa

Okinawa desperately needs new plans to develop a self-sustainable economy. Yet Okinawa is not suited for a manufacturing industry for two reasons. First, an industrial development that destroys the fragile ecosystem of the coral-based ocean environment is not a viable solution. Second, according to Jiro Ushio, a president of *Keizai Dôyûkai* (the Japanese Association of Corporate Executives), one of the four major business groups in Japan, Okinawa is not an attractive market from an investor's perspective. As a manufacturing market, the cost of production is lower than that of the mainland but it is higher than that of neighboring countries, such as Taiwan and the Philippines. It does not take much longer for Japanese on the mainland to fly to Manila than to fly to Okinawa. As a consumer market, Okinawa, with a 1.3 million population, is less attractive than Singapore and Hong Kong. Thus, Ushio concludes that Okinawa's strongest advantage is still tourism. He further suggests that Tokyo help boost Okinawa's tourism, which has been faltering with the increased number of Japanese traveling abroad: The Japanese government can give tax incentives, such as a partial tax exemption for hotel construction in Okinawa, and a reduction in airfares to Okinawa to the equivalent fares to Guam and Saipan.[36]

Thus, new economic development programs should aim for a nonmanufacturing sector that is compatible with the preservation of the fauna and flora surrounding the coral reefs. Cognizant of the need for such development, Okinawa prefecture announced the "Cosmopolitan City Okinawa Formation Concept" in May 1997. The plan promotes self-sufficient economic development for the twenty-first century through the promotion of industry and culture. In essence, by taking advantage of the unique natural environment and geographic location, the cosmopolitan concept is designed to make Okinawa a hub of international cultural, economic, and educational exchanges in the Asia-Pacific region. Okinawa has already established liaison offices with Taiwan and Hong Kong to promote trade and investment. Okinawa has also put forth a basic plan to establish the Okinawa International Peace Research Institute and is planning to create the Okinawa North-South International Center, modeled after the East-West Center in Hawaii.[37]

Along this line, creating more training centers for people from developing countries is a highly viable idea. The existing Okinawa International Center of Japan International Cooperation Agency (JICA) has trained 300 trainees from developing countries every year. Foreign trainees, who would be uncomfortable in Tokyo and other major cities on the mainland, feel at home in Okinawa, because its climate is similar to that of their homeland and the Okinawan people are more open. Governor Ota regards the training center as "the sole pride of Okinawa."[38]

To realize these plans, Okinawa has asked Tokyo to create the Okinawa Special Economic Zone, where corporations can enjoy special preferential tax treatments, and visitors from Taiwan, Hong Kong, and South Korea require no visas. Yet the Japanese government has objected to this idea because it would lead to "one country, two systems." (Special preferential taxes are not given in mainland Japan, and visa are required for Asian visitors to mainland Japan.) So far, the only measures to help Okinawa's development that Tokyo has agreed to implement are (1) the reduction of airfares between Okinawa and the mainland; and (2) training projects for the Okinawan people, such as simultaneous interpretation training and overseas dispatch training.[39]

Haruo Shimada, a professor at Keio University, says that the Japanese government has applied the "one country, two systems" concept to Okinawa in security policy for more than a quarter century (by imposing the uneven burden of the maintenance of the U.S.-Japan Security Treaty on Okinawa and by expropriating private land for the U.S. military bases). Therefore, it is unreasonable for Tokyo to reject the "one country two systems" approach to Okinawa in economic policy.[40]

May 15, 1997 marked the twenty-fifth anniversary of the reversion of Okinawa from the United States to Japan. Yet there were no celebrations in Okinawa to mark the reversion.[41] This was because the memory of subjugation endures in Okinawa, and the Japanese government still considers Okinawa expendable. "People on the mainland have little interest in Okinawa despite the fact that Okinawa is part of Japan," reported one junior high school student in Nagoya City as part of a social science class assignment entitled

"Okinawa 25 Years after the Reversion."[42] This comment by a young mainland Japanese poignantly describes the subjugation of Okinawa. The plight of Okinawa has not changed even a decade after the end of the Cold War, because the Japanese government has subordinated Okinawa's interest, to that of the U.S. government, which is still immersed in the Cold War mentality.

The issues of developing a self-sustainable economy for Okinawa is not a local issue but a national one. Tokyo should take up the issue more seriously and help create a comprehensive and wholesome economy for Okinawa. With the twenty-fifth anniversary of the reversion of Okinawa having passed, the Japanese government should start repaying the burden on Okinawa in earnest. This is a "minimally necessary measure" (to quote Prime Minister Hashimoto when he justified the revision of the land expropriation law) to remedy the sacrifices people in Okinawa made for the sake of Japan's national security for more than half a century.

CHAPTER EIGHT

Kome Kaikoku: Japan's Rice Market Liberalization

Earlier chapters noted that Japan is currently undertaking the third *kaikoku.* With chronic trade imbalances with Japan, the U.S. and European governments have pressured Japan to open its markets and liberalize its trade practices. The first landmark of the third *kaikoku* was the U.S.-Japan Structural Impediments Initiative (SII) Talks that began in 1986 under the Reagan administration. During the SII negotiations, Japan agreed to change its corporate systems and business practices that formed structural impediments to Japanese trade liberalization. Yet changing systems that have been built on the old traditions and customs in Japanese society takes a long time, and the SII has proved to be another political Band-Aid. The Clinton Administration's U.S.-Japan economic framework talks succeeded the SII in 1993, and the United States continues to pressure Japan to open its markets and change its systems. As a result, Japan made a historic decision to open its rice market at the Uruguay Round of the GATT talks in December 1993. *Kome kaikoku* (opening of the rice market) became the second landmark of the third *kaikoku.*

Kome Kaikoku: Background

Since its admission to the GATT in 1955, Japan has substantially removed barriers on agricultural imports. For instance, only 12 items were under agricultural import restrictions for Japan in April 1993, as opposed to 16 for the United States, and 64 for the European Community.[1] Yet Japanese resistance to liberalizing imports of certain agricultural products has occasionally marred GATT negotiations. The prime examples were beef and oranges during the Tokyo Round of the GATT negotiations in the 1970s. In the end, Japan succumbed to foreign pressure. In the case of beef, Japan began to import beef from the United States, Australia, and New Zealand in 1988 under the mandatory import quota, although Japan had 1,700,000 tons of domestic beef inventory. Japan liberalized its beef market in 1991 with a 70 percent tariff on imported beef. Since then, Japan has reduced the tariff rate to 60 percent in 1992 and to 50 percent in 1993.[2]

Japan continued to refuse to open its rice market because of its food self-sufficiency policy. Rice is the Japanese staple food and considered sacrosanct. After the much-publicized liberalization of beef and oranges, rice became the focal point of Japanese liberalization of agricultural imports. As in the case of beef and oranges, Japan eventually succumbed to foreign pressure and agreed to open its rice market in 1993. This is referred to as a "partial" *kome kaikoku* in Japan. It is partial because Japan gained a six-year moratorium on the tariffication (liberalization) of imported rice in exchange for accepting an import quota during the moratorium. This move illustrated the depth of Japanese resistance to rice liberalization. Although partial in nature, the decision to import rice on a regular basis was significant as the first step toward a full liberalization of the Japanese rice market.

U.S. Rice Millers Association

The dispute over the opening of the Japanese rice market can be seen as a tug-of-war between Japan and the United States. Japan has adopted a protectionist rice policy under the pretext of securing the Japanese staple food. Japanese rice agriculture has been heavily subsidized, and the price of rice has been controlled by the Food Agency. Japan grows short-grain rice called *Japonica,* whereas in Southeast Asia and elsewhere in the world, mostly long-grain rice, or *Indica,* is produced. The Japanese like the glutinous and sticky *Japonica* rice and dislike the *Indica* rice, which is not sticky. For Japanese tastes, the stickier the rice, the better.[3]

The United States, mainly California, produces short-grain *Japonica,* the same species as produced in Japan. U.S. rice producers lobbied their government to export their rice to Japan. In the face of mounting pressure to open its rice market, the Japanese Diet, ruled by the Liberal Democratic Party (LDP), passed a resolution to strengthen its food self-sufficiency policy in 1980. A high-ranking LDP official said that rice was a "religious" matter for Japan.[4] He meant that rice is so sacred that it is untouchable. The holiness of rice originated in ancient Japanese culture, when the imperial family used rice in Shinto rituals. In fact, rice was so valuable that only members of the aristocracy, wealthy merchants, and warriors could afford to eat it regularly, whereas the majority of the populace, including rice-producing farmers themselves, ate rice only for special occasions. It was not until the early decades of this century that rice became the staple grain in the

Japanese diet. Thus, rice had mystical significance in Japanese culture, and even today, Japanese consider it "more than just food."[5]

Frustrated by Japan's persistent refusals to open its rice market, the U.S. Rice Millers Association (USRMA) raised the issue with the U.S. trade representatives (USTR) in 1986. The USRMA requested the USTR to apply the Super 301 Article to Japan in 1986. The article empowers the U.S. president to take retaliatory actions against countries that practice unfair trade. The USTR rejected the request. Meanwhile, the Uruguay Round of the GATT started in 1986, and Japan agreed to discuss the liberalization of rice imports at the international forum in 1987. The USRMA requested the USTR for the second time to apply the Super 301 Article to Japan in 1988. The USTR again rejected the request, however, because Japan had agreed to discuss the issue at the Uruguay Round. In response to the USRMA's move, the Japanese Diet passed a resolution to oppose the liberalization of rice imports.

An episode involving the display of American rice in Japan illustrated the extent of the hysteria on the part of the Japanese government against the liberalization of rice imports. In March 1991, Japan hosted the International Food Fair in Chiba City, adjacent to Tokyo. It was designed to promote Japanese food imports, such as tropical fruits, cheese, and wine. At the U.S. exhibition booth, U.S. rice producers displayed cooked rice as samples. Officials of the Japanese Ministry of Agriculture, Forestry, and Fisheries (Agricultural Ministry) who came to inspect the exhibition demanded that the cooked rice be withdrawn. According to the regulations, only raw rice samples were allowed to be displayed. Japanese consumers did not have a chance to taste American rice at the exhibition. At any rate, with the Japanese agreement to discuss liberalization of rice imports at the Uruguay Round, the issue shifted from the bilateral level to the international level.

GATT's Uruguay Round

Since 1987, the Uruguay Round of the GATT has become a major vehicle to lobby for opening the Japanese rice market, and the United States has intensified its drive. In 1989, the United States proposed the "tariffication of non-tariff barriers" of agricultural products. It specifically targeted Japan and rice. It suggested that Japan impose a 700 percent tariff on imported rice to protect domestic rice. The rate was based on the price of Japanese rice, which cost seven times as much as the international market price.

In 1990, the Uruguay Round's Agricultural Committee Chair presented a reconciliation plan to establish a 5 percent "minimum access" import quota on agricultural imports in lieu of tariffication. This formula would impose a mandatory import quota equivalent to 5 percent of the total domestic consumption. In 1991, GATT director-general Arthur Dunkel laid out the final draft agreement of the Uruguay Round (Dunkel Proposal). It called for "comprehensive tariffication of all agricultural imports" and "3–5 percent minimum access import quotas." The Dunkel Proposal was in line with the U.S. tariffication of non-tariff barriers proposal of 1989. The Dunkel Proposal would allow Japan to impose a 700–800 percent tariff on imported rice. The Dunkel Proposal sent a clear signal that the liberalization of Japanese rice imports was inevitable. It was a U.S. victory. Nonetheless, Japan refused to accept the inevitable. In 1992, Japan submitted to the GATT its agricultural market liberalization program's "country tables" that listed which countries Japan would import agricultural products from. The section for rice was left blank. It demonstrated the Japanese nonacceptance of the Dunkel Proposal. In July 1993, at the Tokyo Summit meeting of the Group of Seven (Canada, England, France, Germany, Italy, Japan, the United States, and the European Union), member nations agreed to conclude the Uruguay Round by the end of 1993.[6]

Japanese Domestic Politics

Meanwhile, a new Japanese cabinet was formed in August 1993. The Hosokawa cabinet, led by Morihiro Hosokawa of the Japan New Party (JNP), was born out of Japanese anger over the 38-year-long monopoly of power and corrupt money politics of the LDP. The coalition cabinet was made up of seven political parties and a political group, such as the Renewal Party, the JNP, and the SDPJ. These disparate parties were united by anti-LDP platforms and promises for political reforms. After this unprecedented development in Japanese politics at home, the Uruguay Round negotiations were expected to proceed more smoothly, given that refusal to open the rice market was the pillar of LDP policy. Yet immediately after the creation of the new cabinet, the ruling parties of the coalition cabinet reached an agreement to refuse the tariffication of rice of the Dunkel Proposal. That even the new cabinet, whose raison d'être was being anti-LDP, opposed the opening of the rice market demonstrated the intrinsic parochialism and anachronistic attitude of Japanese politicians and the political strength of rice farming in Japan. In this case, the SDPJ strongly opposed the tariffication of rice. The problem with the Hosokawa cabinet was the fragile nature of the coalition, which included the SDPJ on the left as well as three new splinters of the LDP (the Renewal Party, the JNP, and the NPS) on the right of center. Prime Minister Hosokawa himself seemed not to oppose the tariffication of rice. He was quoted as saying, "I myself am flexible but some party within the coalition [opposes it]."[7] He had to concede to the

SDPJ, the largest party in his coalition cabinet. (Hosokawa's JNP had 35 seats, whereas the SDPJ had 70 in the House of Representatives.) This time, the SDPJ, unprecedentedly teamed up with the LDP, its long-time enemy now in the opposition, opposed the tariffication of rice. Another unexpected turn of events further illustrated that Japanese rice policy was anachronistic and parochial.

Reigai in the Summer of 1993

An event that unfolded in the fall of 1993 was unexpected. Japan was hit by the *reigai* (damage to agricultural products due to cold weather) in the summer of 1993. It was an unusually rainy and cold summer. Sunshine is critical for agriculture. In September, it became clear that the rice production would be the lowest in 60 years. Rice production in 1934 was 7,630,000 tons, whereas that of 1993, was estimated to be 7,932,000 tons. The Japanese consume nearly ten million tons of rice a year. This means that in the fall of 1993, production was more than two million tons low, or a 20 percent shortfall. The rice production index dropped as low as 75 out of 100 on October 15, 1993. The 75-point value denotes "considerably bad," and the index was expected to decrease further. To cope with the shortage of rice, the government decided to import rice on an emergency basis from Thailand and the United States. It decided on 200,000 tons of emergency rice imports to be shipped by December 1993. The rice was earmarked only for use by rice-processing manufacturers to make *mochi* (rice cake) or *sembei* (rice crackers), popular snacks in Japan. In November 1993, the government decided to import an additional 900,000 tons of rice to be shipped by March 1994. This time, it was finally earmarked for use as *shushoku* (main dish) by consumers.[8]

Japan was obliged to import rice and lost face. Had Japan liberalized its rice market earlier, it could have avoided losing face. It seemed as if heaven had sent a message to Japan. Nonetheless, the government did not learn a lesson from this event. The imports were deliberately called "emergency rice imports." Moreover, Japanese politicians continued to strive to gain further concessions in the Uruguay Round. The ensuing desperate attempts to prevent the tariffication of rice revealed that the Hosokawa cabinet was no different from that of the LDP. In September 1993, Japan and the United States reached a tentative agreement to postpone the tariffication of rice in exchange for raising the minimum access import quota. In November 1993, Agricultural Minister Hata requested that Dunkel exclude exceptional items from the comprehensive tariffication program. Later in the same month, Japan had the United States officially agree to postpone tariffication of rice for six years in exchange for raising the minimum access import quota to

4–8 percent. Some might consider this a Japanese victory; it was a Japanese loss in the long run, however. This trade-off indicated the Japanese resolve to refuse the inevitable and the refusal to achieve its prime goals of the third *kaikoku:* liberalization and *kokusaika.*

Hosokawa's Decision to Open the Rice Market

On December 14, 1993, Prime Minister Morihiro Hosokawa announced that his government had decided to accept a compromise plan drafted by Germain Denis, chair of the Market Access Negotiation Group of the Uruguay Round. The GATT compromise proposal was in line with the U.S.-Japan agreement, allowing Japan a six-year grace period for tariffication of rice. This agreement was to take effect in 1995. Japan promised to import 4 percent of its total domestic consumption (400,000 tons) of rice in 1995 and increase the volume to 8 percent (800,000 tons) by 2000. While the Japanese government hailed the agreement as *kome kaikoku,* it was only a partial opening. The six-year moratorium on tariffication of rice was a Japanese strategy to buy time. In the announcement, Prime Minister Hosokawa apologized for making the decision, saying, "I am heartbroken. I am very sorry for failing to preserve the food self-sufficiency policy."[9] Prime Minister Hosokawa's statement reflects the lingering resistance to *kome kaikoku* in Japan.

In preparation for the eventual opening of the market, the Murayama cabinet enacted a new food law in November 1995. The new law repealed the food control law that had lasted more than fifty years. The original food control law, enacted in 1942, stipulated the rationing of rice to deal with the food shortage during World War II. Under the law, the Food Agency bought rice from farmers and distributed it to wholesalers, thereby regulating the price of rice. Despite the law's revisions in 1952 and 1982, the government's direct control system remained unchanged. In contrast, the new law liberalized the production, distribution, and sale of rice from the "control in principle" system to the "free in principle" system. For instance, the new law relaxed the distribution of rice by replacing the strict authorization system (that only authorized dealers can distribute rice in the authorized districts) with a simple registry system. Also, the new law approved the so-called *jiyū-mai* (rice freely distributed in the black market), which had been unofficially distributed outside the government's route since 1969, and allowed farmers to sell rice directly to wholesalers, retailers, and consumers insofar as they registered with the Food Agency in advance. Yet Japanese consumers have not enjoyed the full benefits of the liberalization; the price of rice is still several times higher than in the U.S. market.[10]

The Japanese public has ambivalent views on the partial opening of the rice market. An opinion poll indicated that more than three quarters of respondents accepted the decision; it also revealed their deep concern over *kome kaikoku,* however.

Yomiuri Public Opinion Poll on *Kome Kaikoku*

On December 18, 1993, four days after Prime Minister Hosokawa's decision to accept the GATT compromise plan, the *Yomiuri Shimbun* conducted a public opinion poll on the issue. The poll results showed that 77 percent of the total 3,000 respondents approved of the decision. But only 8.4 percent definitely approved of it, because they thought that "the decision was reasonable," whereas 68.6 percent reluctantly approved of it, thinking that "the decision was unavoidable"; 19.4 percent of the respondents were against the decision. In comparison, in a similar poll conducted in October 1993, 62 percent supported the idea of the rice market opening, whereas 30 percent opposed the idea. The two polls cannot be compared directly, because questions in each were slightly different. (The December 1993 poll asked specifically about the prime minister's decision, whereas the October 1993 poll asked about the idea of opening the rice market in general.) But the 15 percent increase in the number supporting the opening and the 10.6% decrease in the number opposing it seemed to indicate that the public has come to accept the rice market opening as a fact of life.[11]

With regard to the question of whether Japan should allow the tariffication of rice, 34.6 percent of respondents in the December 1993 poll thought that Japan should do so; 43.3 percent thought that Japan should not. The result indicates the ambivalence on the part of the public. The respondents were split between those who thought that tariffication of rice would have a positive impact and those who thought that it would have a negative impact. For instance, 62.3 percent of the respondents thought that tariffication of rice would make the supply of rice stable, whereas 30.8 percent thought that it would make the supply unstable. Also, 50.8 percent of respondents thought that tariffication of rice would improve domestic rice agriculture, whereas 43.6 percent thought that it would ruin rice agriculture. A large number of respondents were also concerned with the safety of foreign rice: 72.2 percent thought that the safety of imported rice would become a major issue, and 30.8 percent thought that it would not be a major issue. In addition, 69.5 percent of respondents thought that the tariffication of rice would not significantly change the price of rice; only 26.4 percent thought that it would reduce the price.[12] The ambivalence and concern about the rice market opening on the part of the public were understandable, given the unreasonable rice policy the government had maintained under the food self-sufficiency policy.

Food Self-Sufficiency Policy

The Japanese government under the LDP encouraged farmers to produce rice to ensure food self-sufficiency. The policy was in principle understandable, given that rice is the Japanese staple and that the Japanese suffered from a severe shortage of food during World War II. As Japan rapidly recovered economically and adopted a Western style of living, however, some critics began to question the rationale of the policy. First, the food self-sufficiency policy is no longer tenable in the electric age, when everything depends on oil and the Japanese cannot eat rice without importing oil. Today, everybody uses electric rice cookers, and having rice self-sufficiency is not enough to secure the survival of the Japanese people. A good analogy is the "paper panic" during the first oil crisis in 1973. With the oil embargo imposed by the Organization of Petroleum Exporting Countries (OPEC), the price of crude oil quadrupled. As a result, the price of toilet paper and tissue paper went sky high in Japan. One roll of toilet paper cost one dollar. One tissue paper carton cost seven dollars. Retailers withheld inventories of these commodities in anticipation of further price increases. Japanese consumers panicked. The bottom line is that the Japanese energy supply is 99 percent dependent on imports. The lesson of the paper panic was that Japan cannot produce anything unless the supply of oil is secured. The food self-sufficiency policy misses the point. The Japanese cannot eat rice without importing oil.[13]

Second, the food self-sufficiency policy is untenable in the increasingly interdependent international economy. Japan has benefited enormously from the international free trade system by exporting its manufactured goods. As a foremost beneficiary of the system, Japan should reciprocate by opening its markets to imports. But Japanese markets are still closed to many foreign goods. This is the major point of foreign accusations about unfair Japanese trade practices. In this situation, opening the Japanese rice market would alleviate American anger directed at Japan. A $120 million import of American rice in itself would not offset a $60 billion U.S. trade deficit with Japan; it has great symbolic meaning, however, and would placate American frustration over chronic U.S. trade deficits with Japan.[14]

Another problem with the food self-sufficiency policy is a new phenomenon called *kome banare* (detachment from rice). Japanese tastes have changed over the past few generations. The older generation eats rice at every meal. In contrast, the younger generation has grown up with bread and milk, and does not have as strong an attachment to rice as the older generation. Recent statistics endorse this. According to the food supply and demand tables issued by the Agricultural Ministry, annual Japanese rice consumption per capita for the fiscal year (FY) 1992 was a record low of 69.7 kilograms—a 0.2-kilogram decrease from the previous year. It is less than 60 percent of the 118.3 kilograms of FY 1962.[15] The policy to secure self-sufficiency in rice as *the* Japanese staple food is becoming obsolete.

Japanese Consumers:
Foremost Victims of Rice *Sakoku*

Japanese consumers are the chief victims of the government's rice policy. The price of rice is regulated by the Food Agency's food control system. The price of rice has been kept high to protect farmers. A 20-pound bag of rice that costs $70 in Japan sells for only $10 in the United States.[16] Japanese consumers were obliged to buy expensive rice but acquiesced. Theoretically, Japanese consumers would benefit greatly from liberalization of the rice market. In the case of liberalization of the beef market, the tariff rate decreased from 70 percent in 1992 to 50 percent in 1993, and the domestic self-sufficiency rate (the ratio of domestic production to the total inventory) dropped to less than 50 percent in 1992. With the excessive inventory and intense price competition, the price of beef decreased. For instance, the price of Australian *baraniku* (loose meat) went down from ¥142 (per 100 grams) in January 1993 to ¥111 in September 1993. As for the liberalization of rice, however, the price did not decrease, as in the case of beef; because the government decided to maintain the food control system during the partial opening of the rice market (1995–2001) and impose a 700–800 percent tariff on imported rice.[17]

It should be noted that the United States is the world's second-largest exporter of rice. Ironically, the United States is referred to as *Beikoku* (Rice Country) in Japan, according to the conventional way of phonetically converting foreign words into the Japanese language. The United States is in fact a "rice country." It produced 7,700,000 tons of rice, whereas Japan produced 7,932,000 tons in 1993. The quality of California rice is as good as that of prime grade Japanese domestic rice and costs only one seventh of the latter's price. Arkansas, President Clinton's home state, also produces quality *Japonica* rice.[18] It makes more sense for Japanese consumers to buy much cheaper rice from the rice country than to buy expensive domestic rice. When California rice went on sale in Tokyo in late February 1994 as a result of the emergency rice imports, the rice was sold out in two hours.[19] Refusing to liberalize rice would only penalize Japanese consumers. Why, then, did the government stick to the obsolete food control system? It did so because the policy was a convenient way for LDP politicians to ensure farmers' votes.

LDP's *Hyôden* Politics

Farmers have traditionally constituted the backbone of the LDP power base. It is generally recognized that farmers are powerful lobbyists in Japan, holding strong voting power referred to as *hyôden* (votes of rice paddy fields). Owing to the disproportionate representation in the Japanese election system, a farmer's vote in a rural constituency counted more than five times as much as a white collar worker's vote in an urban district. In exchange for votes, LDP politicians rewarded rice farmers with agricultural subsidies. The food control system protected the vested interest of Japanese politicians who depended on *hyôden* and that of farmers who benefited from the subsidies.[20] A closer examination of Japanese rice policy, however, defies the conventional notion of collusion of power between LDP politicians and farmers. It reveals that farmers are instead victims of the inconsistent rice policy of the government.

Japanese Farmers:
Invisible Victims of the Rice Policy

Japanese rice policy is characterized by inconsistency. First, the government ordered farmers to grow rice and gave them incentives in the form of agricultural subsidies. The policy worked well, and by the early 1970s, Japan had a large surplus of rice. Japanese do not like to eat old rice. How to consume *komai* (rice stored for more than a year) and *kokomai* (rice stored for more than two years) became a serious issue. Eventually, they were used for public school lunches, as a substitute for bread. In 1971, the LDP adopted a new policy, *gentan* (reduction of rice fields). This time, the government ordered rice farmers to abandon rice cultivation and to produce fruits and vegetables instead. The policy was euphemistically called "production adjustments" or "activation of rice fields." Rice farmers adopted the *gentan* policy and made herculean efforts to make necessary adjustments.

In the summer of 1993, Japan was hit by a record *reigai,* and rice production drastically decreased. Rice inventory decreased from 1,080,000 tons (FY 1991) to 260,000 tons (FY 1992). The Japanese consume nearly ten million tons of rice a year. Faced with the substantial shortage, the government adopted a new policy of *fukuden* (return to rice fields). Now the government wants farmers to go back to rice production. Originally, the *gentan* (reduction of rice fields) goal for FY 1992 was 830,000 hectares; the government reduced the goal by 130,000 hectares to 700,000 hectares, however, and encouraged *fukuden.* The government further reduced the *gentan* goal for FY 1993 to 673,000 hectares.[21]

Yomiuri Opinion Poll of Japanese Farmers

An opinion poll of Japanese farmers revealed their reluctance to join *fukuden*. According to a poll of 230 farmers conducted in December 1993 by the *Yomiuri Shimbun,* more than half of the respondents did not support the *fukuden* policy. Eighty-one respondents said that they approved of *fukuden,* whereas 109 respondents said that they disapproved. Twenty-six respondents were undecided. In comparison to a similar poll conducted two months earlier, the number of undecided farmers increased by 10 from 26 to 36. They were undecided because they distrusted the government. They thought that "the intention of the government [on *fukuden*] is unclear," that "the government's *gentan* policy is inconsistent," and that "the future of Japanese agriculture is uncertain." Those who disapproved of *fukuden* thought that "now that the government has decided to import rice [the government abandoned farmers], there is no reason to obey the government" and that "it is hard to go along with the *fukuden* policy, given the uncertainty as to how long this policy would last." Those who approved of *fukuden* considered that "it is better to have larger rice fields since it is more cost-efficient [insofar as I grow rice.]"[22]

The results reflected farmers' overall distrust of the government. They were first encouraged to produce rice, then discouraged from producing rice, and then were again encouraged to produce rice. They could no longer entrust their livelihood to the vagaries of government. Bureaucrats do not understand how hard it is to actually carry out *fukuden.* It is difficult to return the once-converted dry fields back to muddy paddy fields, called *suiden.* The aging agricultural population makes *fukuden* more difficult; one in three of those who are engaged in agriculture belongs to the "aged population bracket," that is, they are more than 65 years old. Another factor is that "converted products" such as vegetables and fruits yield a higher return. With the coming of *kome kaikoku,* farmers cannot help questioning what will happen if cheap foreign rice dominates the rice market. Will the government ask farmers to reduce rice fields again? Rice farmers are the ones who will be hit hardest by *kome kaikoku.* The *fukuden* drive in the age of *kome kaikoku* is at best short-sighted. In essence, Japanese farmers are invisible victims of the inconsistent rice policy of the government.[23]

An agricultural economist even argued that the government was responsible for last year's record poor harvest. First, the government allowed inefficient and unskilled rice agriculture under the food management system. Under that system, even so-called Sunday farmers, who had nonagricultural full-time occupations, were qualified to receive government subsidies to grow rice. Second, the distribution system of rice was centrally controlled by the Nôkyô (agricultural cooperatives) and the government. This allowed the existence of a black market in rice. This dual distribution system of rice made farmers grow prime-grade "brand" rice that was not resistant to bad weather but sold for high prices on the black market. The cold summer was not the sole cause of the reduction in rice production.[24]

Private Advisory Groups

Some private organizations anticipated the arrival of *kome kaikoku* and advised the government to open the rice market as early as 1987. In January 1987, the *Keidanren* (Federation of Economic Organizations, a big-business group in Japan), published a report stating that it would be difficult for Japan to refuse the import liberalization of rice. In February 1993, 113 university professors and intellectuals issued an urgent appeal to the Miyazawa Cabinet to accept the tariffication of foreign rice. The appeal stated that tariffication was essential for a successful conclusion of the Uruguay Round. The appeal was originally put forward by the Emergency Policy Council of the Japan Forum on International Relations, a private advisory group chaired by Saburo Okita, the former foreign minister in the Ohira Cabinet in the 1970s. The council set up the National Committee to Call for Tariffication of Importation of Rice, to urge Japan to open its rice market.[25]

In hindsight, had the government taken the advice of these private advisory groups seriously and put it into practice, Japan would not have had to make the embarrassing decision to make emergency rice imports in the fall of 1993. It was yet another example of nonaction that characterizes Japanese foreign policy making. As previous chapters showed, the nature of postwar Japanese foreign policy is reactive, being "too little and too late." It was even referred to as *gaikô onchi* (diplomatic tone-deaf). The pattern has been repeated. In the age of an interdependent international economy, liberalization of rice imports is international common sense, but Japan failed to perceive this. Japanese resistance to opening the rice market until faced with such an embarrassing event once again revealed the lack of international common sense, a manifestation of *sakoku* mentality on the part of Japanese decision makers.

Prime Minister Hosokawa's decision to accept the partial *kome kaikoku* symbolized the end of the reign of LDP politics, which lasted for 38 years, from 1955 to 1993. The LDP's rice policy, regarding rice as sacrosanct, epitomized Japanese anachronistic and parochial thinking. However, there are still concerns for *kome kaikoku*. The partial *kome kaikoku* should not be overestimated because it is not a full liberalization. It should be recalled that Japan extracted the concession of a six-year moratorium on the tariffication of rice. It remains to be seen whether tariffication will actually take place in

2001. Moreover, the Hosokawa cabinet, whose platforms were based on reform and change, reaffirmed the LDP's policy of food self-sufficiency at its inception. The Hosokawa government's mismanagement in distributing the emergency imported rice raises doubts for the future. The government first tried to sell imported rice in the form of blend sale (mixing both imported and domestic rice in the same bag). The problem was that the two different kinds of rice cannot be cooked together. The government tried to impose the blend sale to ensure that consumers buy foreign rice. The government did not understand that the best way to encourage consumers to buy foreign rice was to liberalize the market. The government could not do so because it would jeopardize the centrally controlled pricing system for domestic rice. At any rate, the idea of blend sale was so absurd that it caused a furor among consumers.[26] Later, the government accepted, along with the blend sale, the "set sale" (a package sale of domestic and imported rice by using separate bags for each rice). In this way, consumers were still obliged to buy foreign rice, as in the case of the blend sale.

Meanwhile, the price of domestic rice went up (a 20-pound bag of prime brand rice costs more than $200) and caused the current *kome sôdô* (rice panic), reminiscent of the "paper panic" during the first oil crisis. It was even worse, since the issue at stake was a staple food. Theft of rice and hours-long queuing up to buy rice became a common scene. The *kome sôdô* at home had adverse international ramifications. The international price of rice increased from $220 per ton in June 1993 to $285 at the end of October 1993, when Japan decided to make emergency rice imports. The price jumped to $420 in February 1994 in the midst of the *kome sôdô*. This put rice importers among developing countries in a position of hardship.[27]

Japanese consumers have not enjoyed the full benefits of the partial liberalization of the rice market, because the price of rice is still several times higher than that in the U.S. market. They are so used to the old government-controlled system that they still buy expensive rice from the old authorized dealers, instead of buying cheaper *jiyûmai* ("freely distributed rice"), now called *keikakugai ryûtsûmai* ("rice distributed outside the plan") directly from farmers. Under these circumstances, it remains to be seen whether the partial *kome kaikoku* is the beginning of a successful liberalization of the rice market, as an integral part of the third Japanese *kaikoku*, or the end of such an attempt.

CHAPTER NINE

The Japanese Constitution and Military *Kokusaikôken*

Changing Japanese Attitudes toward the Constitution

This chapter examines the issue of constitutional revision. As was discussed earlier, Article 9 of the Japanese peace constitution is deeply related to postwar pacifism in Japan, one of the attributes of the *sakoku* mentality. The latter has been a major obstacle to expanding Japan's role in the maintenance of international peace and security, including Japan's participation in UNPKO. In fact, much of the domestic debate on Japan's international security role has revolved around the constitutional revision. This chapter analyzes what seems to be a changing attitude among Japanese toward the constitution.

On April 3, 1993, the *Yomiuri Shimbun* released the results of a public opinion poll it conducted on March 19–20, 1993. The poll indicated that 50.4 percent of Japanese thought that "it is better to revise the Japanese constitution," whereas 33.0 percent thought that "it is better not to revise it." The result is quite significant in that this was the *first* time support for the idea of revising the constitution had gained the majority since the *Yomiuri Shimbun* began the poll on the constitution in 1981. Figures for those who favored the amendment changed from 27.8 percent (1981), 22.6 percent (1986), 33.3 percent (1991), to 50.4 percent (1993). The numbers that did not favor the amendment changed from 43.9 percent (1981), 56.6 percent (1986), 51.1 percent (1991), to 33.0 percent (1993).[1]

The *Yomiuri Shimbun* is Japan's largest private newspaper within the center-right spectrum of ideology. The company supports constitutional revision. It even came up with a draft revision of the constitution and proposed it to the government in 1995. As will be examined later, another poll by a public broadcasting station showed somewhat different results from that of

Yomiuri. Nevertheless, as Japan's largest daily, it is useful to analyze the *Yomiuri* poll to grasp changing Japanese attitudes.

The issue of constitutional revision originates in the fact that the postwar Japanese constitution was drafted by the U.S. occupation forces, better known as the SCAP. To prevent the recurrence of Japanese militarism, SCAP put an article in the new Japanese constitution, under which Japan renounced war as the right of the nation and as a means of settling international disputes. (This was Article 9, known as the "war-renouncing article"). The article says:

> Aspiring sincerely to an international peace based on justice and order, the Japanese people forever renounces war as a sovereign right of the nation and the threat or use of force as means of settling international disputes.
>
> In order to accomplish the aim of the preceding paragraph, land, sea, and air forces, as well as other war potential, will never be maintained. The right of belligerency of the state will not be recognized.[2]

Under the U.S. occupation, Japan had no choice but to accept the new constitution. General MacArthur erroneously implanted pacifism in the Japanese mind by calling for Japan "to be the Switzerland of the Orient." MacArthur misled the Japanese by stressing Switzerland's neutrality without noting that Switzerland was heavily armed and enforced compulsory conscription. Japanese became oblivious to the fact that armament is the essential prerequisite for neutrality. MacArthur's indoctrination worked, since the Japanese felt guilty about their militarism during World War II. Thus, a solid consensus was created for the peace constitution, which was regarded as a "holy book" by the Japanese.

The ruling Liberal Democratic Party (LDP) adopted a tight pro-U.S. policy and de facto supported the constitution. Certain leaders within the conservative LDP, such as Prime Minister Ichiro Hatoyama, had tried to revise the constitution, calling for a "spontaneous constitution." However, the LDP acquiesced in retaining the U.S.-imposed constitution because there was solid support for the peace constitution among the people. Strong opposition from the left was also a major obstacle to constitutional revision. The Japan Socialist Party (JSP) strongly supported the constitution because of its pacifist beliefs. Conversely, the nationalists on the right demanded constitutional revision. They were resentful that the United States had drafted the Japanese constitution and "imposed" it on Japan. They demanded revision of the "war-renouncing article" that denies a nation's inalienable right to arm itself.

With the outbreak of the Korean War, the United States saw the need to rearm Japan due to its strategic position. *Keisatsu Yobitai* (the National

Police Reserves) were created in 1950 under the directive of SCAP, and Japan became an important base for the United Nations Forces (UNF) in the war. Thus, the Korean War transformed Japan from a former enemy into an important ally for the United States. It was an irony that the United States totally demobilized Japan in 1945 and began rearming Japan as early as 1950. Again, Japan had no say at that time toward the United States. The U.S.-Japan Mutual Security Aid (MSA) Agreement was signed in 1954 to oblige Japan to build up its defense in exchange for U.S. military and economic aid. Also, the *Keisatsu Yobitai* was reorganized as *Hoantai* (National Security Force) in 1952, and then as the *Jieitai* (National Self-Defense Forces, or SDF) in 1954.

The creation of the SDF caused intense controversy with regard to the constitutionality of such armed forces. It should be recalled that Article 9 renounces war as a sovereign right of the nation and relinquishes armed forces. Those on the left argued that the SDF was unconstitutional and demanded its disbandment. Those on the right demanded constitutional revision to make the SDF unequivocally constitutional. In the end, the ruling LDP settled the controversy by a flexible interpretation of the constitution: It was interpreted in such a way that Article 9 does not preclude a nation's inalienable right to defend itself and thereby allows the possession of self-defense forces. This settlement became known as the "expanded interpretation" of the constitution. Also, the SDF was interpreted to be used solely for self-defense, prohibiting overseas operations; this was the establishment of the so-called solely defense principle.

The problem with the expanded interpretation is that the constitutionality of the SDF was left ambiguous to this day. It was a product of compromise on the part of the ruling LDP, caught between opposition to the constitutional revision at home and U.S. pressure to create de facto armed forces. The debate on the revision intensified in the latter half of the 1980s in response to the U.S. demand for Japan to expand its role in the U.S.-Japan alliance in the post–Cold War era. Yet the government still distinguishes the "individual self-defense right" and the "collective self-defense right" and maintains that exercising the former is constitutional, whereas exercising the latter is unconstitutional. Thus, Japan can engage its SDF only in individual defense for its self-defense but cannot participate in the collective defense for its allies when Japan itself is not under attack. This limitation is a major hurdle for the new guidelines for U.S.-Japan defense cooperation.[3]

A constitutional revision requires not only two thirds of both houses of Japan's Parliament but also the majority of the people (Article 96). The *Yomiuri Shimbun* hailed the result of the poll, having reached a threshold of the majority (50.4 percent), as a "watershed" in the postwar constitutional debate.[4]

1993 *Yomiuri* Poll on the Constitution

The *Yomiuri* poll on the constitution was conducted among 3,000 Japanese constituents, with 2,042 responding (68 percent turnout). Of the respondents, 47 percent were men and 53 percent women; 15 percent were in their twenties; 16 percent, in their thirties; 24 percent, in their forties; 21 percent, in their fifties; 15 percent, in their sixties; and 9 percent, in their seventies and above. The poll revealed the following results: More men (55.0 percent) favored the idea of revising the constitution than women (46.3 percent). There was a solid correlation between the result and age. The younger generation favored revision more than the older generation; age twenties (52.5 percent), age thirties (56.2 percent), age forties (51.1 percent), age fifties (49.4 percent), and above (42.2 percent). As to the correlation with the party affiliation, 52.0 percent of the LDP supporters, 57.1 percent of the *Kômeitô* (Clean Government Party) supporters, and 60.7 percent of the newly created Japan New Party supporters, and even 49.3 percent of the SDPJ supporters favored the revision. The result for the SDPJ supporters is quite surprising, given that the party staunchly supports the constitution. Considering the political and psychological taboos imposed by Article 9, the change in Japanese perceptions of constitutional revision is significant.[5]

The respondents who favored the idea to revise the constitution (50.4 percent) cited the following reasons for supporting the idea (the poll offered multiple choices; respondents could choose as many reasons as they deemed appropriate):

Reason #1: "The current constitution cannot deal with new issues such as *kokusaikôken* (international contributions)" (55.7 percent);

Reason #2: "To solve constitutional issues by a mere interpretation or implementation, instead of revising the constitution, creates confusion" (31.1 percent);

Reason #3: "The constitution was imposed by the United States" (23.1 percent);

Reason #4: "There are too many claims for rights while obligations are ignored" (20.8 percent);

Reason #5: "The revision is necessary to claim the nation's right to self-defense and to enable Japan to have a real army" (6.2 percent).[6]

It is important to note that the top reason for support for revision was "the need for *kokusaikôken*" (55.7 percent) rather than "that it was imposed by the United States" (23.1 percent). More than twice the number of respondents thought that revision was necessary for the sake of *kokusaikôken* rather than for the sake of a constitution of Japan's own choosing. It should be recalled that in the past the major advocacy for revision came from nationalists, including Yasuhiro Nakasone, who had argued that Japan should have a constitution of its own choosing and an army of its own as a sovereign nation. Currently, support for constitutional revision comes not only from the traditional pro-revision group on the right but also from a broader spectrum of ideology. Nakasone, after he became the prime minister in 1982, advocated the revision more for the sake of strengthening Japan's relationship with the United States than from a solely nationalistic standpoint. This means that the rationale for revision has changed from "reversion to the prewar time" (nationalism) to a call for establishing Japan's future role in international society. This result clearly reflects the changing Japanese attitudes toward Japan's *kokusaikôken* and its role in international security.[7]

In contrast, those who opposed the idea of revision (33.0 percent) cited the following reasons for not supporting the idea of revising the constitution (multiple choices):

Reason #1: "The peace constitution is a source of pride for Japan in the world" (42.3 percent);

Reason #2: "The constitution has already been established among the people" (39.0 percent);

Reason #3: "The revision could open a road to militarism" (28.8 percent);

Reason #4: "The constitution guarantees fundamental human rights and democracy" (25.1 percent);

Reason #5: "The constitution can be flexibly interpreted and implemented according to changes with time" (18.4 percent).[8]

Another question in the 1993 *Yomiuri* poll asked what the Japanese thought of the constitutional debate. The poll indicated that Japanese who favored the constitutional debate outnumbered by more than three times those who did not favor it. The poll revealed that 66.8 percent of the respondents thought that the increased debate on the constitution among the political parties and intellectuals was desirable, whereas only 19.1 percent thought that debate was undesirable. Among those who favored the constitutional debate (66.8 percent), 57.2 percent favored the debate because "it is necessary to review the constitution according to changes in situations at home and abroad." Further, 25.7 percent favored it because "it is necessary to remove the confusion and inconsistency in the way the constitution has been interpreted," whereas 13.4 percent did so because "it is wrong to regard revising the constitution as taboo." In comparison, among those who did not favor the constitutional debate (19.1 percent), 39.4 percent did not favor it because "it is too political (being motivated by politicians' political agenda)"; 31.2 percent because "the current constitution is functioning adequately"; and 27.1 percent because "the debate is superficial and without substance."[9]

This result is significant given that debate on the constitution had been considered taboo by the majority of the Japanese. The SCAP personnel who drafted the constitution thought that the Japanese would revise it after Japan regained independence in 1952. Contrary to American expectations, the Japanese took the U.S.-drafted constitution seriously and came to regard it as sacrosanct. The "sacred" nature was so firmly attached to the constitution that it was taboo even to debate it.

The question is what changed the Japanese attitude toward the constitution. Three major factors caused the change: first, Japan's growing economic position in the world; second, the Japanese realization of its emerging role in international society; and third, the U.S. pressure on Japan to increase its "burden sharing" in the maintenance of international security.

Cause One: Japan's Growing Global Position

Japan's growing position in the world is the underlying cause for the changing attitudes toward the constitution. At the end of World War II, Japan was totally devastated and its gross national product (GNP) was marginal, on the order of $1 billion in 1946. With U.S. military and economic aid, Japan's economy has recovered rapidly, and its GNP exceeded $100 billion in 1966. Japan's economy continued to grow, and its GNP reached $1 trillion in 1978. Japan achieved its economic miracle and became the number two economic power in the world. Japan caught up with the United States in 1989 in terms of per capita national income, with Japan's per capita national income reaching $23,033, whereas that of the United States was $20,852.[10] Meanwhile, Japan continues to catch up with the United States in terms of GNP. In 1993, Japan's GNP hovered around $3.3 trillion, whereas the U.S. GNP was about $5.5 trillion. An American political scientist stated that a "cross-over point" would occur when Japan's GNP would surpass that of the United States.[11] Yet it is important to take these statistical comparisons with a grain of salt; figures on the Japanese performance fluctuated with the exchange rate and were significantly inflated due to appreciation of the yen from ¥360 in 1971 to ¥110 in 1993.

With this breathtaking economic growth, the Japanese have gradually come to realize the importance of Japan's world position. This is all the more so with the decline and disintegration of the Soviet Union in the late 1980s.

Cause Two: Japan's Emerging Role in International Society

As a corollary to Japan's growing position in the world, Japanese have become more aware of Japan's need to contribute to international society: with power come responsibilities. The issue of *kokusaikôken,* to what extent and how Japan should contribute to the international community, has become a subject of hot debate among politicians, scholars, and opinion leaders, whose influence on the formation of public opinion is considerable.

At the end of World War II, Japan did not have to assume any world responsibility. In fact, Japan was deprived of such responsibility by the former Allied powers. As Japan's economic power grew, Japan contributed in overseas economic development and financial assistance to the Third World, but it maintained a low-key posture in the maintenance of international security. It should be recalled that Article 9 of the Japanese constitution renounces the use of force and that the SDF can only be used for self-defense. Now, with its status as the number two economic power in the world, Japan can no longer be indifferent to the maintenance of international security.

The need for Japan's contribution to international security grew stronger after the collapse of the Soviet Union. The Bush administration tried to establish a new international order in the aftermath of the Cold War. With the escalation of civil wars in the former Soviet Union, Yugoslavia, Cambodia, Somalia, and elsewhere, the need for UNPKO had never been greater. Japan could not participate in the UNPKO, however, due to the constitutional limitation of Article 9.

Thus, debate on *kokusaikôken,* specifically on participation in the UNPKO, revolved around constitutional revision. The debate on the constitution with regard to *kokusaikôken* can be categorized into four schools of thought. The first is the "anti-revision /anti-military *kokusaikôken.*" Its proponents advocate abiding by the "peace constitution" and support only nonmilitary *kokusaikôken.* This position represents the left and the left-of-center of the spectrum of ideology, such as the SDPJ and its splinters. The second school is "anti-revision/pro-military *kokusaikôken.*" It can also be defined as pro-constitution internationalist. This group stresses the prime importance of *kokusaikôken* and maintains that *kokusaikôken* should encompass a military contribution. To enable this, the group recognizes the need for constitutional revision; nevertheless, it deems the flexible interpretation of the constitution to be sufficient, given the practical difficulties of such revision. This position has been taken by a wide spectrum of ideologies from the center to the right-of-center, including former prime minister Kiichi Miyazawa, since it prescribes a realistic approach to meet the increasing need for military *kokusaikôken* in the constitutional impasse.[12]

The third school is the "pro-revision/pro-military *kokusaikôken.*" It is "anti-constitution internationalist," as opposed to the second group's "pro-constitution internationalism." It calls for constitutional revision to make military *kokusaikôken* unequivocally constitutional so as to eliminate the ambiguities of Article 9. This position has been taken by the right and by some on the right-of-center, including former prime minister Nakasone. The fourth school is the "pro-revision/anti-military *kokusaikôken.*" This school represents a minority nationalist group on the extreme right. Among the four schools of thought, although the second has been the mainstream so far, the third school is likely to gain more support among the Japanese in the near future.[13]

As the result of a number of televised debates, the Japanese public has begun to reconsider Japan's role in international peace and security. A public opinion poll conducted by the Prime Minister's Office showed increasing support for the *kokusaikôken* in the maintenance of international peace. The poll taken in October 1990 indicated that 34.7 percent of the respondents thought that "contributions to international peace such as the mediation of regional conflicts" was an important aspect of Japan's role in international society. It ranked second behind the "contribution to global environmental issues and other global issues" (43.2 percent). The number that support the "contributions to international peace" increased by 2.8 percent to 37.5 percent the following year.[14]

However, the realization of Japan's growing role in military *kokusaikôken* on the part of some opinion leaders was not a sufficient factor to change the deep-rooted pacifism and isolationist attitude of the Japanese general public.

Cause Three: U.S. pressure to Increase Japan's "Burden Sharing" in the Maintenance of International Security

The decisive force to change the Japanese stance on the *kokusaikôken* had to come from abroad; this was pressure from the U.S., or *gaiatsu.* It has played a crucial role in the formation of Japan's foreign policy since Japan was opened to the modern world in 1853. As was noted in Chapter 1, Japan opened its door twice in the past, and is currently embarking on the third opening. All three *kaikoku* involve *gaiatsu* from the United States. *Gaiatsu* epitomizes the pattern of postwar Japan's foreign policy.

In Japan's third *kaikoku,* the ultimate objectives can be summarized as *kokusaika* (internationalization) and *kokusaikôken* (international contributions), especially the military *kokusaikôken.* As Japan's economic power grew and relative U.S. economic power began to decline, the benevolent protector of Japan was no longer willing to accept the expense of defending Japan. As U.S. frustration grew, the "free-rider" accusation became louder in the 1980s. Also, the collapse of the Soviet empire decreased the compelling need of the United States to protect Japan. As a result, the U.S. demand for Japan to increase its burden sharing in the maintenance of international security, based on the so-called equal partnership concept, intensified. In response,

Japan has gradually and substantially increased its burden sharing. For example, since 1978 Japan has significantly increased its contribution to the costs for Japanese employees working for the U.S. forces stationed in Japan. According to the U.S.-Japan agreement on the status of forces (SOFA), expenses of local employees working for the U.S. forces in Japan are to be covered by the United States. In response to U.S. requests, however, Japan began to cover the benefit-related costs in 1978 and salary-related costs as well in 1987, as part of Japan's defense budget. The amount has steadily increased to $1.3 billion in 1991, which accounted for approximately 4 percent of Japan's total defense budget for that year. This annual appropriation out of the defense budget toward expenses of U.S. forces is called the *omoiyari-yosan,* which literally means "sympathy budget" but is called "host-nation support" in English. The amount has continued to increase to $2.4 billion in 1997, about 5.5 percent of the total $43.7 billion Japanese defense budget for that year.[15]

Growing U.S. pressure on Japan has not been limited to the maintenance of international security. Along with the free-rider accusation, the charge of closed Japanese economic structures and market systems intensified, reflecting the relative decline of the U.S. economy. In response to mounting attacks on Japan's allegedly unfair trade practices, Japan has grudgingly opened its markets to foreign goods, corporations, and financial institutions. The Structural Impediments Initiative between the United States and Japan was the prime example.

In this context the United States requested that Japan share the burden of the Persian Gulf War. Japan's contribution to that war became a showcase for Japan's third *kaikoku* in terms of military *kokusaikôken.*

Japanese Debate on the Gulf War

As a result of U.S. pressure on Japan to contribute to the Multinational Forces (MNF) engaged in the Gulf War, the issue of *kokusaikôken* became a focal point of the debate among Japanese opinion leaders. There were three major positions on the Japanese involvement in the Gulf War. The first school argued for visible *kokusaikôken,* including military contributions. It proposed that Japan should contribute because the country is a world economic power and also because it depends largely on the Middle East for its oil supply. This position was taken by those on the right and the right of center. It was highly critical of the Japanese government's grudging and belated response to the situation. The second school favored peaceful means and took a long-term perspective. It regarded substantial financial contributions as the optimal means of Japan's *kokusaikôken.* It also proposed the creation of a world network for *kokusaikôken,* such as transportation services by the SDF. Its constituents were largely in the center. The third school took a pacifist standpoint by recourse to Article 9 of the constitution. It opposed military contributions and was even cautious on financial contributions to the MNF. It was against war in principle and was also critical of the U.S. air raids against Iraq (criticizing them as having been premature). This represented the views of the left of center and the left.[16]

Japan's *Kokusaikôken* to the Gulf War

In the fall of 1990, after the Iraqi invasion of Kuwait, the Kaifu cabinet agreed to contribute $2 billion to the Multinational Forces (MNF). In January 1991, with the outbreak of the Gulf War, U.S. treasury secretary Nicholas Brady asked Japan to pay $9 billion as an additional financial contribution to the MNF. Brady asked Japan to cover 20 percent of the total war cost that was estimated at $45 billion. (The daily war cost was estimated to be $500 million and the war was expected to last for three months.) The Kaifu cabinet was not initially willing to pay such a huge amount (Japan's national defense budget was about $30 billion), yet in the end it agreed to pay the $9 billion. It meant about $84 per Japanese citizen. To accomplish this, the government decided to levy contingent special taxes on corporations, gasoline, and cigarettes. Furthermore, the United States asked Japan to pay an additional $500 million to compensate for the loss in value of the dollar due to the depreciation of yen (from ¥130 to ¥137) at the end of the war. The Kaifu cabinet agreed to pay the $500 million, as well. This financial contribution was extraordinary, considering that the annual Japanese contribution to overseas development aid (ODA) has averaged about $10 billion during the last several years.[17]

The problem with the Japanese contribution to the war, however, was that the extraordinary amount of the financial contribution was not enough. Japan was perceived as unwilling to get involved in the war, so that Japan only made "financial contributions" but no "human contributions." With the mounting criticism against this "checkbook diplomacy," Kaifu decided to send SDF transportation equipment for the purpose of transferring possible refugees. This decision met with strong opposition in the Diet, given that the dispatch of the SDF overseas was illegal according to the SDF law. In the end, however, the government issued a special political decree, making applicable to this case the SDF law's Article 100 (paragraph 5), which allows the use of the SDF to transfer national guests overseas. In reality, no occasion arose to utilize the SDF for such purposes.

Further, the Kaifu cabinet agreed to send Maritime SDF (MSDF) minesweepers to the Persian Gulf to clean up after the war. This decision was more controversial than the transfer of refugees because it could not be interpreted as a humanitarian act. The government issued a political statement, justifying the dispatch of the MSDF for the security of Japanese ships, resorting to Article 99 of the SDF law that stipulates the use of the SDF for minesweeping operations. After the war in April 1991, Japan sent a flotilla of six minesweepers, of which the last one returned home in 1992. The international media criticized the dispatch as being too little, too late. There has been no spontaneity on the part of Japan, which led to criticism of Japan's foreign policy as "made in the U.S." All of Kaifu's responses to the U.S. demands epitomize the pattern of Japan's foreign policy formation after the end of World War II. All of the Japanese contributions for the Gulf War, both financial and quasimilitary, were made grudgingly and belatedly. Owing to this lack of spontaneity, these contributions were not appreciated.[18]

One fundamental problem with Japan's contribution to the Gulf War was the absence of a legal framework to justify the use of the SDF in overseas engagements. To legitimize such use of the SDF, legislation was necessary.

International Peace Cooperation Law

In October 1990, just after the Iraqi invasion of Kuwait, the Kaifu Cabinet submitted the Bill Concerning Cooperation for UN Peace Efforts (the UN Peace Cooperation Bill) to the Diet, but the bill was defeated. The LDP then tried a second time. In September 1991, the Kaifu cabinet submitted the Bill Concerning Cooperation for United Nations Peace Keeping Operations and Other Operations (the International Peace Cooperation Bill). The House of Representatives (HR) passed the bill; it did so, however, without sufficient deliberation. The way the bill was adopted was perceived as *kyôkô saiketsu* (forced decision) and caused political turmoil. Thus, the HR had to reconsider the bill and vote again. After the adoption by the HR for the second time, the bill was submitted to the House of Councillors (HC), but the term of the Diet session ended in December 1991, before the HC had time to consider the bill. Meanwhile, the Kaifu cabinet dissolved and was replaced by the Miyazawa cabinet in November 1991. In June 1992, the HC finally passed the bill.

Although the International Peace Cooperation Bill was not enacted in time for the Gulf War, it opened an avenue for the SDF to participate in future UNPKO under a constitutional framework. In fact, no sooner was the International Peace Cooperation Bill enacted than the UNTAC (UN Transitional Administration in Cambodia) was created. Japan could no longer afford to be indifferent to military involvement in the UNPKO after the kind of criticism it received during the Gulf War. The significance of the Gulf War in terms of Japanese *kokusaikôken* is that Japanese postwar pacifism has succumbed to U.S. pressure. The Japanese accepted the de facto enactment of the International Peace Cooperation Law and the engagement in the UNTAC. A recent public opinion poll indicates such Japanese acceptance.

1993 *Yomiuri* Poll on Sending the SDF Overseas

The *Yomiuri* poll taken in early 1993 indicates a changing Japanese attitude toward the role of the SDF. This poll revealed that more Japanese felt that sending the SDF overseas was *not* a problem, as compared to those who felt that it was a problem. To be exact, 45.4 percent of the respondents thought that sending the SDF overseas was not a problem because "it is consistent with the spirit of the constitution that hopes for international peace," whereas 42.6 percent thought that sending the SDF overseas was a problem because "it is against the constitution." As compared to the same poll taken in June 1992 (just after the passage of the International Peace Cooperation Bill), the number of respondents that felt that sending the SDF overseas was not a problem increased by 11.4 percent, from 34 percent to 45.4 percent. Also, the number that felt that sending the SDF overseas was a problem decreased by 13.4 percent, from 56 percent to 42.6 percent. As for the correlation with political party support, 56 percent of the supporters of the LDP (a 10 percent increase from June 1992) and 31 percent of supporters of the SDPJ (an 18 percent increase from June 1992) felt that sending the SDF overseas was not a problem. Also, more than 50% of the supporters of the *Kômeitô* and the Japan New Party thought that sending the SDF overseas was not a problem.[19]

Lingering Ambivalence

The above discussion noted the significant changes in Japanese attitudes toward constitutional revision and military *kokusaikôken*. Yet the turmoil surrounding the deliberations and the final passage of the International Peace Cooperation Bill indicated that U.S. pressure was necessary as an essential catalyst for such changes. As Motohiro Kondo, a former editor of *Chûôkôron* (a major journal of politics), points out, although the Gulf War obliged the Japanese to realize the need for a thorough review of Article 9, Japan missed an opportune occasion to do so during the deliberations on the International Peace Cooperation Bill. The Diet bypassed the issue of the constitutionality of the overseas dispatch of the SDF and left the fundamental problem of the constitutionality of the SDF ambiguous once again.[20]

Despite the results of the *Yomiuri* opinion polls examined above, the Japanese public is still ambivalent about the validity of constitutional revision and Japan's military international contribution. In fact, the number of supporters of constitutional revision decreased by 6 percent to 44 percent in the 1994 *Yomiuri* poll. The number increased to 51 percent in 1995 and decreased again to 47 percent in 1996 in the same poll.[21] Another poll conducted by Nippon Hôsô Kyôkai (NHK) more clearly illustrates the lingering Japanese ambivalence on this issue. According to NHK's poll on Life and Politics in 1993, only 38 percent of the respondents thought that it was necessary to revise the constitution, whereas 34 percent thought that it was unnecessary. The number of supporters of constitutional revision is substantially lower than that of the *Yomiuri* poll of the same year (50 percent).[22]

As mentioned earlier, the *Yomiuri Shimbun,* a private newspaper, takes the center-right spectrum of ideology, whereas NHK, a quasi-governmental public TV broadcasting station, and takes a neutral (centrist) position in politics. The discrepancy in the poll results seems to reflect the difference in the political positions of the two institutions: The results of the *Yomiuri* polls are more pro-change toward revision, whereas those of the NHK poll are more pro-status quo.

The discrepancy is also evident in another poll. Concerning how the Japanese think of the SDF, the *Yomiuri* poll of 1994 showed that 53 percent of the respondents had a favorable impression of the SDF, whereas only 26.4 percent had a good impression of the SDF according to Prime Minister's Office poll in the same year.[23] Again, the gap between the private newspaper poll and the government-sponsored poll is enormous. That at best only half of Japanese citizens had a positive view of the SDF (and, even worse, only a quarter in the government poll) is surprising and seems incomprehensible to foreign observers. This is yet another manifestation of misplaced pacifism (aversion to militarism) and the *sakoku* mentality on the part of the Japanese.

Japanese attitudes toward the constitution and international military contribution are changing. Yet the majority of Japanese are still ambivalent, owing to the legacy of Japanese militarism in World War II and the pacifism implanted by the U.S.-drafted constitution. The resignation of Defense Director-General Keisuke Nakanishi of the Hosokawa cabinet in December 1993, after he expressed his view in favor of constitutional revision, again illustrated how deeply pacifism has permeated the Japanese mind. Prime Minister Hosokawa could not save his cabinet member because his coalition cabinet included the SDPJ, a staunch defender of the peace constitution. Thus, the *sakoku* mentality lives on in the Japanese mind.

Japan's postwar constitution has outlived its original purpose of eradicating the Japanese militarism of World War II. The peace constitution was realistically feasible, insofar as the United States was committed to defend

Japan during the Cold War. But the situation has changed, and the United States wants Japan to share in the maintenance of international security. The constitution must be revised to clearly stipulate the right of self-defense and define Japan's role in the maintenance of international security. This does not mean that Japan will go back to militarism. The former West Germany had its Basic Law (constitution), which also restricted the use of force after the country's defeat in World War II. Nonetheless, West Germany has revised the Basic Law 37 times since 1947 to allow rearmament according to changes in the international situation.[24] Italy also has revised its constitution seven times since World War II, for the same reasons. It is hoped that the new century will open a more candid and earnest debate on constitutional revision.

CHAPTER TEN

Japan and the United Nations: Peacekeeping Operations and Permanent Security Council Seat

This chapter examines the issue of Japanese participation in UN peacekeeping operations as an essential aspect of *kokusaikôken,* which is an integral part of Japan's *kokusaika.* In 1994, Japan officially made a bid for a permanent Security Council seat at the United Nations. The bid reflects Japan's growing influence in the United Nations as the second-largest financial contributor to the regular UN budget and to the UNPKO budget. Moreover, Japan's contribution to the United Nations is no longer limited to the financial realm. Japan has actively participated in UNPKO since it enacted the International Peace Cooperation Law in 1992.

In this context, the Japanese ambassador to the United Nations, Yoshio Hatano, announced that Japan would seek a permanent seat in the Security Council in March 1994. It was the first time the Japanese government had made such an intention official. Japan, along with Germany, is not a permanent Security Council member and was not one of the original members of the United Nations. Japan was admitted to the United Nations in 1956, and Germany in 1973. In nearly half a century since the inception of the United Nations, Japan has become the second-largest world economic power and the second-largest financial contributor to the world organization. Japan paid $127 million, or 12.45 percent of the total UN regular budget for 1993, and had agreed to increase its contribution to 15.65 percent for 1997. West Germany has also achieved a remarkable economic recovery and became an 8.93 percent contributor to the UN regular budget. With the relative decline of American economic power and the demise of the Soviet Union, the international expectation for Japan and Germany to play a more active role in the United Nations has increased. In the past, Japan has served the Security Council seven times as a nonpermanent member, including the term from 1991 to 1993, whereas Germany has served twice. A nonpermanent member's decision-making power is limited, however, because it does not have the veto power given to the five permanent members.[1]

Under these circumstances, Japan and Germany began a bid for permanent Security Council seats. Japan appointed Hisashi Owada, the former administrative vice-foreign minister, as UN ambassador in June 1994. Yet neither a sizable financial contribution nor sending a seasoned diplomat to the United Nations has been sufficient to gain a permanent seat. Japan has to clear a constitutional barrier that limits the overseas use of force and restricts participation in UNPKO.

Japan's Past Contribution to UNPKO

As was noted in earlier chapters, because of the constitutional constraint, Japan's contribution to UNPKO has remained largely financial. Although Japan has become the second-largest financial contributor to the UNPKO budget, contributing $394 million for 1993, it was criticized for not contributing enough. Japan sent six civilian UNPKO missions between 1988 and 1992, but they were inconspicuous. These missions included one political officer each to UNGOMAP (Afghanistan/Pakistan), UNIIMOG (Iran/Iraq), UNIKOM (Iraq/Kuwait), and UNAMIC (Cambodia) for several months during that period, as well as 27 election supervisors to UNTAG (Namibia) in 1989 and three electoral observers to UNAVEM II (Angola) in September 1992, each for a month (see Table 10.1).[2]

More visible participation was required to meet international expectations. This necessitated establishment of a legal framework that would enable the SDF to participate in UNPKO. The outbreak of the Gulf crisis in August 1990 provided Japan with the first opportunity to create such a framework. In the fall of 1990, the government submitted the Bill Concerning Cooperation for UN Peace Efforts (the UN Peace Cooperation Bill). Deliberations in Parliament rekindled the old debate on the constitutionality of the SDF, however, and the bill was abandoned before deliberations were completed. Even though Japan was then serving on the Security Council as a nonpermanent member, and Ambassador Hatano was chairing the council during the war, Japan did not join the multinational forces. Although Japan made a huge financial contribution of $13 billion to the MNF (the entire UNPKO budget is $3 billion a year) by levying special taxes on its citizens, this gesture was criticized as checkbook diplomacy. Only after the war's end in April 1991 did Japan send the Maritime SDF to the Gulf for minesweeping operations, an action that was criticized as being "too little and too late."[3]

Table 10.1 Japan's Participation in UNPKO

Mission	Period of Stay	Number of Personnel and Duty
UNGOMAP (Afghanistan/ Pakistan)	June 1988– November 1989	1 political officer
UNIIMOG (Iran/Iraq)	August 1988– November 1989	1 political officer
UNTAG (Namibia)	October 1989– November 1989	27 election supervisors
UNIKOM (Iraq/Kuwait)	May 1991–November 1991	1 political officer
UNAMIC (Cambodia)	December 1991– September 1993	1 political officer
UNAVEM II (Angola)	September 1992– October 1992	3 electoral observers
UNTAC (Cambodia)	September 1992– September 1993	8 (16 total)* SDF cease-fire observers 75 civilian police unit 600 (1,200 total)* SDF engineering unit 41 electoral observers
ONUMOZ (Mozambique)	May 1993–January 1995	5 (10 total)* SDF staff officers 48 (144 total)* SDF movement control unit 15 electoral observers
ONUSAL (El Salvadore)	March 1994–April 1994	15 (30 total)* electoral observers
UNPROFOR (former Yugoslavia)	March 1994– December 1995	1 political officer
UNAMIR (Rwanda)	October 1994– December 1994	260 GSDF soldiers for refugee relief assistance
UNDOF (Golan Heights)	February 1996–present	2 (4 total)* SDF staff officers 43 (172 total)* transport unit

*The number refers to the total number of personnel on a rotation system.
Sources: "Building Peace: Japan's Participation in UNPKO," Ministry of Foreign Affairs, Tokyo, July 1994, p. 9, and MFA, Tokyo, September 1997.

International Peace Cooperation Law

In September 1991, a year after the failure of the UN Peace Cooperation Bill, the cabinet submitted another bill, the Bill Concerning Cooperation for UN Peacekeeping Operations and Other Operations, to Parliament. The so-called International Peace Cooperation Bill passed in June 1992 after stormy deliberations in Parliament. On the second try, Japan enacted a law that enabled the SDF to participate in UNPKO. The Law was not free from limitations, however. First, the SDF's participation required the approval of Parliament. Second, the law only allowed the SDF to participate in logistical operations, banning participation in peacekeeping forces (PKF). The law also set forth preconditions for participation in UNPKO. The so-called five principles are as follows: (1) the parties in the armed conflict have agreed on a cease-fire; (2) the parties in the armed conflict and host countries have given consent to deployment for the operation and to Japan's participation in the operation; (3) the operation must ensure strict impartiality; (4) the Japanese contingent must withdraw should any of the above requirements cease to be satisfied; and (5) the use of weapons is limited to the minimum amount necessary to protect the personnel's lives. No sooner had the law taken effect in August 1992 than the government sent the SDF to Cambodia.[4]

UNTAC (Cambodia)

The United Nations established the UN Transitional Authority in Cambodia (UNTAC) in March 1992, with the mandate of monitoring the cease-fire and supervising the existing administration in conducting a general election for the constitutional assembly. Reflecting the complex nature of the Cambodian civil war, UNTAC had become a large and costly operation, involving 22,000 personnel. This became the SDF's first full-fledged participation in UNPKO. Since September 1992, Japan sent a total of 1,216 SDF personnel (two dispatches of eight military observers, and two dispatches of 600-man construction units), 75 civilian police, and 41 polling station officers. Another point to be noted is that the UNTAC was headed by a Japanese diplomat, Akashi Yasushi, who has served in the United Nations since 1957. Two Japanese, a civilian policeman and a young male volunteer, died in the mission, which caused a sensation in Japan. In contrast, such deaths did not receive national attention in European countries, even though 58 English and 51 French personnel had died in various UNPKO missions in the past. This indicated that the Japanese have not accepted UNPKO as a fact of life. With the successful completion of the UNTAC in September 1993, Japan next sent the SDF to Mozambique.[5]

ONUMOZ (Mozambique)

After the end of the civil war in Mozambique, the United Nations established the UN Operation in Mozambique (ONUMOZ) in December 1992. The mission had a wide range of mandates: to monitor and verify the cease-fire; to supervise and monitor the peace process; to monitor a general election scheduled in October 1994; and to supervise the supply of humanitarian aid and food. About 6,700 military personnel from 21 countries have participated in the operation. Since May 1993, Japan has sent a total of 202 SDF personnel (two dispatches of five staff officers and four dispatches of 48-man movement control units), as well as a dozen electoral officers.[6]

When ambassador Hatano made a bid for a permanent Security Council seat in March 1994, Japan was participating only in the ONUMOZ operation, which was scheduled to terminate at the end of 1994. Thus, Japan hurriedly sent 15 electoral observers to the UN Observer Mission in El Salvador (ONUSAL) in March 1994. The mission stayed only for a week, followed by another week-long mission in April. Japan had to look for other UNPKO to participate in, for the sake of the bid.[7]

UNDOF (Golan Heights)

In June 1994, Prime Minister Tsutomu Hata sent an investigation team to Syria to examine whether it was feasible for Japan to participate in the UN Disengagement Observer Force (UNDOF) in the Golan Heights. UNDOF was created in June 1974, in the buffer zone between Israel and Syria after the fourth Middle East war. Given that its mandate was primarily peacekeeping and that there existed a cease-fire agreement by the parties to the armed conflict, the Hata cabinet considered that UNDOF met the five principles of the International Peace Cooperation Law. It planned to send 80 ground SDF personnel in August 1994 to replace the Canadian movement control unit. Had the mission materialized, it would have been the SDF's third UNPKO mission.[8]

As seen earlier, however, the mission was not sent in August due to the change in the Japanese government in June. The new coalition cabinet head, socialist prime minister Tomiichi Murayama, was not as enthusiastic about the mission as his predecessor. One of his coalition's concerns was that the mission might violate the five principles of the International Peace Cooperation Law because the task of the movement control unit would involve the transportation of ammunition and possibly the use of force. Another concern was that UNDOF was an indefinite mission. Opponents argued that Japan should not participate in such a dangerous and long-term mission, and criticized the Ministry of Foreign Affairs (MFA) for being too anxious to participate in UNPKO for the sake of obtaining a permanent Security Council seat. Prime Minister Murayama finally sent an SDF mission to UNDOF in late January 1996, a year and a half later than his predecessor's original plan.[9]

UNAMIR (Rwanda)

In August 1994, Japan sent a $3 million financial contribution and in-kind supplies to the UN Assistance Mission for Rwanda (UNAMIR) to help Rwandan refugees. According to the five principles of the International Peace Cooperation Law, Japan could not send military personnel to Rwanda because the parties in the armed conflict had neither agreed to the creation of a UNPKO nor to Japanese participation in the operation. However, the Murayama cabinet decided to send a medical team, including SDF personnel, to Zaire and Tanzania, considering that sending a mission to Rwanda's neighboring countries that were not parties to the conflict did not violate the five principles. The first SDF contingent for Rwandan refugee relief assistance, consisting of 100 ground SDF soldiers, arrived in Goma, Zaire, in October 1994. It was followed by the second contingent, consisting of 124 personnel, and the third, consisting of 36 soldiers. This became the SDF's first humanitarian deployment.[10]

The key for more active SDF participation in UNPKOs hinged on whether the government could remove the ban on PKF participation. The review of the International Peace Cooperation Law concerning PKF was scheduled to take place in 1995. However, the Murayama cabinet did not review the law. With the SDF's actual participation in UNPKO, an increasing number of Japanese have come to accept its overseas engagement. Meanwhile, Japan revised its 19-year-old national defense program outline in 1995. The new outline stipulates Japan's contribution to the maintenance of international peace and security, through its participation in international peacekeeping operations and in international emergency assistance activities.[11]

Prime Minister's Office Poll on UNPKO

According to a poll conducted by the Prime Minister's Office, the number of respondents who were in favor of continued SDF participation in UNPKO have changed from 20.6 percent (1991), to 17.1 percent (1994), and to 31.0 percent (1996). Correspondingly, the numbers of those who were against it have decreased from 18.8 percent (1991), to 10.8 percent (1994), and to 3.0 percent (1996). These results indicate increasing support for the SDF's engagement on the part of the Japanese. Yet as many as 44.1 percent gave only reluctant approval in the poll, whereas 11.3 percent still leaned toward disapproval. This meant that the majority of Japanese still did not positively support the SDF's participation in UNPKO even in 1996.[12] This result is consistent with that of another Prime Minister's Office poll examined in Chapter 2 (see Table 2.3). An international opinion poll also showed a similar result.

Yomiuri/Gallup Poll on UNPKO

An international opinion poll by the *Yomiuri Shimbun,* with the cooperation of the Gallup Poll, demonstrated that a greater percentage of Americans and Europeans supported Japan's SDF mission to UNTAC (Cambodia) than for the Japanese themselves (see Table 10.2). The poll also revealed that more Americans and Europeans thought their respective country's army should participate in UNPKO as well as in prevention of regional conflicts than for the Japanese. The poll showed a wide gap between the Japanese and the Americans/Europeans on international security. Many Japanese are still affected by the war experience (the atomic bombings of Hiroshima and Nagasaki) and support the "war-renouncing" constitution. The Japanese expect the United Nations to maintain international peace and security, but they are unwilling to commit themselves to such a role. The international comparison clearly illustrated Japan's *sakoku* mentality.[13]

Germany and UNPKO

After World War II, the Allied powers' occupation forces divided Germany into West Germany and East Germany. During the height of the Cold War, West Germany joined the North Atlantic Treaty Organization (NATO), whereas East Germany joined the Warsaw Pact Treaty. West Germany revised its Basic Law (constitution) in 1949 and restored its independence in 1955. Although the preamble of the new Basic Law obligates Germany to serve world peace as an equal partner in a united Europe, Article 87 forbids the use of armed forces for purposes other than self-defense. Although Article 24 allows Germany to become a party to a system of collective security, it has been interpreted that it allows only for deployment within NATO territories.[14]

Within this constitutional framework, West Germany has actively participated in UNPKO since its admission to the United Nations in 1973, providing financial, logistical, and personnel support. The record is impressive. From 1973 to 1990, it participated in more than nine UNPKOs, including UNEF II (Suez Canal/Sinai Peninsula), UNIFIL (Lebanon),

Table 10.2 *Yomiuri*/Gallup Poll on UNPKO

Support for the Japanese SDF's participation in UNTAC (Cambodia):

Japanese	59%	
Americans	71%	
British	69%	
Germans	68%	
French	73%	(April 30, 1993)

My country should send its army to UNPKO as part of contribution to international society:

Japanese	16%	
Americans	34%	
British	47%	
Germans	23%	
French	20%	(April 30, 1994)

My country's army should cooperate in prevention of regional conflicts other than UNPKO:

Japanese	9%	
Americans	12%	
British	23%	
Germans	12%	
French	17%	(April 30, 1994)

The United Nations should do more to prevent and solve regional conflicts:

Japanese	50%	
Americans	22%	
British	28%	
Germans	39%	
French	29%	(April 30, 1994)

Sources: "*Nichibeiô gokakoku seron chôsa*" (U.S./Europe/Japan five-nation public opinion poll), *Yomiuri Shimbun*, April 30, 1993, and April 30, 1994.

UNTAG (Namibia), ONUCA (Central America), ONUSAL (El Salvador), ONUVEN (Nicaragua), ONUVEH (Haiti), MINURSO (Western Sahara), and UNAVEM (Angola). After its unification in 1990, Germany was expected to play a more active role at the United Nations. Germany has become the fourth-largest contributor to the UN regular budget as well as to the UNPKO budget. Despite the U.S. request, however, Germany could not join the MNF during the Gulf War due to constitutional restrictions. Since then, Chancellor Helmut Kohl's coalition government, comprising the Christian Democratic Union (CDU), the Christian Social Union (CSU), and the Free Democratic Party (FDP), has sought in vain to revise the Basic Law to allow the dispatch of German troops outside NATO territories.[15]

Finally, responding to international pressure, Chancellor Kohl sent armed missions to the UN Protection Force (UNPROFOR) in Bosnia-Herzegovina in 1992 and to the UN Operation in Somalia II (UNOSOM II) in 1993, by interpreting Article 24 as allowing Germany to participate in collective security outside NATO territories. Specifically, he committed German troops to the surveillance of the Adriatic in July 1992 as part of the naval embargo of the former Yugoslavia and to the aerial surveillance of the no-fly zone over Bosnia in April 1993. Both operations were conducted by NATO and the Western European Union (WEU) under UN supervision. Germany also dispatched a contingent of 1,700 soldiers, including, for the first time, a *Bundeswehr* (self-defense force) battalion to UNOSOM II to provide logistical support.[16]

These armed missions provoked opposition; the largest opposition party, the Social Democratic Party (SPD), denounced them as unconstitutional and brought the case before the Constitutional Court, Germany's highest court. In July 1994, the Constitutional Court ruled that Germany was at liberty to assign its armed forces in NATO/WEU operations to implement UNSC resolutions and in UN peace-enforcing missions, and that the three out-of-area missions in dispute were constitutional. The court's ruling removed the two-decades-long constitutional ban on participation in UNPKF. The ruling will enable more active German participation in UNPKO and enhance its bid for a permanent Security Council seat. Currently, Germany is engaged in four UNPKO: MINURSO (Western Sahara), UNPROFOR (former Yugoslavia), UNIKOM (Iraq), and UNOMIG (Georgia).[17]

Changes in the UNPKO mandate also call for more active participation by Germany and Japan.

Evolution of UNPKO

UNPKO have undergone a quantitative and qualitative expansion over the four decades since the inception of the first UNPKO in 1948. Thirteen missions were created between 1948 and 1978, with the mandate of monitoring truces and preventing the recurrence and aggravation of conflicts. Examples include UNTSO (Jerusalem) and UNMOGIP (India/Pakistan). Nations such as Austria, Finland, and Fiji, which were not directly involved in the Cold War, actively participated in UNPKO. They sent small-scale contingents to disputed areas. No new missions were sent until 1988. Then, 21 new missions were created between 1988 and 1994. This means that more than two thirds of the total 34 missions were created after 1988, with six established in 1993 alone. The mushrooming of civil wars in Eastern Europe, Africa, and elsewhere in the post–Cold War era increased the need for such missions.[18]

Along with the increase in the number of missions, the size of each mission has expanded. The lessened likelihood of a superpower confrontation in the post–Cold War era has enabled the major powers to participate in UNPKO and has enabled an increase in the size of each mission. For example, UNSOM II involved almost 30,000 personnel, including U.S. military, and UNTAC involved more than 22,000 personnel, including Japan's SDF. UNPKO's operating budget has increased to $3 billion, roughly three times the UN regular budget. The most important difference between traditional and new missions, however, lies in the qualitative expansion. New missions are entrusted with a much larger mandate than old ones, consisting not only of military tasks but also of a wide range of nonmilitary tasks. Such civilian tasks include overseeing the establishment of new governments, election monitoring, national reconstruction and rehabilitation, human rights monitoring, and refugee repatriation. UNTAC and ONUMOZ are prime examples. The expansion of UNPKO into a larger civilian mandate necessitates more active Japanese participation in UNPKO.[19]

Domestic Support for Japan's Bid

As Japan's full-fledged participation in UNPKO commenced, its potential to become a permanent Security Council member has improved, and the government made its bid public in March 1994 at the United Nations. A recent opinion poll conducted by the MFA showed that the majority of Japanese citizens now support Japan's bid. According to the poll, 52.9 percent of respondents thought Japan should become a permanent member, whereas only 14.8 percent thought Japan should not. It should be noted that some of the reasons for supporting the bid were naïve, such as that Japan, a peace-loving nation, could contribute to world peace. The major reasons for supporting Japan's bid were (out of 52.9 percent):

- "Japan should actively participate in the creation of world peace" (41.2 percent);
- "Japan should participate in decision-making and get veto power" (25 percent);
- "Japan's permanent membership will promote world peace because it is a peace-loving nation" (27.5 percent);
- "Japan could make a larger financial contribution if it becomes a permanent member" (5.5 percent).

Major reasons for opposition were (out of 14.8 percent):

- "Japan should not get involved in decision-making concerning the use of force" (60.7 percent);
- "a permanent member has to assume a greater responsibility" (36.9 percent);
- "Japan is not yet qualified to become a permanent member" (23.8 percent);
- "the UN itself has problems" (20.2 percent).[20]

International Support for Japan's Bid

UN secretary-generals, both the former, Boutros Boutros-Ghali, and the incumbent, Kofi Annan, support Japan's bid for a permanent Security Council seat. In addition, four permanent council members, the United States, Great Britain, France, and Russia, have so far expressed their support for the bid; China has not expressed its views. During a visit to Japan in December 1993, the then secretary-general Boutros-Ghali expressed his support for Japan's bid and requested that Japan participate in UNPKO more actively. Boutros-Ghali had earlier suggested that Japan should consider revising its constitution so that Japan could participate in UNPKO more actively, but he retracted the statement when it caused an uproar in Japan. Showing an understanding for Japan's constitutional limitation on the use of force, Ghali this time said that such participation was not a requirement for Japan to become a permanent member and that it would not have to assume any new military responsibility if it became one.[21]

The then-U.S. ambassador to Japan, Walter Mondale, also strongly supported the bid in May 1994, stating that it was anachronistic for Japan not to be a permanent member, and that the U.S. government would not seek Japanese military contributions beyond its constitutional limitation. Yet it should be noted that the U.S. Senate passed two resolutions, in January and July 1994, requesting that the United States should not support Japan's bid unless Japan commits itself to engage fully in UN peacekeeping and peacemaking operations. Senator William Roth, Jr., a Republican from Delaware, stated that a permanent member's responsibilities include peacekeeping and peacemaking, and that Japan had no intention of removing obstacles to its full engagement in such operations.[22]

According to the *Yomiuri*/Gallup poll conducted in April 1993, a near majority of American and European respondents supported the idea that Japan and Germany should become permanent UNSC members. The combined figures for both "only Japan and Germany should be added to the SC" and "Japan, Germany, and other countries should be added to the SC" were

47 percent for the Japanese, 46 percent for the Americans, 49 percent for the British, 51 percent for the Germans, and 52 percent for the French, respectively. Also, Americans and Europeans expect Japan to play a greater role in international politics. According to the 1994 *Yomiuri*/Gallup Poll, 47 percent of Americans, 51 percent of British, 28 percent of Germans, and 50 percent of French respondents thought that Japan's leadership in international politics would strengthen in the twenty-first century, whereas only 25 percent of Japanese thought so. Similarly, more Americans and Europeans thought Japan's economic and military powers would grow in the next century than did the Japanese (see Table 10.3).[23]

Even Southeast Asian countries, which suffered under Japanese militarism during World War II and have been concerned with the SDF's overseas engagements, support Japan's bid. Singapore president Ong Teng Cheong told Prime Minister Murayama, who was visiting Southeast Asia in August 1994, that Japan should seek a permanent Security Council seat to play its role as a global power. Malaysian prime minister Mahathir Mohamad told Murayama that Japan should stop its "redemptive diplomacy" and encouraged Japan to become a permanent council member and promote the peace and prosperity of Asia. Thailand also supports Japan's bid. South Korea, which was annexed by Japan during 1910–1945, seems not to oppose giving Japan a permanent seat but opposes giving it veto power. The Korean objection apparently derives from the lack of Japanese commitment to international security. It is conceivable that South Korea fears Japan would veto a UN effort to protect Korea, like the one mounted during the Korean War.[24]

There is reasonable international support for the Japanese bid. As of the end of September 1994, 42 countries have expressed their support for it. Yet Japan has to clear a few more hurdles to obtain the seat. China, a permanent council member, might object to the Japanese bid. Brazil, Egypt, India, Indonesia, and Nigeria expressed their intention of seeking permanent seats at the forty-ninth session of the UN General Assembly in September 1994. A fundamental problem, however, lies with the lack of commitment to UN peacemaking efforts on the part of Japan.[25]

Japanese Domestic Politics

Foreign Minister Yohei Kono of the Murayama cabinet told the UN General Assembly in September 1994 that while it is ready to fulfil the responsibilities of a permanent Security Council member, Japan would not take part in constitutionally prohibited military actions requiring the use of arms. This statement was regarded as Japan's official bid for a permanent seat by UN officials concerned. Murayama's cabinet secretary denied this, however, saying that the foreign minister's speech was not intended as such a bid.[26]

Table 10.3 *Yomiuri*/Gallup Poll on Japan's Leadership, 1994

Japan's leadership in international politics would strengthen in the twenty-first century:

Japanese	25%
Americans	47%
British	51%
Germans	28%
French	50%

Japan's economic power will grow in the twenty-first century:

Japanese	25%
Americans	46%
British	56%
Germans	38%
French	50%

Japan's military power will grow in the twenty-first centry:

Japanese	17%
Americans	46%
British	38%
Germans	20%
French	40%

Sources: "*Nichibeiô gokakoku seron chôsa*" (U.S./Europe/Japan five-nation public opinion poll), *Yomiuri Shimbun,* April 30, 1994.

The problem was that Prime Minister Murayama was a socialist, and his coalition cabinet was composed of the SDPJ, the LDP, and the NPS. This coalition government was unusual in that the SDPJ joined with the conservative LDP. The coalition's problem was that the SDPJ had been a staunch supporter of the constitution and denounced the SDF as unconstitutional. Murayama was reluctant to commit the SDF to UN peacemaking efforts. The tone of his inaugural speech in July 1994 was more cautious than enthusiastic with regard to Japan's commitment to the UN. He said that the government would keep its stance of actively cooperating in UNPKO efforts abroad within the bounds of the constitution, and it would seek a permanent SC seat if there was enough support in the international community and among the Japanese. In reality, Murayama had no reason to be hesitant.[27]

In August 1994, a private advisory council report to the prime minister urged Murayama to end the ban on the SDF's participation in UNPKF. The

Defense Problems Study Council, led by Hirotaro Higuchi, recommended that Japan adopt active defense policies and create a UNPKO office within the National Defense Agency in order to contribute more to UNPKO. It was hoped that Murayama would take the council's advice seriously, but his cabinet fell short of committing Japan to UN peacemaking operations at the General Assembly.[28]

Some cautious views still exist concerning the Japanese bid. Critics argued, given that Japan has yet to establish a clear legal framework for the SDF to participate in UNPKF, it was premature for Japan to seek a permanent seat and it was a mistake for the MFA to hastily seek such a position. Although former UN secretary-general Boutros-Ghali said that such participation was not a precondition for becoming a permanent member, it is odd for a permanent member not to be able to use its armed forces in UNPKF. Germany cleared this obstacle with the recent Constitutional Court ruling. Masashi Nishihara, a professor at Japan's Defense Academy, said that Japan would be ridiculed for having "bought" the permanent seat if it refuses to participate in UNPKF.[29]

Another concern is the uncertainty over Japan's ability to assert itself in the international arena. Japan has been a loyal follower of the United States during the post–World War II era. Yoshihiro Tsurumi, business professor at Baruch College, argued that it was the U.S. strategy to let Japan become a permanent member without veto power and to make Japan pay the costs of UNPKO. In a similar vein, Ronald Dore, professor at the University of London, doubted that Japan would be able to promote global interests rather than U.S. national interests if it became a permanent member. After the experience in Somalia, the United States distanced itself from the United Nations by reducing its PKO contribution from 32 percent to 25 percent and by requesting reimbursement for goods and services it provided.[30]

All the critics' concerns derived from Japan's indecisiveness and lack of clear vision in its global policy. Lastly, the Japanese bid also involves Security Council reforms.

Security Council Reforms

In December 1992, the forty-seventh session of the UN General Assembly adopted a consensual resolution concerning the "Question of the Equal Distribution on and the Increase in the Membership of the SC" and established a working group on the SC reforms. One of the issues was the increase in the number of permanent members that would have veto power. The rationale is that despite drastic changes in the global balance of power from the inception of the UN to the present, the number of permanent members has remained at five. As Ambassador Hatano stated, the emergence of new global powers that have attained levels of influence equal to that of the current permanent members calls for an increase in permanent members to enhance the Security Council's legitimacy and credibility. In response to the Third World leaders' bid for permanent seats at the forty-ninth session of the General Assembly in September 1994, the United States argued that new permanent members should have global economic and political power, being actually able to contribute to world security, and that Japan and Germany were the only two countries that had such qualifications.[31]

Another issue was the expansion of the number of nonpermanent members. The rationale for this enlargement was that there was a dramatic increase in UN member states from the original 51 in 1945 to 185 in 1997. Although the number of nonpermanent members increased from the original six to ten in 1965, the quadrupled number of UN members calls for a further increase in nonpermanent SC members to secure an equitable geographical representation. There also existed the idea of creating a third category of membership, "semi-permanent members." Such members would not be permanent but would serve longer than the present two-year nonpermanent-member term.[32]

The working group on the SC reforms met in September 1994 but did not reach any consensus on how many new permanent and non-permanent members should be added to the council. To break the stalemate, the U.S. ambassador to the United Nations, Bill Richardson, announced in July 1997 that the United States would accept three permanent members from developing countries in addition to Germany and Japan, without a veto power. A consensus has been formed at the United Nations that three members should be chosen from Asia, Africa, and Latin America, respectively, to secure an equitable geographic representation. Although Brazil, Egypt, Germany, India, and Japan, which were considered likely candidates, expressed their support for the U.S. proposal, Italy, Mexico, and Pakistan were opposed to it. Italy is opposed to the idea of Germany becoming a permanent member; Mexico, to that of Brazil; and Pakistan, to that of India, respectively. Thus, the new U.S. proposal triggered an intense rivalry between the supporters of the powerful candidates and their opposition groups. The UN working group hopes that it will work out a consensus plan by the end of the century.[33]

Changes in the composition of Security Council members require amendments to Article 23 of the UN Charter. Such amendments require adoption by a two-thirds majority of the General Assembly, which has 185 member states as of July 1997, and ratification by a two-thirds majority of the United Nations, including all the permanent SC members.

The international and domestic factors examined in this chapter justify the Japanese bid. At the international level, Japan's influence at the United

Nations is growing as the second-largest financial contributor, for both the regular and the PKO UN budgets. Moreover, Japan enacted the International Peace Cooperation Law and has actively participated in UNPKO, sending four SDF missions and a number of civilian missions. Yasushi Akashi successfully supervised UNTAC (Cambodia) and oversaw UNPRO-FOR (the former Yugoslavia), as a special envoy of the UN Secretary-General. Sadako Ogata, who heads the UN High Commissioner for Refugees (UNHCR), coordinates refugee works with UNPKO personnel in Bosnia, Somalia, Rwanda, and elsewhere. Japan should increasingly play such a visible leadership role, as exemplified by Akashi and Ogata.

In an interview in Bosnia, Akashi said that Japan's contribution to UNPKO was its international "obligation," and that fulfilling such an obligation was a requirement for Japan to become a permanent SC member. It is high time for Japan and Germany to become permanent SC members and wield global leadership commensurate with their economic and political standings. In the meantime, Japan should remove obstacles to its bid by articulating its commitment to UN peacemaking operations and should consolidate public opinion at home and abroad.[34]

CONCLUSION

Prospects for Japan's *Kokusaika*

The preceding chapters demonstrated that the Japanese attitudinal prism is characterized by the *sakoku* mentality. Japanese perceptions of other countries and their people are filtered through this parochial mind-set. The narrow-minded mentality also permeates the outlook of Japanese policy decision makers. Their distorted perceptions, along with the bureaucratic inertia and inactivity on the part of Japanese politicians, adversely affect a wide range of Japanese public policy making initiatives, from economic policy to security policy. This invisible structure helps sustain Japanese isolationism and protectionism, and resists the changes sought by the United States and by European countries. Thus, along with the uncertainty in the leadership ability of the Japanese politicians, the *sakoku* mentality constitutes the most formidable impediment to Japan's *kokusaika*. Although Japan is only slowly and reluctantly moving toward internationalization, its Asian neighbors, notably South Korea and Taiwan, have undertaken globalization in earnest.

Comparative Analysis:
Globalization of South Korea and Taiwan

President Kim Young Sam of South Korea (the Republic of Korea) declared the creation of a New Korea as his foremost goal in his inaugural speech in 1993 and named 1995 as the kick-off year in his country's push toward globalization (*segyehwa,* in Korean). President Kim called *segyehwa* "the quickest way to build the Republic into a first-rate nation in the twenty-first century" and identified six goals to that end: improved government efficiency, the implementation of local autonomy, better quality of life for all South Koreans, a sharper competitive edge for South Korean products, reconciliation and cooperation with North Korea, and South Korea's assumption of a role on the international stage.[1]

The Kim administration has already undertaken sweeping political reforms to eradicate political corruption and create a clean government. It revised the Public Officials' Ethics Law in 1993, which requires high-ranking public officials to register and make public their personal assets in order to discourage the illegal and unethical accumulation of wealth. At President Kim's urging, the South Korean National Assembly passed a package of three political reform bills in 1994. The Law for Electing Public Officials and Preventing Electoral Irregularities is designed to ensure the transparency of campaign financing. The amended Political Fund Law controls fundraising by political parties and individual politicians. The revised Local Autonomy Law provides for the election of the chief executives of local governments to restore local autonomy after a 30-year hiatus. The arrest of former president Roh Tae Woo, involving the illegal slush fund scandal, along with the arrest of former president Chun Doo Hwan concerning the 1979 military coup and the 1980 Kwangju massacre, epitomize the sweeping political reforms undertaken by the Kim administration. Such prosecution of former heads of state was inconceivable in the past in South Korea.[2]

In terms of economic reforms, the Kim administration has committed itself to liberalization, decentralization, and deregulation of the economic system. Among other things, it has enforced a number of measures, such as new approval procedures for starting a business; amended government decrees regarding the use of land for foreign businesses; simplified regulations on production, distribution, and trade; tax incentives for foreign investment in high-tech industries; and stronger protection of intellectual property rights.[3]

Meanwhile, Taiwan (the Republic of China) is promoting its globalization in earnest. At his inaugural speech in 1990, President Lee Teng-hui articulated Taiwan's commitment to globalization in order to make the republic a useful member of the global community. Its goals encompass democratization of political systems and economic development at the domestic level, the peaceful unification of China at the regional level, and reentry into the United Nations and admission into other international organizations at the international level.[4]

Under President Lee's leadership, Taiwan has accelerated its democratization process. It transacted two rounds of constitutional reforms to modernize the central and local governments. Also, the new constitution provides that the republic's president shall be elected by a direct and popular vote. Its first direct presidential election took place in March 1996. As for economic development, President Lee implemented a six-year national development plan to expedite Taiwan's modernization process. Taiwan has also achieved breathtaking progress in economic liberalization. Under Lee's guidance, for instance, it lifted interest rate controls, eased restrictions on the export of gold, deregulated entry into the banking system, and established a foreign currency call loan market. Taiwan also promised to reduce tariffs on more than 700 items and to deregulate foreign investment, transportation, finance, and import approval, as its "initial action" at the APEC (Asia-Pacific Economic Cooperation forum) meeting in Osaka, in November 1995. Taiwan is currently building an Asia-Pacific regional operations center, comprising financial, manufacturing, sea and air transportation, telecommunications, and media sectors.[5]

At the regional level, the Taiwanese government has adopted a more open policy vis-à-vis Communist China. As a result, cross-Straits exchanges have been expanded to include cultural, educational, and economic activities. President Lee also launched the "southward policy" in 1994, which is designed to promote economic and trade cooperation with ASEAN and enhance the economic integration of the region. Taiwan's acceptance in the global community is growing as well. For example, the Republic of China obtained observer status in GATT in 1992. At the United Nations, twelve countries formally proposed the creation of an ad hoc committee to consider the republic's participation in the United Nations in 1994. President Lee reiterated Taiwan's determination to play a more positive role in the global community during his recent trip to the United States in June 1995. At Cornell University, his alma mater, Lee stated that the Republic of China has a "yearning" for international recognition commensurate with its economic power.[6]

A comparative analysis demonstrates that both South Korea and Taiwan, the world's twelfth- and the thirteenth-largest trading economies, respectively, are more willing to change domestic systems and globalize themselves than is Japan. They are keen to catch up with the world's leading advanced industrialized countries, such as the United States and Japan. Also, being "divided nations," both South Korea and Taiwan eagerly seek acceptance by the international community and admission into major international organizations. Therefore, both the South Korean and Taiwanese governments seriously promote globalization, seek to play a greater role on the international stage, and mobilize their citizens toward that goal.

It is, however, necessary to understand that their globalization will take time, given that their democratization process has just started and that they are still middle-size economies or so-called NIES (newly industrialized economies). In the case of South Korea, President Kim is the first civilian and the second popularly elected president of the country. As for Taiwan, it lifted the martial law decree only in 1987 and has yet to have a popularly elected president. Violent fights in the Taiwanese Parliament indicate that Taiwan's political reforms have a long way to go. While it remains to be seen whether their globalization drives will fully succeed in the future, the South Korean and Taiwanese governments have a strong determination to achieve such goals and have undertaken their resolutions in earnest.

In contrast, the Japanese government has no such zeal for its own internationalization and is only reluctantly pursuing it due to external pressure. While a superficial internationalization, or quantitative *kokusaika,* as exemplified by the glut of foreign goods in the daily life of Japanese and the unprecedented number of Japanese tourists going abroad, has made certain progress, *kokoro no kokusaika* (internationalization of the mind), or qualitative *kokusaika,* has not taken root in the hearts of Japanese. This is so despite the fact that former prime minister Yasuhiro Nakasone declared the creation of *kokusai kokka Nihon* (an internationalized Japan) at the Japanese Parliament in 1984.

Although Japan achieved its status as the world's second-largest economy more than a decade ago, it still has not been able to demonstrate international leadership abilities or earn international respect. On the contrary, the Japanese government is still reluctant to promote trade liberalization and economic deregulation. Not surprisingly, foreign governments' complaints and demands have not ceased at all. For instance, at the APEC meeting in Osaka in November 1995, Japan staunchly resisted the liberalization of imports of agricultural products to the end. Its performance as the host country of the conference was embarrassing.[7] In a joint meeting of the representatives of the European Union (EU) Parliament and the Japanese Parliament held in Tokyo in November 1995, the EU stated that Japan has made insufficient progress in realizing trade deregulation and in playing an active role at the United Nations.[8] In March 1996, the United States released its latest annual report on foreign trade barriers. The report listed 49 items in eight sectors as Japanese trade barriers. They included anticompetitive customs (Japan's ineffective antimonopoly policy), import policies (such as those of agricultural products), government procurement (including computers, supercomputers, medical equipment, and Nippon Telegraph and Telephone Corporation's [NTT] anticompetitive selection of its dealers), protection of intellectual property rights, and barriers in the service sectors (such as financial services and the insurance business). The report's newest additions to the list of Japanese trade barriers included rice imports, electric communication services, and port transportation.[9]

In addition, Japan has still been unable to settle the postwar compensation issues, both tangible and intangible, with its Asian neighbors, involving its acts of aggression during World War II. As examined earlier, the Japanese government refused to pay formal compensation to the former *jûgun ianfu* (comfort women) of the war. The Asia Peace and Friendship Fund, a private fund created in lieu of an official one, has paid a temporary compensation only to 25 victims as of July 1997. As late as May 1996, Prime Minister Hashimoto repeated the same government view—that the state compensation issue has already been settled legally.[10] Worse yet, Japanese political leaders have repeatedly denied Japan's acts of aggression. As a result of the protests by the Asian governments concerned, five incumbent ministers resigned during 1986–1995 alone, with the most recent one being Management and Coordination Agency director-general Takami Eto in November 1995.

Even former socialist prime minister Murayama said at the House of Councillors in October 1995 that the Japan-Korea Annexation Treaty of 1910 was concluded legally.[11] Both the South and North Korean governments believe that the treaty was forcibly imposed upon the Koreans and was in principle null and void, whereas the Japanese government considers the treaty legally effective. Chinese president Jiang Zemin and South Korean president Kim Young Sam issued an unprecedented joint statement, requesting Japan to correct its view of history, in the first Chinese presidential visit to Seoul in November 1995.[12] In return, Ichiro Ozawa, secretary-general of New Frontier Party, criticized anti-Japanese history education in China and South Korea at a political seminar in December 1995. He said that Chinese and South Korean anti-Japanese history education with political intentions in mind would not bring anything positive in the future.[13]

With these anachronistic attitudes of its political leaders, Japan will lose out to its "little brothers" in Asia unless it takes *kokusaika* seriously and pursues it in earnest. Not surprisingly, the *Yomiuri Shimbun* poll conducted in late 1994 revealed that overseas leaders and intellectuals are pessimistic about Japan's internationalization. The newspaper interviewed 100 leading politicians, high-ranking government officials, and literary intellectuals throughout the world.

According to the poll, the respondents view the present Japan as "an economic animal," "culturally closed," and "not accepting of cultural diversity"; they also think that Japan "does not know where it wants to head" and is "having an identity crisis." In addition, the poll reported a wide gap between what the respondents expect from Japan in the twenty-first century and what they think Japan will actually accomplish. According to the poll, 78 percent said that they hoped that Japan would become an open country in the next century, whereas only 28 percent thought that Japan would become an open country. Similarly, 77 percent said they hoped that Japan would become a democratic country, whereas only 53 percent thought that Japan would become a democratic country. Also, 62 percent hoped that Japan would become a country that other nations could trust, but only 25 percent really thought that it would. As for Japanese responsibilities involving World War II, 37 percent thought that Japan had almost solved the wartime settlement problem. Conversely, 22 percent thought that "Japan has hardly solved the matter," and 16 percent thought that

"Japan has not solved the matter at all," whereas 10 percent thought that "Japan has already solved the matter."[14]

Prospects for Japan's *Kokusaika*

Despite the negative indications of the prospects for Japan's internationalization and the slow pace at which the country is moving in that direction, the tide of Japan's *kokusaika* is irreversible. Japanese policy makers realize that they should promote *kokusaika* because they recognize that the country will be isolated from the rest of the world unless it opens itself more to foreigners and foreign entities. However, it would be difficult for Japan to change its policies and practices because of cultural fundamentals, such as Japan's national characteristics in general and the *sakoku* mentality in particular. Yet this is not impossible. Just as South Korea and Taiwan are promoting globalization, Japan can carry out its internationalization only if its policy makers and people realize the essential need for *kokusaika* and exert more conscious and serious efforts to that end. In particular, policy makers must overcome the status quo mentality and implement more effective legislation for *kokusaika*. They should realize that replacing protectionism with internationalism would benefit Japanese consumers (by increasing their choice of merchandise and raising their standard of living) as well as Japanese business sectors in the long run (by enhancing competitiveness and revitalizing the Japanese economy).

In fact, the Hashimoto coalition cabinet revised the existing three-year deregulation program (1995–1997 fiscal years) in March 1996. The revised plan added more than 569 new measures in housing and land, distribution, information and telecommunications, finance, securities and insurance, and employment and labor. This revision, along with the existing 1,116 programs and 112 measures allegedly already implemented by various ministries and agencies during fiscal 1995, brought to 1,797 the total number of deregulation programs in 11 sectors. The revision included a drastic review of the Building Standards Law to facilitate importation of housing products, a liberalization "in principle" of foreign exchange transactions, and an initial review of the ban on the employment of Japanese lawyers by foreign law firms. Other measures included deregulation of the taxi business, changing the sale of salt from a license system (monopoly) to a no-license system for retailers, and altering cellular phone rates from an approval system to an advance notification system.[15]

Nonetheless, just listing items does not actually deregulate Japanese systems. Despite the impressive number of programs, the revised plan delayed important measures due to the difficulty of making adjustments among the ruling coalition of the LDP, SDPJ, and NPS. For instance, the new plan failed to lift the ban on holding companies and to break up Nippon Tele-graph and Telephone Corporation (NTT), which monopolizes the domes-tic telephone network. (Japanese phone bills are two to five times those of the United States.) Also, the plan failed to include progressive repeal of the Large Retailers' Law (which restricts large retailers' entry for the protection of smaller retailers). The U.S. and European governments, as well as Japan's big business group, have repeatedly requested the repeal.[16]

Yet a more fundamental problem with the deregulation program is that it did not specify when these measures actually would be implemented and how long it would take. For instance, the plan only promised to start a re-view of the Building Standards Law. A review does not guarantee any ac-tual change. Also, the plan promised liberalization of foreign exchange transactions only in principle. The authorities concerned could mandate as many exceptions to the liberalization as they would like. In essence, the new plan still left a lot of leeway in the implementation of the deregula-tion measures.[17]

Under these circumstances, the application of *gaiatsu* (external pressure) is still necessary to bring these deregulation measures into reality. The United States should continue to pressure Japan to liberalize its markets and internationalize its society. The pressure does not necessarily have to be ap-plied in a confrontational or adversarial fashion, as it sometimes has been in the past; it can be applied in a more collaborative and persuasive manner, as one of the Aesop's fables, "The Wind and the Sun," tells us. The United States should try to convince the Japanese people that *kokusaika* will benefit those who have sacrificed their private interests for the sake of national eco-nomic growth in the postwar period.

For example, the United States should make the point to Japanese con-sumers and consumer advocacy groups that market liberalization will greatly reduce the cost of goods and services, ranging from the price of rice, Japan's number-one staple (a new law concerning food just took effect in February 1996, and Japanese consumers have yet to benefit from the GATT rice liberalization agreement in 1993), to phone service. The United States should also collaborate with proponents of *kokusaika* in Japan. For example, it can work with the associations of Korean residents in Japan and groups of foreign residents who seek Japanese nationality and equal rights. The United States should also mobilize professional groups at home, such as academic institutions, bar associations, the press, and sports interests to pressure their Japanese counterparts and the Japanese government to adopt more open-door policies for professional labor. The United States also should cooperate with the press, both at home and abroad, and launch mas-sive publicity campaigns for Japan's labor *kaikoku* in particular and overall *kokusaika* in general.

Finally, the United States not only should use bilateral channels but also should make concerted efforts with European and Pacific rim countries through the Group of Seven summits and APEC meetings. In addition, the U.S. government should be patient and seek long-term and sustainable solutions rather than quick and superficial results. It should be recalled here that the United States also has employed exclusionist and protectionist policies in the past. Moreover, the Founding Fathers, the Republican Party, and even most free traders believed that protectionism promoted national growth. For instance, the Hoover administration enforced strong protectionist measures under the Hawley-Smoot Tariff Act of 1930, the highest tariff enacted since 1828. The Arthur administration enacted the Chinese Exclusion Act in 1882, while the Coolidge administration banned Japanese immigration through the Immigration Act of 1924.[18]

In this sense, Japan's *sakoku* policy is not an exception but rather is a manifestation of the nationalism employed by other countries, including the United States and Europe. Given its own *sakoku* practices in the past, the U.S. government should recognize that it will take a long time for Japan and other traditional Asian societies to open up.

In essence, the third *kaikoku* opened a Pandora's box and exposed the closed nature of the Japanese psyche to the world. Strong political leadership and effective *gaiatsu* pressure are necessary if the third *kaikoku* is ever to succeed. It should be noted here that all past U.S. efforts to open Japan brought unintended consequences. The first *kaikoku* (Commodore Perry's economic open-door policy) made Japan a military rival of the United States, and the second *kaikoku* (General MacArthur's political open-door policy) made it an economic rival. The third *kaikoku* (highlighted by Commerce Secretary Mickey Kantor's economic open-door policy and Defense Secretary William Perry's military open-door policy) could, at least theoretically, make Japan a political rival of the United States. Should the Japanese government somehow manage to overcome the domestic political contentions and take up *kokusaika* in earnest, Japan could become a major political power in the world.

As of August 1997, it seems unlikely that Japan will become a major political rival of the United States in the foreseeable future. To quote Masaru Tamamoto, who teaches at the American University School of International Service in Washington, D.C., "Japan is a power without purpose . . . it is a nation obsessed with its uniqueness, fundamentally incapable of responsible international leadership." He states that because of the Japanese inability to relate to the world, outside observers are mystified by the behavior of the great power that refuses to act like one. Tamamoto argues that Japan should revamp the two pillars of its Cold War policy stance: pacifism and political isolationism, or what he calls "a willful innocence of international politics." He also says that before Japan can assume greater international responsibilities, it must change some of its fundamental characteristics. Should Japan remain resistant to opening its markets and changing its military policy, the United States, which has acted as "the primary impetus for change on the part of Japan," will grow impatient. Yet in the words of Tamamoto, Japan seeks to redefine its relationship with the United States in the post–Cold War context, while preserving as much as possible the Cold War benefits of that relationship. Ironically, the U.S. global military strategy in the post–Cold War era calls for a more active Japanese engagement in the maintenance of international peace and security and the formation of a more bilateral partnership with the United States in this arena. Failure to do so will jeopardize the strong relationship both nations have enjoyed in the post–World War II period.[19]

The tide of Japan's globalization is irreversible. Japan is in the midst of the daunting task of redefining its national identity to fit its international status. Given the extreme difficulty of changing the characteristics of the nation in general and of the Japanese *sakoku* mentality in particular, conscious and serious efforts by both the Japanese government and its citizens are the crucial prerequisite for the success of the third *kaikoku*. To achieve this goal is to enhance the welfare of the majority of the Japanese who have sacrificed their private happiness for the sake of national economic growth in the postwar period. If human civilization is evolving, then mankind should eliminate all forms of racial discrimination in the twenty-first century. Go Sengen, a master of *Igo* (Chinese chess), suffered from discrimination by his two home countries. Go was born in China in 1914 and went to Japan to study *Igo* in 1928. He obtained Japanese citizenship but was deprived of it with the outbreak of the Sino-Japanese War in 1937. He did not regain Japanese citizenship until 1979. In China, Mr. Go was labeled a traitor because he was naturalized in Japan. The 81-year-old *Igo* master sincerely hopes that the twenty-first century will become a truly equal world, one without racial prejudice.[20]

As for the Japanese, they should overcome their inferiority complex toward the West and their superiority complex toward Asia. By the next century, Japan must become an open society in which all *gaijin* residents can enjoy the benefits and entitlements accorded the Japanese. Suh Yong-dal, a Korean professor at Momoyama Gakuin University in Tokyo, stated that "the litmus test for Japan's internationalization is whether it can create a society in which both the Japanese and foreigners can coexist."[21] Japan's government and its people should make every effort to pass this test. Otherwise, Japan will be left behind by its Asian neighbors and will be isolated from the rest of the world.

Notes

Introduction

1. *"Goran PKO kyô tôchaku"* (Golan PKO arrives today), *Yomiuri Shimbun,* February 1, 1996.
2. *"Shuppatsu semaru Goran PKO"* (Golan PKO departs soon), *Yomiuri Shimbun,* January 26, 1996, and *"Goran PKO"* (Golan PKO), *Chûnichi Shimbun,* January 24, 1996.
3. *"Goran Kôgen PKO"* (Peacekeeping in Golan Heights), *Yomiuri Shimbun,* February 3, 1996.
4. *"Watanabe hatsugen wa môgen"* (Watanabe statement is paranoiac), *Yomiuri Shimbun,* June 5, 1995.
5. *"'Ianfu kikin'"* (Fund for comfort women), *Yomiuri Shimbun,* April 8, 1996.
6. *"Moto ianfu e nennai shikyû wa konnan"* (Unable to pay the former comfort women before the yearend), *Yomiuri Shimbun,* November 28, 1995.
7. *"'Ianfu' baishô o kankoku"* (Recommendations of compensation for "comfort women"), *Yomiuri Shimbun,* November 23, 1994.
8. *"Nihon wa kokka hoshô o"* (Japan should provide state compensation), *Yomiuri Shimbun,* February 7, 1996.
9. *"'Ianfu kikin'"* (Fund for comfort women), *Yomiuri Shimbun,* April 8, 1996, and *"'Ajia josei kikin' hossoku nishûnen"* (Two years since the creation of "Asia Women's Fund"), *Yomiuri Shimbun,* July 19, 1997.
10. *"Kojin mienu Nihon, kojin ni sareta kao"* (Japan without individuals; a face treated as the deceased), *Yomiuri Shimbun,* April 3, 1996.
11. Comprehensive Planning Bureau, Japan's Economic Planning Agency, ed., *Sekai no naka no Nihon* (Japan in the world) (Tokyo: Ministry of Finance, 1984), p. 1, and Ryuhei Hatsuse, *Uchinaru Kokusaika* (Internal internationalization) (Tokyo: Sanrei Shobô, 1985), p. iii.
12. For a detailed definition of *kokusaika,* see Yasushi Sugiyama, "Internal and External Aspects of Internationalization," in Glenn D. Hook and Michael A. Weiner, eds., *The Internationalization of Japan* (New York: Routledge, 1992), pp. 72–103.
13. For a further definition of *kokusaika,* see Toru Yano, *Nihon no kokusaika o kangaeru* (A Thought on Japan's internationalization) (Tokyo: Nikkan Kôgyô Shimbunsha, 1988), and Yano, *Kokusaika no imi* (The meaning of internationalization) (Tokyo: NHK, 1986).

14. Seisaku Kagaku Kenkyûjo, ed., *Nakasone Yasuhiro Shuyô Enzetsushû* (Collection of major speeches of Yasuhiro Nakasone) (Tokyo: Seisaku Kagaku Kenkyûjo, 1984), pp. 32–37.

15. *"Kokuren no jinshu sabetsu teppai jôyaku"* (UN treaty on the elimination of racial discrimination), *Yomiuri Shimbun*, May 20, 1995, and *"Jinshu sabetsu teppai jôyaku o Sanin shônin"* (The House of Councillors approves treaty on the elimination of racial discrimination), *Yomiuri Shimbun,* December 2, 1995.

16. Robert Jervis, *Perception and Misperception in International Politics* (Princeton, N.J.: Princeton University Press, 1976), pp. 3–31.

17. Harold Sprout and Margaret Sprout, *An Ecological Paradigm for the Study of International Politics,* Center for International Studies, Princeton, N.J., Monograph No. 30 (1968), pp. 11–42.

18. "Decision-making as an Approach to the Study of International Politics," in Richard C. Snyder, H. W. Bruck, and Burton Sapin, eds., *Foreign Policy Decision-Making* (New York: The Free Press, 1963), pp. 14–74.

19. Michael Brecher, B. Steinberg, and J. Stein, "A Framework for Research on Foreign Policy Behavior," *Journal of Conflict Resolution,* Vol. XIII, No. 1 (March 1969), pp. 75–101. For an application of Brecher's model, refer to Brecher, *The Foreign Policy System of Israel: Setting, Images, Process* (New Haven: Yale University Press, 1977).

20. Yano, *Nihon no kokusaika o kangeru,* pp. 25, 34–42, and 53.

21. Yasuaki Onuma, *Wakoku to Kyokutô no aida: rekishi to bunmei no naka no "kokusaika"* (Between Japan and Far East: "internationalization" in history and civilization) (Tokyo: Chûô Kôronsha, 1988), p. 67, and Onuma, "Pitfalls of Internationalization," *International House of Japan (IHJ) Bulletin,* Vol. 4, No. 4 (Autumn, 1984), p. 5., and Onuma, ed., *Kokusaika: utsukushii gokai ga umu seika* (Internationalization: the outcome of unintentional misunderstandings) (Tokyo: Tôshindô, 1990).

22. Examples include Malcolm Trevor, ed., *The Internationalization of Japanese Business: European and Japanese Perspectives* (Boulder, Colo.: Westview Press, 1987); Toru Iwami and Houndmills Basingstoke, *Japan in the International Financial System* (New York: St. Martin's Press, 1995); and Charles J. McMillan, ed., *The Japanese Industrial System* (New York: Walter de Gruyter, 1996).

23. Hiroshi Mannari and Harumi Befu, eds., *The Challenge of Japan's Internationalization* (Tokyo: Kôdansha International, 1983). Another earlier study is Ronald Dore, "The Internationalization of Japan," *Pacific Affairs,* Vol. 52, No. 4 (Winter 1979), pp. 594–611.

24. Hook and Weiner, eds., *The Internationalization of Japan.*

25. *"Kokoro no kokusaika wa mada"* (Internationalization of the heart has yet to be seen), *Asahi Nenkan* (Asahi Almanac), (Tokyo: Asahi Shimbunsha, 1995), p. 46, and Soseki Natsume's speech quoted in Tamotsu Aoki, *"Nihon bunkaron" no henyô* (Evolution of the "discourse on Japanese culture") (Tokyo: Chûô Kôronsha, 1990), pp. 7–9.

26. Aoki, *"Nihon bunkaron,"* pp. 11–13.

27. Ibid., pp. 17–19.

28. Ibid., pp. 27–28; Chie Nakane, *"Nihon teki shakai-kôzô no hakken"* (A new light on Japanese social structure), Chûô Kôron (May 1964), pp. 48–85; Keiichi Sakuta, *Haji no bunka saikô* (Reexamination of culture of shame), Shisô no Kagaku (April 1964), pp. 2–11; Kunio Odaka, *Nihon no keiei* (Japan's Management) (Tokyo: Chûô Kôronsha, 1965); Eshun Hamaguchi, *"Nihon rashisa" no saihakken* (Rediscovery of "Japaneseness"), (Tokyo: Nihon Keizai Shimbunsha, 1977); Yasusuke Murakami, Shumpei Kumon, and Seizaburo Sato, *Bunmei to shite no ie shakai* (*Ie* society as a pattern of civilization) (Tokyo: Chûô Kôronsha, 1979; and Ezra Vogel, *Japan as Number One,* (Cambridge, Mass.: Harvard University Press, 1979).

29. Harumi Befu, "Internationalization of Japan and Nihon Bunkaron," in Mannari and Befu, eds., *op. cit.,* pp. 260–263.

30. Chalmers Johnson, "The Internationalization of The Japanese Economy," in ibid., pp. 32–34.

31. Chalmers Johnson, *The MITI and the Japanese Miracle* (Stanford: Stanford University Press, 1982); James Fallows, "Containing Japan," *Atlantic Monthly,* Vol. 263, No. 5 (May 1989), pp. 40–54; Karel van Wolferen, "The Japan Problem," *Foreign Affairs,* Vol. 65, No. 1 (Winter 1986–1987), pp. 288–304; Wolferen, *The Enigma of Japanese Power* (New York: Knopf, 1989); Richard J. Samuels, *"America no 'Nihonjin ron' o sôtenken suru"* (A comprehensive survey of "Japanese studies" in the United States), Chûô Kôron (May 1992), pp. 134–159; and Samuels, *"Nihon ishitsu ronja tachi no kôzai"* (Pluses and Minuses of the revisionists on Japanese studies), Chûô Kôron (June 1992), pp. 190–207.

32. Aoki, *op. cit.,* pp. 126–128; Kunio Odaka, *Nihon teki keiei: sono shinwa to genjitsu* (Japanese style management: its myth and reality) (Tokyo: Chûô Kôronsha, 1984).

33. Masaru Tamamoto, "The Ideology of Nothingness: A Meditation on Japanese National Identity," *World Policy Journal,* Vol. XI, No. 1 (Spring 1994), p. 89.

34. Bruce Stronach, *Beyond the Rising Sun: Nationalism in Contemporary Japan* (Westport, Conn.: Praeger, 1995), pp. 55–56.

35. The Japanese general public's perceptions of *kokusaika* is examined in Chapter 2.

36. *"Kokuren kamei yonjûnen o kataru"* (Speaking about the forty years of Japan's admission to the United Nations), *Yomiuri America,* April 3, 1996.

37. Kent E. Calder, "Japanese Foreign Economic Policy Formation: Explaining the Reactive State," *World Politics* (July 1988), pp. 517–541, and Dennis T. Yasutomo, *The New Multilateralism in Japan's Foreign Policy* (New York: St. Martin's Press, 1995), pp. 34–42.

38. Hisashi Owada, then director-general of the Treaties Bureau, MFA, interview by the author, Tokyo, November 18, 1986.

39. Minoru Tamba, then Japanese consul-general at Boston, interview by the author, Boston, August 25, 1986.

40. Takehito Seki, *"Nihon no taiso seisaku o kangaeru"* (Thinking about Japanese foreign policy toward the Soviet Union), *Sekai,* No. 501 (May 1987), p. 146.

41. Shinji Sudo, *"Nihon no gaikô seisaku"* (Japan's foreign policy), in Hitoshi Hanai, ed., *Hikaku gaikô seisakuron* (Discourse on comparative foreign policy) (Tokyo: Gakuyô Shobô, 1983), pp. 30–31.

42. Shinsaku Hogen, *Nihon no gaikô senryaku* (Strategy for Japan's diplomacy) (Tokyo: Hara Shobô, 1981), pp. 3–4, and interview by the author, Tokyo, October 22, 1986.

Chapter 1

1. Toru Yano, *Nihon no kokusaika o kangaeru* (A thought on Japan's internationalization) (Tokyo: Nikkan Kôgyô Shimbunsha, 1988), p. 41, and *"Oshii yûjin"* (an irreplaceable friend) *Chûnichi Shimbun*, December 15, 1996.

2. Mark Borthwick, *Pacific Century: The Emergence of Modern Pacific Asia* (Boulder, Colo.: Westview Press, 1992), pp. 119–122.

3. Ibid., pp. 127–129, and Richard J. Samuels, *"Rich Nation Strong Army": National Security and the Technological Transformation of Japan* (Ithaca: Cornell University Press, 1994), pp. 84–88.

4. Yano, *op. cit.,* pp. 213 and 218.

5. Frank Gibney, *The Pacific Century: America and Asia in a Changing World* (New York: Maxwell Macmillan, 1992), pp. 104–118 and 147–156.

6. John K. Fairbank, Edwin O. Reischauer, and Albert M. Craig, *East Asia: Tradition and Transformation,* rev. ed., (Princeton, N.J.: Houghton Mifflin, 1989), pp. 817–825.

7. Ibid., pp. 826–827.

8. *"Nichibei bôeki masatsu"* (U.S.-Japan trade friction), *Yomiuri Shimbun,* January 31, 1994.

9. Ryutaro Komiya and Motoshige Itoh, "Japan's International Trade and Trade Policy, 1955–1984," in Takashi Inoguchi and Daniel I. Okimoto, eds., *The Political Economy of Japan,* Vol. 2., *The Changing International Context* (Stanford: Stanford University Press, 1988), pp. 190–193.

10. Koichi Hamada and Hugh T. Patrick, "Japan and the International Monetary Regime," in ibid., pp. 111–118, and *"Amerika, futago no akaji no jittai"* (The reality of the American twin deficits), *Chûnichi Shimbun,* August 22, 1993.

11. Major protagonists of this view include Clyde Prestowitz, Jr., *Trading Places: How We Allowed Japan to Take the Lead,* (New York: Basic Books, 1988), and Karel van Wolferen, *The Enigma of Japanese Power* (New York: Knopf, 1989).

12. *"Maekawa repôto"* (Maekawa report), in Jiyû Kokuminsha, ed., *Gendai yôgo no kiso chishiki 1992* (Basic knowledge of contemporary jargons 1992) (Tokyo: Jiyû Kokuminsha, 1992), p. 387.

13. Ibid.

14. *"Nichibei kôzô kyôgi hajimaru"* (The U.S.-Japan structural talks begin), *Yomiuri Shimbun,* September 16, 1989.

15. *"Kôzô shôheki nakushitara"* (If the structural barriers are removed), *Chûnichi Shimbun,* May 4, 1990.

16. "Japanese ends U.S. Talks; Is Said to Vow Trade Action," *New York Times,* March 4, 1990.

17. Asahiko Isobe, "*'Shihyô' ni tekisanu kawase sôba*" (The exchange rate is not a suitable "index"), *Yomiuri Shimbun,* March 16, 1994.

18. "*Bei, bunya betsu no shijô kaihô o semaru*" (The U.S. demands opening of markets for specific sectors), *Yomiuri Shimbun,* April 18, 1993.

19. "*Nihongata shisutemu sôtenken: seiji, keizai henkaku no michi saguru*" (Overhaul of the Japanese systems: in search of political and economic reforms), *Yomiuri Shimbun,* February 15, 1994.

20. "*Nichibei keizai kyôgi monowakare*" (U.S-Japan economic talks collapsed), *Yomiuri Shimbun,* February 13, 1994.

21. "*Shatô, renritsu seiken o ridatsu*" (The SDPJ left the coalition), *Yomiuri Shimbun,* April 27, 1994. The coinage "perpetual opposition" was quoted from Gerald L. Curtis, *The Japanese Way of Politics* (New York: Columbia University Press, 1988), p. 117.

22. "*Nichibei, hôkatsu kyôgi no saikai happyô*" (Announcement of the resumption of the U.S.-Japan economic framework talks), *Yomiuri Shimbun,* May 25, 1994.

23. Chalmers Johnson, "Artificial Cartels of the Mind Justify Distrust of Japan," *International Herald Tribune,* June 16, 1993 and "*Nihon 'maindo' no karuteru*" (Japanese "mind" cartel), *Global Business,* August 1, 1993, p. 58.

24. Stephen P. Gibert, *Northeast Asia in U.S. Foreign Policy,* (Washington, D.C.: Center for Strategic and International Studies, Georgetown University, 1979), pp. 16–28.

25. Shintaro Ishihara and Morita Akio, "*Nô" to ieru Nihon* (The Japan that can say "no") (Tokyo: Kôbunsha, 1989), pp. 116–130; Chalmers Johnson and E. B. Keehn, "The Pentagon's Ossified Strategy," *Foreign Affairs,* Vol. 74, No. 4 (July-August, 1995), pp. 104–108; and Hisashi Owada, then director-general of the Treaties Bureau, MFA, interview by the author, Tokyo, November 18, 1986.

26. "*Heisei 8-nendo ikô ni kakeru bôei keikaku no taikô ni tsuite*" (On the defense program outline for fiscal year 1996 and thereafter), Defense Agency, November 28, 1995.

27. "*Nichibei yûji kyôryoku kentô e*" (Japan to review U.S.-Japan military cooperation), *Yomiuri Shimbun,* April 30, 1996, and "*Nichibei, shin gaidorain kettei*" (U.S.-Japan new guidelines decided), *Yomiuri Shimbun,* September 24, 1997.

28. "*Hashimoto naikaku stâto*" (Hashimoto cabinet starts), *Yomiuri Shimbun,* January 12, 1996.

29. "*Oshii yûjin*" (an irreplaceable friend) *Chûnichi Shimbun,* December 15, 1996.

Chapter 2

1. "*'Masatsu' ga kikikan zôfuku*" ("Frictions" multiply a sense of crisis), *Asahi Shimbun,* June 28, 1995.

2. Chalmers Johnson, "Artificial Cartels of the Mind Justify Distrust of Japan," *International Herald Tribune,* June 16, 1993.

3. Chie Nakane, *Japanese Society* (Berkeley: University of California Press, 1970), pp. 3–8, and Edwin O. Reischauer, *The Japanese Today* (Cambridge, Mass.: Harvard University Press, 1988), pp. 31–36 and 395.

4. Reischauer, *op. cit.,* pp. 395–400, and *"21 seiki eno josô: rensai 10"* (A warming-up for the twenty-first century: series 10), *Yomiuri Shimbun,* January 4, 1995.

5. *"Nakusô gaikokujin sabetsu"* (Let's remove discriminations against foreigners), *Yomiuri Shimbun,* March 1, 1994.

6. Public Information Division, Prime Minister's Office, ed., *Seron chôsa: gaikô* (public opinion polls: diplomacy), Vol. 28, No. 4 (April 1996), pp. 3–4.

7. Ibid.

8. Ibid.

9. Ibid.

10. Ibid., pp. 5–6.

11. Ibid.

12. Ibid.

13. Ikutaro Shimizu, *"Kaku no sentaku: Nihon yo kokka tare"* (Options for nuclear armament: Japan, be a sovereign nation), *Shokun,* Vol. 12, No. 7 (July 1980), p. 100.

14. Ibid., pp. 37–40.

15. Public Information Division, Prime Minister's Office, *op. cit.,* pp. 15–16.

16. Ibid.

17. *"Goran PKO no anzen taisaku wa"* (Are there safety measures for Golan PKO?), *Yomiuri Shimbun,* April 20, 1996.

Chapter 3

1. T. R. Reid and Paul Blustein, "Japanese View U.S. with New Negativity," *Washington Post,* March 1, 1992, p. 1, author's emphasis.

2. *"Bubei"* (Contempt for the United States), *Yomiuri Shimbun,* March 2, 1992.

3. Don Oberdorfer, "U.S.-Japan Relations Seen Suffering Worst Downturn in Decades," *Washington Post,* March 1, 1992.

4. Reid and Blustein, *op. cit.*

5. Public Information Division, Prime Minister's Office, ed., *Seron chôsa: gaikô* (Public opinion polls: diplomacy) Vol. 28, No. 4 (April 1996), pp. 51–52. The four answers in the original Japanese were *"shitashimi o kanjiru"* (feel friendly*),* *"dochirakatoiuto shitashimi o kanjiru"* (feel somewhat friendly), *"dochirakatoiuto shitashimi o kanjinai"* (do not really feel friendly), and *"shitashimi o kanjinai"* (do not feel friendly at all). The author used English translations by the MFA, "Summary of a Public Opinion Survey," October 1994.

6. Ibid.

7. Reid and Blustein, *op. cit.*

8. Public Information Division, Prime Minister's Office, ed., *op. cit.,* pp. 57–58.

9. Ibid., pp. 53–54.

10. Reid and Blustein, *op. cit.*

11. Kenji Suzuki, *"Hôdô ga odoraseru Nichibei 'kiki'"* ("Crisis" in U.S.-Japan relations made by the mass media), *Chûô Kôron* (May 1992), pp. 76–88.

12. Kenji Suzuki, letter to the author, July 8, 1992, author's emphasis.

13. Yasuo Tanaka and Akira Asada, *"Yûkoku hôdan"* (Foolish talks on the nation), *CREA,* May 1991, pp. 27–29.

14. Ibid., author's emphasis.

15. Ibid., p. 28.

16. Jun Eto and Nagayo Homma, *"'Shinbei' to 'hanei' no aida: Nihonjin wa naze Amerika ga kiraika?"* (In-between "pro-U.S." and "anti-U.S.": why do the Japanese dislike the U.S.?), *Bungei Shunjû,* June 1991, pp. 95–102, author's emphasis.

17. Ibid., pp. 101–103.

18. Interviews, Richard B. Matthews and Motohiro Kondo, March 26, 1993, Los Angeles, California.

19. Ibid.

20. Eto and Homma, *op. cit.,* pp. 95–106, author's emphasis.

21. Ibid., p. 96.

22. Ibid.

23. Paul Kennedy, *The Rise and Fall of the Great Powers: Economic Change and Military Conflict from 1500 to 2000* (New York: Random House, 1987).

24. NHK hôsô yoron chôsosajo, ed., *Sengo yoronshi* (History of postwar public opinion), Vol. 2 (Tokyo: Nippon hôsô shuppan kyôkai, 1982), p. 205; NHK yoron chôsabu, ed., *Gendai nihonjin no ishikikôzô* (The structure of contemporary Japanese consciousness), Vol. 3 (Tokyo: Nippon hôsô shuppan kyôkai, 1992), p. 98; Masaru Tamamoto, "The Ideology of Nothingness: A Meditation on Japanese National Identity," *World Policy Journal,* Vol. XI, No. 1 (Spring 1994), p. 98; and Shintaro Ishihara and Akio Morita, *"Nô" to ieru Nihon* (The Japan that can say "no") (Tokyo: Kôbunsha, 1989).

25. Shintaro Ishihara, *The Japan That Can Say "No"* (New York: Simon and Schuster, 1989).

26. Kiichi Miyazawa, quoted in David E. Sanger, "Japan Premier Joins Critics of Americans' Work Habits," *New York Times,* February 4, 1994.

27. Toshio Ishiwata, *"Kotoba no 'dentatsuryoku' ubau 'gokai' gairaigo no kôzui"* (Flood of "mistaken" foreign words that usurp "communicability" of word"), *Yomiuri Shimbun,* July 18, 1995.

28. Public Information Division, Prime Minister's Office, ed., *op. cit.,* pp. 55–56.

29. Oberdorfer, *op. cit.,* author's emphasis.

30. Armacost, Michael H. *Friends or Rivals?* (New York: Columbia University Press, 1996), p. 254.

Chapter 4

1. *"Taiheiyô sensô wa shinryaku ito nai"* (The Pacific War was not a war of aggression), *Yomiuri Shimbun,* August 13, 1994.

2. Michael Brecher, B. Steinberg, and J. Stein, "A Framework for Research on Foreign Policy Behavior," *Journal of Conflict Resolution,* Vol. XIII, No. 1 (March 1969), pp. 75–101.

3. Ibid.

4. Mark Borthwick, *Pacific Century: The Emergence of Modern Pacific Asia* (Boulder, Colo.: Westview Press, 1992), pp. 119–122.

5. Toru Yano, *Nihon no kokusaika o kangaeru* (A thought on Japan's internationalization) (Tokyo: Nikkan Kôgyô Shimbunsha, 1988), pp. 213, 218, and 221–230.

6. Yasuaki Onuma, *Wakoku to Kyokutô no aida: rekishi to bunmei no naka no 'kokusaika'* (Between Japan and Far East: "internationalization" in history and civilization) (Tokyo: Chûô Kôronsha, 1988), pp. 101–103.

7. Frank Gibney, *The Pacific Century: America and Asia in a Changing World* (New York: Maxwell Macmillan, 1992), pp. 111–112.

8. Chalmers Johnson, *Meiji: Asia's Response to the West,* Vol. 2, *The Pacific Century,* videocassette, The Annenberg/CPB Collection, 1992.

9. Yasuaki Onuma, ed., *Kokusaika: utsukushii gokai ga umu seika* (Internationalization: the outcome of unintentional misunderstandings) (Tokyo: Tôshindô, 1990), p. 218.

10. David A. Titus, "Accessing the World: Palace and Foreign Policy in Post-Occupation Japan," in Gerald L. Curtis, ed., *Japan's Foreign Policy* (Armonk, N.Y.: M. E. Sharpe, 1993), pp. 66–67.

11. Ibid.; *"Tennô hochû"* (Emperor visits China), *Chûnichi Shimbun,* October 24, 1992; and Prasert Chittiwatanapong, "Japan's Roles in the Posthegemonic World: Perspectives from Southeast Asia," in Tsuneo Akaha and Frank Langdon, eds., *Japan in the Posthegemonic World* (Boulder, Colo.: Lynne Rienner, 1993), pp. 214–215.

12. *"Jimin, dakyôan saguru"* (LDP seeks a compromise draft), *Yomiuri Shimbun,* May 21, 1995, and Nicholas D. Kristof, "Japan Expresses Regret of a Sort for the War," *New York Times,* June 7, 1995.

13. *"Nankin daigyakusatsu no kiroku"* (Records of the Nanjing Massacre), *Yomiuri America,* January 14, 1995.

14. *"Sensô sekinin o meguru saikin no kakuryô no hatsugen"* (Recent ministers' comments on war responsibilities), *Yomiuri Shimbun,* August 14, 1994.

15. Ibid. The statements involving Korea in Table 4.1 are discussed later in the chapter.

16. *"'Nankin daigyakusatsu wa Chûgoku no decchiage'"* (The Nanjing massacre is a fabrication by China), *Chûnichi Shimbun,* November 11, 1990.

17. *"Hosô hatsugen & tekkai"* (Justice minister's statement and retraction), *Yomiuri Shimbun,* May 7, 1994.

18. Public Information Division, Prime Minister's Office, ed., *Seron chôsa: gaikô* (Public opinion polls: diplomacy), Vol. 28, No. 4 (April 1996), pp. 61–64. The poll on the Republic of China (Taiwan) was not available.

19. Ibid., pp. 51–52 and 61–64.

20. "A Stickler for History, Even If It's Not Very Pretty," *New York Times,* May 27, 1993, and Allen S. Whiting, *China Eyes Japan* (Berkeley: University of California Press, 1989), pp. 46–51.

21. Jiyû Kokuminsha, ed., *Gendai yôgo no kiso chishiki 1992* (Basic knowledge of contemporary jargons 1992) (Tokyo: Jiyû Kokuminsha, 1992), pp. 907 and 913.

22. Ibid.; *"Daisanji Ienaga kyôkasho soshô: Kuni no ichibu haiso kettei e"* (The third Iyenaga textbook lawsuit: government's partial loss established), *Yomiuri Shimbun,* May 12, 1994; and *"Daisanji Ienaga kyôkasho soshô: Kentei no sankasho ihô"* (The third Iyenaga textbook lawsuit: screening of three accounts ruled unconstitutional), *Yomiuri Shimbun,* October 21, 1993.

23. *"Daisanji Ienaga kyôkasho soshô: Saikôsai, kuni ni baishô meirei"* (The third Iyenaga textbook lawsuit: Supreme Court ordered the government to pay compensation), *Chûnichi Shimbun,* August 30, 1997; T. R. Reid, "Japan's Lessons in History," *Washington Post National Weekly Edition,* September 5–11, 1994, p. 25; and Saburo Ienaga, *The Pacific War, 1931–1945* (New York: Pantheon Books, 1978).

24. Jiyû Kokuminsha, ed., *op. cit.,* p. 328.

25. Ibid., and *"Zanryû koji 36 nin ga rinichi"* (36 orphans left in China leave Japan) *Yomiuri Shimbun,* December 7, 1994.

26. Jiyû Kokuminsha, ed., *op. cit.,* p. 328, and *"Kotoba no kabe, shûshoku nan . . . koji nisei kakutôki"* (Language barrier, difficulty in finding jobs, etc.: second generation orphans' battle) *Yomiuri Shimbun,* December 5, 1994.

27. Kyodo News Service, Tokyo, December 5, 1994, and Seiichi Morimura, *Akuma No Hôshoku* (Insatiable appetite of a devil) (Tokyo: Kadokawa Shoten, 1983 and 1985).

28. Kyodo News Service, ibid.

29. *"Kyû Nihongun dokugasu, Chûgoku ni 200 manpatsu"* (Japan's former army left two million poisonous gas bombs in China), *Yomiuri Shimbun,* January 5, 1995.

30. Ibid., and Kyodo News Service, Hiroshima, December 5, 1994.

31. Jiyû Kokuminsha, ed., *op. cit.,* pp. 327–328.

32. *"Taiwan kakutei saimu shiharai kaishi"* (Payments of established liabilities toward Taiwanese starts), *Yomiuri Shimbun,* December 30, 1994.

33. *"Hosô hatsugen & tekkai"* (Justice minister's statement and retraction), *Yomiuri Shimbun,* May 7, 1994, and *"Taiheiyô sensô wa shinryaku ito nai"* (The Pacific War was not a war of aggression), *Yomiuri Shimbun,* August 13, 1994.

34. *"Watanabe hatsugen wa môgen"* (Watanabe remarks were paranoiac), *Yomiuri Shimbun,* June 5, 1995.

35. *"Eto sômuchô chôkan ofureko hatsugen"* (Management & Coordination Agency director-general Eto's off-the-record remarks), *Yomiuri Shimbun,* November 10, 1995.

36. Public Information Division, Prime Minister's Office, ed., *op. cit.,* pp. 65–58. The poll on the Democratic People's Republic of Korea (North Korea) was not available.

37. Jiyû Kokuminsha, ed., *op. cit.*, p. 329, and *"Nakamura giin ga shazai"* (Nakamura apologized), *Yomiuri Shimbun*, February 10, 1995.

38. "Japan Eases Rule on Korean Aliens," *New York Times*, January 11, 1991.

39. *"Nicchô Kôshô: saikai jitsugen nao kyokusetsu"* (Japan-North Korea negotiations: difficult resumptions), *Yomiuri Shimbun*, October 25, 1994.

40. *"Jûgun ianfu: minkan kikin ni kuni mo shusshi"* (Comfort women: the government will also donate to a private fund), *Yomiuri Shimbun*, November 17, 1994. For details on *ianfu*, refer to George Hicks, *The Comfort Women* (New York: W. W. Norton, 1995).

41. *"Minkan kikin, Nisekki ni secchi"* (A private fund will be created at Japan Red Cross), *Yomiuri Shimbun*, December 7, 1994.

42. *"'Ianfu' baishô o kankoku"* (Recommendation for "comfort women" compensation), *Yomiuri Shimbun*, November 23, 1994; *"Ianfu kikin"* (Fund for comfort women), *Yomiuri Shimbun*, April 8, 1996; and *"Ajia josei kikin' hossoku nishûnen"* (Two years since the creation of "Asia Women's Fund"), *Yomiuri Shimbun*, July 19, 1997.

43. *"'Aimaina Nihon' no watashi"* ("Ambiguous Japan" and I), *Yomiuri Shimbun*, December 8, 1994.

44. *"21 seiki eno josô"* (A warming-up for the twenty-first century), *Yomiuri Shimbun*, January 10, 1995.

Chapter 5

1. This chapter examines the original five ASEAN nations and excludes nonoriginal members such as Bhurnei, Laos, Myanmar, and Vietnam, because the data for the latter were not available.

2. Michael Brecher, B. Steinberg, and J. Stein, "A Framework for Research on Foreign Policy Behavior," *Journal of Conflict Resolution*, Vol. XIII, No. 1 (March 1969), pp. 75–101.

3. Robert O. Keohane and Joseph S. Nye, Jr., *Power and Interdependence: World Politics in Transition* (Boston: Little, Brown, 1977), pp. 23–27.

4. Ibid.

5. Public Information Division, Prime Minister's Office, ed., *Seron chôsa: gaikô* (Public opinion polls: diplomacy), Vol. 27, No. 4 (April 1995), p. 46. The poll asked Japanese perceptions of ASEAN as a whole, not individual states of ASEAN.

6. Ibid., pp. 30, 38, and 41.

7. Ibid., pp. 32, 40, 43, and 46–47.

8. Akira Iriye, *China and Japan in the Global Setting*, (Cambridge, Mass.: Harvard University Press, 1992), p. 45.

9. Chaiwat Khamchoo, "Japan's Role in Southeast Asian Security," *Pacific Affairs*, Vol. 64, No. 1 (Spring 1991), p. 8.

10. Sueo Sudo, *The Fukuda Doctrine and ASEAN* (Singapore: Institute of Southeast Asian Studies, 1992), pp. 1–4 and 230–231.

11. Keizai Kôhô Center, ed., *Japan 1995: An International Comparison* (Tokyo: Keizai Kôhô Center, 1995), p. 42. The data for Thailand were not available.

12. Ibid., pp. 38–39.

13. Ibid., p. 55.

14. Robert Neff et al., "Japan's New Identity," *Business Week,* April 10, 1955, p. 111.

15. Economic Cooperation Bureau, Ministry of Foreign Affairs, ed., *Japan's ODA: Annual Report 1994* (Tokyo: Association for Promotion of International Co-operation, 1995), pp. 291–313.

16. Chaiwat Khamchoo, *op. cit.,* p. 21.

17. *"Tônan Ajia no tainichikan"* (Southeast Asian perceptions of Japan), *Chûnichi Shimbun,* January 1, 1995.

18. Ibid.

19. Ibid.

20. Ibid.

21. Ivan P. Hall, "Japan's Asia Card," *National Interest,* No. 38 (Winter 1994–95), p. 24.

22. Johnson, Chalmers, *"Ajia no kyôdaika o dôyomuka"* (Empowerment of Asia), *Sekai,* February 1995, p. 67, and Chaiwat Khamchoo, *op. cit.,* pp. 18–19.

23. *"Nihon no jôninri iri shiji"* (Support for Japan's bid for a permanent SC member), *Yomiuri Shimbun,* August 28, 1994.

24. *"Hi kara zanryûkoji, iji 32 nin"* (Thirty-two Japanese orphans from the Philippines), *Yomiuri Shimbun,* June 13, 1995.

Chapter 6

1. *"Kokusaika ni gyakkô hanketsu"* (Sentence goes against internationalization), *Yomiuri Shimbun,* January 27, 1995.

2. Ibid.

3. Jiyû Kokuminsha., ed., *Gendai yôgo no kiso chishiki 1992* (Basic knowledge of contemporary jargons 1992) (Tokyo: Jiyû Kokuminsha, 1992), pp. 330 and 386, and Masahiro Shimizu, letter to author, August 24, 1995.

4. Ministry of Labor, ed., *Rôdô hakusho 1994* (Labor white paper 1994) (Tokyo: Japan Labor Research Institute, 1994), pp. 51–54.

5. Ibid.

6. Ibid.

7. *"Gaikokujin rôdôsha"* (Foreign workers), *Yomiuri Shimbun,* February 21, 1995.

8. *"'Masatsu' ga kikikan zôfuku"* ("Frictions" multiply a sense of crisis), *Asahi Shimbun,* June 28, 1995.

9. International Press Division, Ministry of Foreign Affairs, "Survey Reveals Wide Acceptance of Foreign Workers," July 7, 1991, pp. 1–4.

10. Ibid.

11. *"'Kokusekijôkô' ni kokusaika no nami"* (Waves of internationalization on the "nationality clause"), *Yomiuri Shimbun,* May 2, 1996.

12. Ibid., and *"Chihôjichitai no kokusekijôkô teppai"* (Local governments repeal the nationality clause), *Yomiuri Shimbun,* January 10, 1997.
13. *"Zainichi kankokujin hokenfu teiso e"* (A Korean health nurse in Japan files a lawsuit), *Yomiuri Shimbun,* September 12, 1994.
14. *"Gaikokujin kyohi wa iken"* (To reject foreigners is unconstitutional), *Yomiuri Shimbun,* November 27, 1997.
15. Ivan Hall, "Academic Apartheid at Japan's National Universities," Japan Policy Research Institute (JPRI) Working Paper No. 3 (October 1994), pp. 4–6, and "Academic Apartheid Revisited," JPRI Working Paper No. 9 (May 1995), pp. 1–3.
16. Ibid., and Shimizu, *op. cit.*
17. Masao Kunihiro, "Strengths and Weaknesses of Education in Japan," JPRI Working Paper No. 3 (October 1994), pp. 1–3.
18. Nele Freedman, letter to James W. Lamare, September 15, 1995; Jiyû Kokuminsha., *op. cit.,* p. 377; Johnson, *op. cit.; "Gaikoku bengoshi"* (Foreign lawyers), *Yomiuri Shimbun,* August 23, 1995; and Shimizu, *op. cit.*
19. Chalmers Johnson, *op. cit.,* Yoshiko Sakurai, *"Konnanimo aru Mosukuwa tokuhain no 'tabû'"* (So many "taboos" for correspondents in Moscow), *Shokun* (January 1987), pp. 75–76, and Shimizu, *op. cit.*
20. Masahiro Shimizu, letter to author, September 13, 1995.
21. Frank Blackman, "Neel Not Hitting It Off With Japan," *San Francisco Examiner,* May 14, 1995.

Chapter 7

1. Steve Rabson, "Assimilation Policy in Okinawa: Promotion, Resistance, and 'Reconstruction,'" JPRI Occasional Paper No. 8 (October 1996), p. 1. Strictly speaking, Okinawa is a name of an island in Okinawa prefecture; however, Okinawa prefecture is referred to as Okinawa unless specified otherwise.
2. George H. Kerr, *Okinawa: The History of an Island People* (Rutland, Vt.: Charles E. Tuttle Co., 1958), pp. 62–70.
3. Ibid., pp. 136 and 152–159.
4. Rabson, *op. cit.,* p. 2.
5. Kerr, *op. cit.,* pp. 398–399.
6. Rabson, *op. cit.,* pp. 3–4.
7. Ibid., pp. 4–5.
8. Ibid., and *Battle of Okinawa* (TV documentary), 1996, A & E Network.
9. Koji Taira, "The United States, Japan and Okinawa: Conflict and Compromise, 1995–1996," JPRI Working Paper No. 28 (January 1997), p. 2.
10. *"Zainichi Beigun kichi no genjô"* (The reality of U.S. military bases in Japan), *Chûnichi Shimbun,* November 12, 1995.
11. Ibid.
12. Ibid.
13. Ibid.

14. *"Okinawa Beigun, 1,520 patsu gosha"* (U.S. military in Okinawa mistakenly fired 1,520 bullets), *Yomiuri Shimbun,* February 11, 1997.
15. Ibid.
16. *"Okinawa kichi: Kenan saikaidan ni sakiokuri"* (Talks on Okinawa base Issues postponed to the next meeting), *Yomiuri Shimbun,* February 18, 1997.
17. *"Kankyô chôsa raishû kyôdô de"* (To conduct joint environmental research next week), *Yomiuri Shimbun,* February 18, 1997.
18. *"Kaisei Tokusohô ga seiritsu"* (Revised special measures law established), *Yomiuri Shimbun,* April 18, 1997.
19. *"Tokusohô kaisei, nokoru gimonten"* (Remaining questions on the revised special measures law), *Chûnichi Shimbun,* April 8, 1997.
20. *"Shushô hôbei e 'mentsu' o tamotsu"* (Prime minister's face saved for his visit to the U.S.), *Yomiuri Shimbun,* April 11, 1997; *"Tokusohô kaisei shûin tsûka"* (The House of Representatives passed the revised special measures law), *Yomiuri Shimbun,* April 12, 1997; and *"Kaisei Tokusohô seiritsu"* (Revised special measures law established), *Yomiuri Shimbun,* April 18, 1997.
21. *"Kaisei Tokusohô seiritsu"* (Revised special measures law established), *Yomiuri Shimbun,* April 18, 1997.
22. Mike M. Mochizuki, "Toward a New Japan-U.S. Alliance," *Japan Quarterly,* Vol. 43, No. 3 (July-September 1996), pp. 5–6.
23. Ibid., and *"Tokusohô kaisei, nokoru gimonten"* (Remaining questions on the revised special measures law), *Chûnichi Shimbun,* April 8, 1997.
24. *"Nago shichô ga chôsa yônin"* (Nago mayor accepts the research), *Yomiuri Shimbun,* April 9, 1997.
25. *"Jitsudan kunren iten ukeire kettei"* (Relocation of live firing exercises accepted), *Yomiuri Shimbun,* May 2, 1997.
26. *"Korekara no Okinawa"* (Okinawa's future), Series No. 6, *Yomiuri Shimbun,* May 5, 1997.
27. Joseph S. Nye, Jr., "The Case for Deep Engagement," *Foreign Affairs,* Vol. 74, No. 4 (July-August 1995), pp. 90–102; Tsuneo Akaha, "U.S.-Japan Security Alliance Adrift?," paper delivered at the annual meeting of Asian Studies on the Pacific Coast, Asilomar, Calif., June 1997, p. 7; *"Chûngoku kyôi ron' no fumô"* (The futility of "Chinese threat"), *Yomiuri Shimbun,* June 3, 1997; and *"Nihon no jôninri' shiji o hatsu hyômei"* ([Russia's] first support for "Japan's bid for a permanent SC seat"), *Yomiuri Shimbun,* June 22, 1997.
28. Chalmers Johnson and E. B. Keehn, "The Pentagon's Ossified Strategy," *Foreign Affairs,* Vol. 74, No. 4 (July-August 1995), pp. 104–108, and Chalmers Johnson, "The Failure of Japanese and American Leadership After the Cold War: The Case of Okinawa," paper delivered at the annual meeting of Asian Studies on the Pacific Coast, Asilomar, Calif., June 1997, pp. 5–8.
29. Mike M. Mochizuki and Michael O'Hanlon, "The Marines Should Come Home," *Brookings Review,* Vol. 14, No. 2 (Spring 1996), pp. 10–13, and *"Okinawa Kaiheitai no tettai kanô"* (Withdrawal of marines on Okinawa is possible), *Chûnichi Shimbun,* June 5, 1996.
30. Ibid.

31. *"Korekara no Okinawa"* (Okinawa's future), Series No. 2, *Yomiuri Shimbun,* April 30, 1997, and Akaha, *op. cit.,* p. 8.

32. Masamichi Inoki, *"Okinawa no kôgi ni kotaeru michi,"* (The way to answer Okinawa's protest), *Yomiuri Shimbun,* November 22, 1995, and Akaha, *op. cit.,* p. 9.

33. *"Nichibei kankei ga gaikô no kijiku"* (Relationship with the U.S. is the pivot of Japan's diplomacy), *Chûnichi Shimbun,* April 17, 1997, and *"Okinawa shinkô mosaku tsuzuku"* (Continuing search for Okinawa's development), *Yomiuri Shimbun,* May 15, 1997.

34. *"Korekara no Okinawa"* (Okinawa's future), Series No. 5, *Yomiuri Shimbun,* May 4, 1997. The exchange rate is calculated at $1 = ¥115 as of July 1, 1997.

35. *"Okinawa shinkô mosaku tsuzuku"* (Continuing search for Okinawa's development), *Yomiuri Shimbun,* May 15, 1997.

36. *"Korekara no Okinawa"* (Okinawa's future), Series No. 5, *Yomiuri Shimbun,* May 4, 1997.

37. *"Korekara no Okinawa"* (Okinawa's future), Series No. 4, *Yomiuri Shimbun,* May 3, 1997.

38. Ibid.

39. *"Okinawa shinkô motatsuku gutaisaku"* (Stumbling measures for Okinawa's development), *Yomiuri Shimbun,* June 2, 1997.

40. Haruo Shimada, *"Okinawa jiritsu hatten no tamei"* (For Okinawa's independent development), *Yomiuri Shimbun,* May 14, 1997.

41. Johnson, "The Failure of Japanese and American Leadership After the Cold War," pp. 3 and 7.

42. *"NIE no sekai"* (World of "newspaper in education"), *Yomiuri Shimbun,* June 9, 1997.

Chapter 8

1. *"Kome sensô Part 3: Shijô kaihô no eikyô yosoku"* (Rice war part 3: forecasts for effects of the market liberalization), *Chûnichi Shimbun,* April 11, 1993.

2. *"Yunyû mai: 'onkei' wa tômen futômei"* (The unclear "benefit" of imported rice), *Yomiuri Shimbun,* December 14, 1993.

3. Yasuhiko Nakamura, *Kome kaihô* (Rice liberalization) (Tokyo: NHK Shuppan, 1994), pp. 28–30.

4. Interview with Koichi Kato (then-LDP deputy director-general of the Policy Research Council, the party's top decision-making organ), November 10, 1986. His district is the "rice belt" in Miyagi prefecture.

5. "Rice as a Part of Everyday Life," *Japan Pictorial,* Vol. 19, No. 2 (1996), p. 9.

6. Nakamura, *op. cit.,* pp. 53–78, and 105–130, and *"Kome kaihô kettei e"* (Toward the decision on rice liberalization), *Yomiuri Shimbun,* December 14, 1993.

7. *"Kome kaikoku: shin raundo to Nihon"* (Opening of rice: the new round and Japan), Part 3, *Yomiuri Shimbun,* December 16, 1993.

8. *"Sakkyo shisû 75"* (Rice production index 75), *Yomiuri Shimbun,* December 22, 1993.

9. *"Kome bubun kaihô o kettei"* (Decision on the partial opening of rice), *Yomiuri Shimbun,* December 15, 1993.

10. *"'Kome hanbai' gensoku jiyû ni"* ("Rice sale" free in principle), *Yomiuri Shimbun,* November 1, 1995.

11. *"Kome bubun kaihô o 77% yônin"* (Seventy-seven percent approved the partial opening of rice), *Yomiuri Shimbun,* December 24, 1993.

12. Ibid.

13. Proponents of this argument include Kenichi Ohmae, *"Kome mondai: tan-chô-ki no kaiketsu saku"* (Rice issue: short-term and long-term solutions), *Yomiuri Shimbun,* March 29, 1994, and Kenichi Takemura, *Nichibei kyôzon no Jôken* (Conditions for U.S.-Japan coexistence), (Tokyo: Taiyô Kikaku Shuppan, 1990).

14. The figure is based on an assumption that Japan imports 400,000 tons of American rice at $300 a ton.

15. *"Fukuden? mitei' yureru nôka"* ("Undecided *fukuden:*" swayed farmers), *Yomiuri Shimbun,* December 23, 1993. The Japanese fiscal year starts in April and ends in March of the following year.

16. The data are as of March 1994 and are calculated at the exchange rate of $1 = ¥104.

17. *"Yunyû mai: 'onkei' wa tômen futômei"* (The unclear "benefit" of imported rice), *Yomiuri Shimbun,* December 24, 1993.

18. *"Nihon nôka ni kyôteki!?"* (Strong rival of Japanese farmers!?), *Yomiuri Shimbun,* December 13, 1992.

19. *"Okome ga kaenai"* (There is no rice to buy), *Yomiuri Shimbun,* March 6, 1994.

20. Kent E. Calder, *Crisis and Compensation: Public Policy and Political Stability in Japan, 1949–1986* (Princeton: Princeton University Press, 1988), Chapter 5.

21. *"Fukuden"* (Return to rice fields), *Yomiuri Shimbun,* December 25, 1993.

22. *"Fukuden? mitei' yureru nôka"* ("Undecided *fukuden:*" swayed farmers), *Yomiuri Shimbun,* December 23, 1993.

23. *"Kome kaikoku: korekara no kadai"* (Rice opening: new issues), Part 2, *Yomiuri Shimbun,* December 23, 1993.

24. Saburo Yamada, *"Kome sôdô' to shokkan seido"* ("Rice panic" and the food control system), *Chûnichi Shimbun,* March 29, 1994, and Nakamura, *op. cit.,* pp. 42–50.

25. *"Kome kanzei ka: Seifu ketsudan o"* (The government should decide rice tariffication), *Yomiuri Shimbun,* February 3, 1993, and *"Kome kaihô kettei e"* (Toward the decision on rice liberalization), *Yomiuri Shimbun,* December 14, 1993.

26. *"'Burendo,' 'setto,' and 'gentan': chôrei bokai 'Nôsuishô' no shûtai"* (Embarrassing behavior of the "Agricultural Ministry": inconsistent policy of "blend sale," "set sale," and *"gentan"*), *Shûkan Shinchô* (March 24, 1994).

27. *"Kome bôeki"* (Rice trade), *Yomiuri Shimbun,* April 4, 1994, and Nakamura, *op. cit.,* p. 31.

Chapter 9

1. *"Kenpô seron chôsa"* (Opinion polls on the constitution), *Yomiuri Shimbun,* April 3, 1993.

2. Management and Coordination Agency, Prime Minister's Office, ed., *The Organization of The Government of Japan* (Tokyo: 1985), p. 126.

3. *"Nichibei bôei kyôryoku gaidorain minaoshi"* (Review of the guideline for U.S.-Japan defense cooperation"), *Chûnichi Shimbun,* May 13, 1997.

4. Ibid.

5. Ibid.

6. Ibid.

7. *"Kenpô honsha seron chôsa"* ([*Yomiuri*] opinion polls on the constitution), *Yomiuri Shimbun,* April 8, 1993.

8. *"Kenpô seron chôsa"* (Opinion polls on the constitution), *Yomiuri Shimbun,* April 3, 1993.

9. Ibid.

10. Keizai Kôhô Center, ed., *Japan: An International Comparison,* (1993), and Economic Planning Agency, ed., *Kaigai Keizai Data* (Overseas economic data) (1993).

11. *"Nichibei kankei saiteigi"* (Redefining U.S.-Japan relations), *Nikkei Shimbun,* January 28, 1993.

12. Motohiro Kondo, *"Rondan kara"* (From opinion columns), *Gakuyû* (May 1993), pp. 36–37.

13. Ibid.

14. Public Information Office, Prime Minister's Office, ed., *Seron chôsa: gaikô* (Public opinion polls: diplomacy) Vol. 25, No. 4 (April 1993), pp. 7–8.

15. *Asahi Nenkan 1992* (Asahi Almanac) (Tokyo: Asahi Shimbunsha, 1992), p. 71, and *"Omoiyari yosan gengaku"* (The host-nation budget to be reduced), *Yomiuri Shimbun,* August 4, 1997. The exchange rate was calculated at $1 = ¥113 as of August 1997.

16. Kondo, *op. cit.,* April 1991, pp. 36–37.

17. *Asahi Nenkan 1992, op. cit.,* pp. 72–74 and p. 88.

18. Kondo, *op. cit.* (April 1991), p. 36, and *op. cit.* (May 1991), p. 37.

19. *"Kenpô honsha seron chôsa"* ([*Yomiuri*] opinion polls on the constitution), *Yomiuri Shimbun,* April 8, 1993.

20. Kondo, *op. cit.* (August 1992), p. 36.

21. *"Kenpô kaisei honsha seron chôsa"* ([*Yomiuri*] opinion polls on the constitutional revision), *Yomiuri Shimbun,* April 5, 1996.

22. Nippon Hôsô Kyôkai, ed., *Seikatsu to seiji* (Life and politics) (Tokyo: NHK, 1993).

23. *"Jieitai yônin 53%"* (Fifty-three percent accept the SDF), *Yomiuri Shimbun,* June 9, 1994, and Prime Minister's Office, *Jieitai-bôei mondai ni kansuru seron chôsa* (Public opinion poll on the SDF and defense issues) (Tokyo: Prime Minister's Office, May 15, 1994), p. 33.

24. *"Doitsu no kenpô kaisei"* (Germany's constitutional revisions), *Yomiuri Shimbun,* May 2, 1993.

Chapter 10

1. *"Nihon no jônin rijikoku iri"* (Japan's bid for a permanent member), *Yomiuri Shimbun,* April 20, 1994; "Germany in the United Nations," the German Press and Information Office, Bonn, September 1993, pp. 3–6; and *"Kokuren yosan buntan ritsu, gôi yori 0.1% zô"* (UN budget share, 0.1 percent more than Japan agreed), *Yomiuri Shimbun,* July 17, 1994.

2. Japanese Ministry of Foreign Affairs, ed., "Building Peace: Japan's Participation in United Nations Peace-Keeping Operations" (Tokyo: July 1994), pp. 8–9.

3. Japanese Ministry of Foreign Affairs, *Diplomatic Bluebook 1992,* (Tokyo: 1993), pp. 48–52.

4. Ibid., pp. 53–54.

5. Ibid., pp. 54–55.

6. "Building Peace," p. 9, and *"Mozanbîku ni senkyo kanshiin haken"* (Japan sends election monitors to Mozambique), *Yomiuri Shimbun,* August 13, 1994.

7. *"Jônin rijikoku iri ni iyoku"* (Japan is enthusiastic about becoming a permanent member), *Yomiuri Shimbun,* May 7, 1994.

8. *"'Goran' haken hôshin"* (Japan plans to send SDF to "Golan"), *Yomiuri Shimbun,* June 1, 1994.

9. *"Jiki PKO 'kankyô seibi' o"* (Japan needs to develop readiness for future PKO), *Yomiuri Shimbun,* August 4, 1994.

10. *"Ruwanda shien"* (Support for Rwanda), *Yomiuri Shimbun,* August 4, 1994; *"Ruwanda PKO"* (Rwandan PKO), *Yomiuri Shimbun,* August 13, 1994; and *"Ruwanda haken, rikuji hontai hyaku nin"* (100 ground SDF personnel dispatched to Rwanda), *Yomiuri Shimbun,* October 3, 1994.

11. *"Heisei 8-nendo ikô ni kakeru bôei keikaku no taikô ni tsuite"* (On the defense program outline for fiscal year 1996 and thereafter), Defense Agency, November 28, 1995.

12. Prime Minister's Office, ed., *Jieitai, bôei mondai ni kansuru seron chôsa* (Public opinion poll on the SDF and defense issues) (July 1994), p. 37, and ibid., (February 1996), p. 6.

13. *"Nichibeiô gokakoku seron chôsa"* (U.S./Europe/Japan five- nation public opinion poll), *Yomiuri Shimbun,* April 30, 1993, and April 30, 1994.

14. "Germany in the United Nations" *(op. cit.),* pp. 4–8; "Germany: Constitution and Legal System," German Press and Information Office, November 1993, pp. 6–7, and "Federal Constitutional Court Approves Expanded International Role for German Military," *The Week in Germany,* July 15, 1994, pp. 1–2.

15. Wolf, J. Bell, "German UN Membership 20 Years Old," *Inter Nationes Bonn,* SO 7 (1993), pp. 1–3.

16. "Participation of Germany in the United Nations Missions/Peace-Keeping Operations," German Permanent Mission to the United Nations, Press Release No. 28/94, July 15, 1994, pp. 1–7, and Bell, *op. cit.,* p. 4.

17. "Constitutional Court on Military Missions Abroad," German Federal Constitutional Court, Press Release No. 29/94, (in German), July 12, 1994.

18. "United Nations Peace-Keeping" *(op. cit.),* and Hisashi Owada, "A Japanese Perspective on Peace-Keeping," paper delivered at the International Collo-

quium on New Dimensions of Peace-Keeping, Graduate Institute for International Studies, Geneva, Switzerland, March 10, 1994, pp. 2–4.

19. Owada, ibid.

20. Japanese Ministry of Foreign Affairs, ed., *"Kokuren anzenhoshô rijikai ni kansuru ishiki chôsa"* (Public opinion poll on the UN Security Council) (Tokyo: June 1994), pp. 10–18.

21. "Question of Equitable Representation on and Increase in the Membership," UN General Assembly, Document A/48/264, July 20, 1993; *"Nihon no jônin iri shiji"* (Support for Japan's bid for a permanent member), *Yomiuri Shimbun,* May 21, 1994; and *"Gari kokuren sôchô, kugatsu rainichi"* (UN secretary-general Ghali visits Japan in September), *Yomiuri Shimbun,* July 18, 1994.

22. William V. Roth, Jr., "Japan and the Security Council: Special Responsibilities," *Japan Digest,* October 5, 1994, p. 5.

23. *"Nichibeiô gokakoku seron chôsa"* (U.S./Europe/Japan five-nation public opinion poll), *Yomiuri Shimbun,* April 30, 1993, and April 30, 1994.

24. *"Nihon no jôninri iri shiji"* (Support for Japan's bid for a permanent member), *Yomiuri Shimbun,* August 28, 1994; *"Jôninri iri tsuyoku shiji"* (Strong support for Japan's bid for a permanent member), *Yomiuri Shimbun,* August 30, 1994; "South Korea Objects to Giving Japan Veto Even If It Gets UNSC Seat," *Japan Digest,* October 5, 1994, p. 1; and Chalmers Johnson, "Japan/UN paper," e-mail letter to the author, October 5, 1994.

25. *"Nihon no jôninri iri, kôki nogasuna"* (Japan should not lose an opportunity for becoming a permanent member), *Yomiuri Shimbun,* September 13, 1994, and *"Nihon no jôninri iri mondai"* (Issues on Japan's bid for a permanent member), *Yomiuri Shimbun,* October 1, 1994.

26. *"Jôninri iri, Kokuren sôkai de hyômei e"* (Japan expresses its bid for a permanent seat at the UN General Assembly), *Yomiuri Shimbun,* September 28, 1994.

27. *"Murayama shushô shoshin hyômei"* (Prime Minister Murayama's inaugural address), *Yomiuri Shimbun,* July 19, 1994.

28. *"'Nôdôteki anpo' unagasu"* ("Active" security policies urged), *Yomiuri Shimbun,* August 13, 1994.

29. *"Owada Hisashi shi 'kokuren taishi' kiyô wa shippai"* (Appointment of Mr. Hisashi Owada to the UN ambassador was a mistake), *Shûkan Shinchô* (March 24, 1994), pp. 140–141.

30. Ibid., and Ronald Dore, *"Shakaitô sôri no mujun"* (Contradictions of the socialist prime minister), *Chûnichi Shimbun,* July 22, 1994.

31. "Statement by Ambassador Yoshio Hatano at the 5th Meeting of the Open-ended Working Group on the Question of Equitable Representation on and Increase in the Membership of the Security Council," Japanese Permanent Mission to the United Nations, March 16, 1994, p. 2.

32. *"Kawaru Kokuren: Kadai to tembô"* (Changing United Nations: problems and prospects), *Yomiuri Shimbun,* April 30, 1994.

33. *"Jôninri iri,"* (Japan's bid for a permanent seat), *Yomiuri Shimbun,* September 29, 1994, and *"Jôninri kakudai Bei teian,"* (U.S. proposal for the expansion of the Permanent Security Council), *Yomiuri Shimbun,* July 19, 1997.

34. *"Kôken' wa ima ya kokusai gimu ni"* ("Contribution" has now become an international obligation), *Chûnichi Shimbun,* August 10, 1994, and "Statement by Ambassador Yoshio Hatano . . ." p. 5.

Conclusion

1. "A New Korea Via Globalization," Korean Overseas Information Service, July 1995, pp. 1–2.
2. "Globalization: Korea's New Challenge," *Washington Post National Weekly,* September 4–10, 1995, pp. S1–S4.
3. Ibid.
4. Lee Teng-hui, *Creating The Future* (Taiwan: Government Information Office, 1993), pp. 3–9 and 162–168.
5. "Republic of China on Taiwan in the Global Community," Advertising Section, *Foreign Affairs* (September–October 1994), and "An Initiative into the Next Century," Taiwan Coordination and Service Office for Asia-Pacific Regional Operations Center (March 1995), pp. 3–9.
6. Ibid., and Lee Teng-hui, "Always in My Heart," Taiwan's Government Information Office (June 1995), pp. 7–13.
7. *"APEC Osaka kaigi"* (APEC Osaka conference), *Yomiuri Shimbun,* November 15, 1995.
8. *"Nihon no kiseikanwa fujûbun EU shiteki"* (EU notes that Japanese deregulation insufficient), *Yomiuri Shimbun,* November 22, 1995.
9. *"Bei no Bôeki shôheki hôkoku"* (The U.S. report on trade barriers), *Yomiuri Shimbun,* March 31, 1996.
10. *"Jûgun ianfu eno kokka hôshô o yôbô"* (Request for the state compensation for the army's comfort Women), *Yomiuri Shimbun,* May 3, 1996.
11. *"Kankoku hanpatsu no 'heigô jôyaku' Murayama hatsugen"* (South Korea protests Murayama's "annexation treaty" statement), *Yomiuri Shimbun,* October 31, 1995.
12. *"Chûkan kyôdô seimei"* (Sino-South Korean joint communiqué), *Yomiuri Shimbun,* November 28, 1995.
13. *"Hannichiteki na rekishi kyôiku niwa fuman"* (Dissatisfied with anti-Japanese history education), *Yomiuri Shimbun,* December 19, 1995.
14. *"21 seiki eno josô"* (A warming-up for the twenty-first century), *Yomiuri Shimbun,* January 4, 1995.
15. *"Kisei kanwasaku kaitei"* (Revised deregulation policies), *Yomiuri Shimbun,* March 30, 1996.
16. Ibid.
17. Yoshihide Ishiyama, *"Fujûbun na kisei kanwa keikaku"* (Insufficient deregulation plans), *Yomiuri Shimbun,* March 28, 1996.
18. Roger Daniels, *Asian America* (Seattle: University of Washington Press, 1988), pp. 55–56 and 149–151, and Elliot W. Brownlee, *Dynamics of Ascent: A History of the American Economy,* 2nd ed. (New York: Knopf, 1979), pp. 418–420. For a detailed account of U.S. trade policy, refer to Alfred E. Eckes,

Jr., *Opening America's Market: U.S. Foreign Trade Policy Since 1776* (Chapel Hill, N.C.: University of North Carolina Press, 1995).

19. Masaru Tamamoto, "The Ideology of Nothingness: A Meditation on Japanese National Identity," *World Policy Journal,* Vol. XI, No. 1 (Spring 1994), pp. 89–91.

20. *"Shôgai geneki"* (Lifetime work), *Yomiuri Shimbun,* July 23, 1995.

21. *"'Nihon no gaikokujin mondai' kôgi"* (Lectures on "foreigners issues in Japan"), *Yomiuri Shimbun,* June 22, 1995.

Selected Bibliography

Government Publications

Germany

"Constitutional Court on Military Missions Abroad." German Federal Constitutional Court, Press Release No. 29/94 (translation), July 12, 1994.

"Federal Constitutional Court Approves Expanded International Role for German Military." *The Week in Germany,* July 15, 1994.

"Germany in the United Nations." German Press and Information Office, Bonn, September 1993.

"Germany: Constitution and Legal System." German Press and Information Office, November 1993.

"Participation of Germany in the United Nations Missions/Peace-Keeping Operations." German Permanent Mission to the United Nations, Press Release No. 28/94, July 15, 1994.

Japan

Comprehensive Planning Bureau, Economic Planning Agency, ed. *Sekai no naka no Nihon* (Japan in the world). Tokyo: Ministry of Finance, 1984.

Economic Cooperation Bureau, Ministry of Foreign Affairs, ed. *Japan's ODA: Annual Report 1994.* Tokyo: Association for Promotion of International Cooperation, 1995.

Economic Planning Agency, ed. *Kaigai keizai data* (Overseas economic data). Tokyo: Economic Planning Agency, 1993.

International Press Division, Ministry of Foreign Affairs, ed. "Survey Reveals Wide Acceptance of Foreign Workers." Tokyo: MFA, July 7, 1991.

Japan's Defense Agency, ed. *Defense White Book 1995.* Tokyo: JDA, 1995.

Keizai Kôhô Center, ed. *Japan 1993: An International Comparison.* Tokyo: Keizai Kôhô Center, 1993.

Keizai Kôhô Center, ed., *Japan 1995: An International Comparison,* Tokyo: Keizai Kôhô Center, 1995.

Management and Coordination Agency, Prime Minister's Office, ed. *The Organization of the Government of Japan.* Tokyo: Prime Minister's Office, 1985.

Ministry of Foreign Affairs, ed. *Diplomatic Bluebook 1992.* Tokyo: MFA, 1993.

————, ed. "*Kokuren anzenhoshô rijikai ni kansuru ishiki chôsa*" (Public opinion poll on the UN Security Council). Tokyo: MFA, June 1994.

————, ed. "Building Peace: Japan's Participation in United Nations Peace-Keeping Operations." Tokyo: MFA, July 1994.

————, ed. *Diplomatic Blue Book 1995.* Tokyo: MFA, 1995.

Ministry of Labor, ed. *Rôdô hakusho 1994* (Labor white paper 1994). Tokyo: Japan Labor Research Institute, 1994.

Prime Minister's Office, ed. *Jieitai, bôei mondai ni kansuru seron chôsa* (Public opinion poll on the SDF and defense issues). Tokyo: Prime Minister's Office, July 1994.

————. *Jieitai, bôei mondai ni kansuru seron chôsa* (Public opinion poll on the SDF and defense issues). Tokyo: Prime Minister's Office, February 1996.

Public Information Office, Prime Minister's Office, ed. *Seron chôsa: gaikô* (Public opinion polls: diplomacy). Tokyo: Prime Minister's Office, Vol. 25, No. 4 (April 1993).

————, ed. *Seron chôsa: gaikô* (Public opinion polls: diplomacy). Tokyo: Prime Minister's Office, Vol. 28, No. 4 (April 1996).

South Korea

"A New Korea Via Globalization." Korean Overseas Information Service, July 1995.

Taiwan

"An Initiative into the Next Century." Taipei: Coordination and Service Office for Asia-Pacific Regional Operations Center, March 1995.

Lee Teng-hui. *Creating the Future.* Taipei: Government Information Office, 1993.

————. "Always in My Heart." Taipei: Government Information Office, June 1995.

UN Documents

"Charter of the UN and Statute of the International Court of Justice." UN Office of Public Information, DPI/511–175M, 1980.

"Question of Equitable Representation on and Increase in the Membership." UN General Assembly, Document A/48/264, July 20, 1993.

"United Nations Peace-Keeping." UN Department of Public Information, DPI/1306/Rev. 3, June 1994.

Books

Abe, Kiyoshi, William Gunther, and Harold See, eds. *Economic Industrial and Managerial Coordination Between Japan and the U.S.A.* New York: St. Martin's Press, 1993.

Akaha, Tsuneo, and Frank L. Langdon, eds. *Japan in the Posthegemonic World.* Boulder, Colo.: Lynne Rienner, 1993.

Aoki, Tamotsu. *"Nihon bunkaron" no henyô* (Changes in the "discourse on Japanese culture"). Tokyo: Chûô Kôronsha, 1990.

Armacost, Michael H. *Friends or Rivals?: The Insider's Account of U.S.-Japan Relations.* New York: Columbia University Press, 1996.

Atlantic Council of the United States, ed. *The United States and Japan: Cooperative Leadership for Peace and Global Prosperity.* Lanham, Md.: University Press of America, 1990.

Bienen, Henry, ed. *Power, Economics, and Security: The U.S. and Japan in Focus.* Boulder, Colo.: Westview Press, 1992.

Borthwick, Mark. *Pacific Century: The Emergence of Modern Pacific Asia.* Boulder, Colo.: Westview Press, 1992.

Brecher, Michael. *The Foreign Policy System of Israel: Setting, Images, Process.* New Haven: Yale University Press, 1977.

Brownlee, Elliot W. *Dynamics of Ascent: A History of the American Economy.* 2nd ed. New York: Knopf, 1979.

Buckley, Roger. *US-Japan Alliance Diplomacy, 1945–1990.* New York: Cambridge University Press, 1992.

Calder, Kent E. *Crisis and Compensation: Public and Political Stability in Japan.* Princeton: Princeton University Press, 1988.

————. *Strategic Capitalism: Private Business and Public Purpose in Japan.* Princeton: Princeton University Press, 1993.

Christelow, Dorothy B. *When Giants Converge: The Story of U.S.-Japan Direct Investment.* Armonk, N.Y.: M. E. Sharpe, 1993.

Clyde Prestowitz, Jr. *Trading Places: How We Allowed Japan to Take the Lead.* New York: Basic Books, 1988.

Curtis, Gerald L. *The Japanese Way of Politics.* New York: Columbia University Press, 1988.

————, ed. *Japan's Foreign Policy After the Cold War.* Armonk, NY: M. E. Sharpe, 1993.

————, ed. *The United States, Japan, and Asia.* New York: W. W. Norton, 1994.

Daniels, Roger. *Asian America.* Seattle: University of Washington Press, 1988.

Eckes, Alfred E., Jr. *Opening America's Market: U.S. Foreign Trade Policy Since 1776.* Chapel Hill, N.C.: University of North Carolina Press, 1995.

Fairbank, John K., Edwin O. Reischauer, and Albert M. Craig. *East Asia: Tradition and Transformation.* Rev. ed. Princeton: Houghton Mifflin, 1989.

Feinburg, Walter. *Japan and the Pursuit of a New American Identity: Work and Education in a Multicultural Age.* New York: Routledge, 1993.

Frankel, Jeffrey A., and Miles Kahler, eds. *Regionalism and Rivalry: Japan and the United States in Pacific Asia.* Chicago: University of Chicago Press, 1993.

Fraser, Andrew, R. H. P. Mason, and Philip Mitchell. *Japan's Early Parliaments, 1890–1905: Structure, Issues and Trends.* New York: Routledge, 1995.

Gibert, Stephen P. *Northeast Asia in U.S. Foreign Policy.* Washington, D.C.: Center for Strategic and International Studies, Georgetown University, 1979.

Gibney, Frank. *The Pacific Century: America and Asia in a Changing World.* New York: Maxwell Macmillan, 1992.

Goodman, Grant K. ed. *Japanese Cultural Policies in Southeast Asia During World War II.* New York: St. Martin's Press, 1991.

Grant, Richard L., ed. *Strengthening the U.S.-Japan Partnership in the 1990s.* Boulder, Colo.: Westview Press, 1992.

Green, Michael J. *Arming Japan.* New York: Columbia University Press, 1995.

Hamaguchi, Eshun. *'Nihon rashisa' no saihakken* (Rediscovery of 'Japaneseness'). Tokyo: Nihon Keizai Shimbunsha, 1977.

Hanai, Hitoshi., ed. *Hikaku gaikô seisakuron* (Discourse on comparative foreign policy). Tokyo: Gakuyô Shobô, 1983.

Hatsuse, Ryuhei. *Uchinaru Kokusaika* (Internal internationalization). Tokyo: Sanrei Shobô, 1985.

Hellmann, Donald C. *The United States and Japan After the Cold War.* Lanham, Md.: AEI Press, 1992.

Herzog, Peter J. *Japan's Pseudo-Democracy.* New York: New York University Press, 1993.

Hicks, George. *The Comfort Women.* New York: W. W. Norton, 1995.

Hogen, Shinsaku. *Nihon no Gaikô Senryaku* (Strategy for Japan's diplomacy). Tokyo: Hara Shobô, 1981.

Holland, Harrison M. *Japan Challenges America: Managing an Alliance in Crisis.* Boulder, Colo.: Westview Press, 1992.

Hook, Glenn D., and Michael A. Weiner, eds. *The Internationalization of Japan.* New York: Routledge, 1992.

Ibe, Hideo. *Japan Thrice-Opened: An Analysis of Relations Between Japan and the United States.* New York: Praeger, 1992.

Ienaga, Saburo. *The Pacific War, 1931–1945.* New York: Pantheon Books, 1978.

Inoguchi, Takashi. *Japan's Foreign Policy in an Era of Global Change.* New York: St. Martin's Press, 1993.

―――, and Daniel I. Okimoto, eds. *The Political Economy of Japan.* Vol. 2. *The Changing International Context.* Stanford: Stanford University Press, 1988.

Iriye, Akira. *China and Japan in the Global Setting.* Cambridge, Mass.: Harvard University Press, 1992.

Ishihara, Shintaro, and Akio Morita. *"Nô" To Ieru Nihon* (The Japan That Can Say "No"). Tokyo: Kôbunsha, 1989.

Ishihara, Shintaro. *The Japan That Can Say "No."* New York: Simon and Schuster, 1989.

Iwami, Toru, and Houndmills Basingstoke, *Japan in the International Financial System.* New York: St. Martin's Press, 1995.

Jacob, Jo Dee. *Beyond the Hoppo Ryodo: Japanese-Soviet-American Relations in the 1990s.* Lanham, Md.: The AEI Press, 1991.

Jervis, Robert. *Perception and Misperception in International Politics.* Princeton, N.J.: Princeton University Press, 1976.

Johnson, Chalmers. *MITI and the Japanese Economic Miracle: The Growth of Industrial Policy, 1925–1975.* Stanford: Stanford University Press, 1982.

―――. *Japan: Who Governs: The Rise of the Developmental State.* New York: W. W. Norton, 1995.

Kennedy, Paul. *The Rise and Fall of the Great Powers: Economic Change and Military Conflict from 1500 to 2000.* New York: Random House, 1987.

Keohane, Robert O., and Joseph S. Nye, Jr. *Power and Interdependence: World Politics in Transition.* Boston: Little, Brown, 1977.

Kerr, George H. *Okinawa: The History of An Island People.* Rutland, Vt.: Charles E. Tuttle, 1958.

Lincoln, Edward J. *Japan's Unequal Trade.* Washington, D.C.: Brookings Institution, 1990.

———. *Japan's New Global Role.* Washington, D.C.: Brookings Institution, 1993.

Mannari, Hiroshi, and Harumi Befu, eds. *The Challenge of Japan's Internationalization.* Tokyo: Kôdansha International, 1983.

Mason, T. David, and Abdul M. Turay, eds. *U.S.-Japan Trade Friction: Its Impact on Security Cooperation in the Pacific Basin.* New York: St. Martin's Press, 1991.

McMillan, Charles J., ed. *The Japanese Industrial System.* New York: Walter de Gruyter, 1996.

Miyoshi, Masao. *Off Center: Power and Culture Relations Between Japan and the United States.* Cambridge, Mass.: Harvard University Press, 1991.

Morimura, Seiichi. *Akuma no hôshoku* (Insatiable appetite of a devil). Vols. 1 and 2. Tokyo: Kadokawa Shoten, 1983 and 1985.

Morris, Jonathan, ed. *Japan and the Global Economy.* New York: Routledge, 1991.

Murakami, Yasusuke, Shumpei Kumon, and Seizaburo Sato. *Bunmei to shite no ie shakai* (Ie society as a civilization), Tokyo: Chûô Kôronsha, 1979.

Nakamura, Yasuhiko. *Kome Kaihô* (Rice liberalization). Tokyo: NHK Shuppan, 1994.

Nakane, Chie. *Tate shakai no ningen kankei* (English title: Japanese Society). Berkeley: University of California Press, 1970.

Nester, William R. *The Foundation of Japanese Power: Continuities, Changes, Challenges.* Armonk, N.Y.: M. E. Sharpe, 1990.

NHK hôsô yoron chôsosajo, ed. *Sengo yoronshi* (History of postwar public opinion), Vol. 2. Tokyo: Nippon hôsô shuppan kyôkai, 1982.

NHK yoron chôsabu, ed. *Gendai nihonjin no ishikikôzô* (The structure of contemporary Japanese consciousness), vol. 3. Tokyo: Nippon hôsô shuppan kyôkai, 1992.

Nippon Hôsô Kyôkai, ed. *"Seikatsu to seiji"* (Life and politics). Tokyo: NHK, 1993.

Odaka, Kunio. *Nihon no keiei* (Japan's management). Tokyo: Chûô Kôronsha, 1965.

———. *Nihon teki keiei: Sono shinwa to genjitsu* (Japanese style management: its myth and reality). Tokyo: Chûô Kôronsha, 1984.

Onuma, Yasuaki. *Wakoku to Kyokutô no aida: rekishi to bunmei no naka no "kokusaika"* (Between Japan and Far East: "internationalization" in history and civilization). Tokyo: Chûô Kôronsha, 1988.

———, ed. *Kokusaika: Utsukushii gokai ga umu seika* (Internationalization: The outcome of unintentional misunderstandings). Tokyo: Tôshindô, 1990.

Prestowitz, Clyde, Jr. *Trading Places: How We Allowed Japan to Take the Lead.* New York: Basic Books, 1988.

Pyle, Kenneth B. *The Japanese Question: Power and Purpose in a New Era.* Lanham, Md.: AEI Press, 1992.

Reishauer, Edwin O. *The Japanese Today: Change and Continuity.* Cambridge, Mass.: Harvard University Press, 1988.

Rix, Alan. *Japan's Foreign Aid Challenge: Policy Reform and Aid Leadership.* New York: Routledge, 1993.

Rozman, Gilbert. *Japan's Response to the Gorbachev Era, 1985–1991: A Rising Superpower Views a Declining One.* Princeton, N.J.: Princeton University Press, 1992.

Samuels, Richard J. *"Rich Nation Strong Army": National Security and the Technological Transformation of Japan.* Ithaca, N.Y.: Cornell University Press, 1994.

———, and Myron Weiner, eds. *The Political Culture of Foreign Area and International Studies.* New York: Brassey's, 1992.

Sato, Seizaburo, and Trevor Taylor, eds. *Prospect for Global Order.* Washington, D.C.: Brookings Institution, 1993.

Seisaku Kagaku Kenkyûjo, ed. Nakasone Yasuhiro Shuyô Enzetsushû (Collection of major speeches of Yasuhiro Nakasone). Tokyo: Seisaku Kagaku Kenkyûjo, 1984.

Sprout, Harold, and Margaret Sprout. *An Ecological Paradigm for the Study of International Politics.* Monograph No. 30. Princeton, N.J.: Center for International Studies, 1968.

Stronach, Bruce. *Beyond the Rising Sun: Nationalism in Contemporary Japan.* Westport, Conn.: Praeger, 1995.

Sudo, Sueo. *The Fukuda Doctrine and ASEAN: New Dimensions in Japanese Foreign Policy.* Singapore: Institute of Southeast Asian Studies, 1992.

Takemura, Kenichi. *Nichibei Kyôzon no Jôken* (Conditions for U.S.-Japan coexistence). Tokyo: Taiyô Kikaku Shuppan, 1990.

Tokunaga, Shojiro, ed. *Japan's Foreign Investment and Asian Economic Interdependence: Production, Trade, and Financial Systems.* Tokyo: University of Tokyo Press, 1992.

Trevor, Malcolm, ed. *The Internationalization of Japanese Business: European and Japanese Perspectives.* Boulder, Colo.: Westview Press, 1987.

Unger, Danny, and Paul Blackburn, eds. *Japan's Emerging Global Role.* Boulder, Colo.: Lynne Rienner, 1993.

van Wolferen, Karel. *The Enigma of Japanese Power.* New York: Knopf, 1989.

———. *Ningen o kôfuku ni shinai Nihon to iu sisutemu* (The Japanese system that does not make people happy). Tokyo: Mainichi Shimbunsha, 1995.

Vogel, Ezra. *Japan as Number One.* Cambridge, Mass.: Harvard University Press. 1979.

Whiting, Allen S. *China Eyes Japan.* Berkeley: University of California Press, 1989.

Yamamura, Kozo, and Yasukichi Yasuba, eds. *The Political Economy of Japan.* Vol. 1, *The Domestic Transformation.* Stanford: Stanford University Press, 1987.

Yano, Toru. *Kokusaika no imi* (The meaning of internationalization). Tokyo: NHK, 1986.

———. *Nihon no kokusaika o kangaeru* (A thought on Japan's internationalization). Tokyo: Nikkan Kôgyô Shimbunsha, 1988.

Yasutomo, Dennis T. *The New Multilateralism in Japan's Foreign Policy.* New York: St. Martin's Press, 1995.

Articles

Befu, Harumi. "Internationalization of Japan and Nihon Bunkaron." In Hiroshi Mannari and Harumi Befu, eds., *The Challenge of Japan's Internationalization.* Tokyo: Kôdansha International, 1983, pp. 232–266.

Brecher, Michael, B. Steinberg, and J. Stein. "A Framework for Research on Foreign Policy Behavior." *Journal of Conflict Resolution*, Vol. XIII, No. 1 (March 1969), pp. 75–101.

Calder, Kent E. "Japanese Foreign Economic Policy Formation: Explaining the Reactive State." *World Politics* (July 1988), pp. 517–541.

Chittiwatanapong, Prasert. "Japan's Roles in the Posthegemonic World: Perspectives from Southeast Asia." In Tsuneo Akaha and Frank Langdon, eds., *Japan in the Posthegemonic World*. Boulder, Colo.: Lynne Rienner, 1993, pp. 201–231.

Dore, Ronald. "The Internationalization of Japan." *Pacific Affairs*, Vol. 52, No. 4 (Winter 1979), pp. 594–611.

Eto, Jun and Nagayo Homma. "'Shinbei' to 'hanei' no aida": Nihonjin wa naze Amerika ga kiraika?" (In-between "pro-U.S." and "anti-U.S.": why do the Japanese dislike the U.S.?). *Bungei Shunjû* (June 1991), pp. 95–102.

Fallows, James. "Containing Japan." *Atlantic Monthly* (May 1989), pp. 40–54.

————. "After Centuries of Japanese Isolation, A Fateful Meeting of East and West." *Smithsonian* (July 1994), pp. 20–33.

Hall, Ivan P. "Japan's Asia Card." *National Interest*, No. 38 (Winter 1994/95), pp. 19–27.

————. "Academic Apartheid at Japan's National Universities." Japan Policy Research Institute (hereafter JPRI) Working Paper No. 3 (October 1994), pp. 4–6.

————. "Academic Apartheid Revisited," JPRI Working Paper No. 9 (May 1995), pp. 1–3.

Hamada, Koichi and Hugh T. Patrick. "Japan and the International Monetary Regime." In Takashi Inoguchi and Daniel I. Okimoto, eds., *The Political Economy of Japan*. Vol. 2, *The Changing International Context*. Stanford: Stanford University Press, 1988, pp. 190–193.

Johnson, Chalmers. "The Internationalization of The Japanese Economy." In Hiroshi Mannari and Harumi Befu, eds., *The Challenge of Japan's Internationalization*. Tokyo: Kôdansha International, 1983, pp. 31–58.

————. "Ajia no kyôdaika o dôyomuka" (Empowerment of Asia), *Sekai* (February 1995), pp. 64–77.

————. and E. B. Keehn. "The Pentagon's Ossified Strategy." *Foreign Affairs*, Vol. 74, No. 4 (July–August, 1995), pp. 103–114.

Khamchoo, Chaiwat. "Japan's Role in Southeast Asian Security." *Pacific Affairs*, Vol. 64, No. 1 (Spring 1991), pp. 7–22.

Komiya, Ryutaro, and Motoshige Itoh. "Japan's International Trade and Trade Policy, 1955–1984." In Takashi Inoguchi and Daniel I. Okimoto, eds., *The Political Economy of Japan*. Vol. 2, *The Changing International Context*. Stanford: Stanford University Press, 1988, pp. 173–224.

Kondo, Motohiro. "Rondan kara" (From opinion columns). Gakuyû, April 1991, pp. 36–37, and May 1993, pp. 36–37.

Kunihiro, Masao. "Strengths and Weaknesses of Education in Japan." JPRI Working Paper No. 3 (October 1994), pp. 1–3.

Mochizuki, Mike M. "Japan's Search for Strategy." *International Security*, No. 8 (Winter 1983/84), pp. 153–181.

————. "Toward a New Japan-U.S. Alliance." *Japan Quarterly,* Vol. 43, No. 3 (July–September 1996), pp. 4–16.

————, and Michael O'Hanlon. "The Marines Should Come Home." *Brookings Review,* Vol. 14, No. 2 (Spring 1996), pp. 10–13.

Nakane, Chie. *"Nihon teki shakai-kôsô no nakken"* (A new light on Japanese social structure). Chûô Kôron (May 1964), pp. 48–85.

Nye, Joseph, Jr. "The Case for Deep Engagement." *Foreign Affairs,* Vol. 74, No. 4 (July–August 1995), pp. 90–102.

Onuma, Yasuaki. "Pitfalls of Internationalization." *International House of Japan (IHJ) Bulletin,* Vol. 4, No. 4 (Autumn, 1984), pp. 1–5.

Rabson, Steve. "Assimilation Policy in Okinawa: Promotion, Resistance, and 'Reconstruction.'" JPRI Occasional Paper No. 8 (October 1996), pp. 1–6.

Sakurai, Yoshiko. "Konnanimo aru Mosukuwa tokuhain no 'tabû'" (So many "taboos" for correspondents in Moscow). *Shokun* (January 1987), pp. 70–79.

Sakuta, Keiichi. *"Haji no bunka saikô"* (Reexamination of culture of shame). Shisô Kagagu (April 1964), pp. 2–11.

Samuels, Richard J. "America no 'Nihonjin ron' o sôtenken suru" (A comprehensive survey of "Japanese studies in the United States"). *Chûô Kôron* (May 1992), pp. 134–159.

————. "Nihon ishitsu ronja tachi no kôzai" (Pluses and minuses of the revisionists on Japan). *Chûô Kôron* (June 1992), pp. 190–207.

————. "Japanese Political Studies and the Myth of the Independent Intellectual." In Samuels and Myron Weiner, eds., *The Political Culture of Foreign Area and International Studies.* New York: Brassey's, 1992, pp. 17–56.

Sato, Yoichiro. "Sticky Efforts: Japan's Rice Market Opening and U.S.-Japan Transnational Lobbying." *Japan Studies,* No. 1 (1996), pp. 73–99.

Seki, Takehito. "Nihon no taiso seisaku o kangaeru" (Thinking about Japanese foreign policy toward the Soviet Union). *Sekai,* No. 501 (May 1987), pp. 135–146.

Shimizu, Ikutaro. "Kaku no sentaku: Nihon yo kokka tare" (Options for nuclear armament: Japan, be a sovereign nation). *Shokun,* Vol. 12, No. 7 (July 1980), pp. 1–110.

Snyder, Richard C., H. W. Bruck, and Burton Sapin. "Decision-making as an Approach to the Study of International Politics." In Richard C. Snyder, H. W. Bruck, and Burton Sapin, eds., *Foreign Policy Decision-Making.* New York: Free Press, 1963, pp. 14–74.

Sudo, Shinji. "Nihon no gaikô seisaku" (Japan's foreign policy). In Hitoshi Hanai, ed., *Hikaku gaikô seisakuron* (Discourse on comparative foreign policy). Tokyo: Gakuyô Shobô, 1983, pp. 16–35.

Sugiyama, Yasushi. "Internal and External Aspects of Internationalization." In Glenn D. Hook, and Michael A. Weiner, eds., *The Internationalization of Japan.* New York: Routledge, 1992, pp. 72–103.

Suzuki, Kenji. "Hôdô ga odoraseru Nichibei 'kiki'" ("Crisis" in U.S.-Japan relations made by the mass media). *Chûô Kôron* (May 1992), pp. 76–88.

Taira, Koji. "The United States, Japan and Okinawa: Conflict and Compromise, 1995–1996." JPRI Working Paper No. 28 (January 1997), pp. 1–3.

Tamamoto, Masaru. "The Ideology of Nothingness: A Meditation on Japanese National Identity." *World Policy Journal,* Vol. XI, No. 1 (Spring 1994), pp. 89–99.

Tanaka, Yasuo, and Akira Asada. "Yûkoku hôdan" (Foolish talks on the nation). *CREA* (May 1991), pp. 27–29.

Titus, David A. "Accessing the World: Palace and Foreign Policy in Post-Occupation Japan." In Gerald L. Curtis, ed., *Japan's Foreign Policy.* Armonk, N.Y.: M. E. Sharpe, 1993, pp. 62–89.

van Wolferen, Karel. "The Japan Problem." *Foreign Affairs,* Vol. 65, No. 1 (Winter 1986/1987), pp. 288–304.

Conference Papers

Akaha, Tsuneo. "U.S.-Japan Security Alliance Adrift?" Paper delivered at the annual meeting of Asian Studies on the Pacific Coast, Asilomar, Calif., June 1997, pp. 1–16.

Johnson, Chalmers. "The Failure of Japanese and American Leadership After the Cold War: The Case of Okinawa." Paper delivered at the annual meeting of Asian Studies on the Pacific Coast, Asilomar, Calif., June 1997, pp. 1–19.

Hatano, Yoshio. "Statement by Ambassador Yoshio Hatano at the 5th Meeting of the Open-ended Working Group on the Question of Equitable Representation on and Increase in the Membership of the Security Council." Japanese Permanent Mission to the UN, March 16, 1994, pp. 1–5.

Owada, Hisashi. "A Japanese Perspective on Peace-Keeping." Paper delivered at the International Colloquium on New Dimensions of Peace-Keeping, Graduate Institute for International Studies, Geneva, Switzerland, March 10, 1994, pp. 1–12.

Reference Books

Asahi Nenkan (Asahi Almanac). Tokyo: Asahi Shimbunsha, 1992, 1995.

Jiyû Kokuminsha, ed. *Gendai yôgo no kiso chishiki 1992* (Basic knowledge of contemporary jargons 1992). Tokyo: Jiyû Kokuminsha, 1992.

Magazines

Business Week
Global Business
Japan Digest
Japan Pictorial
Shûkan Shinchô
Newspapers
Asahi Shimbun
Chûnichi Shimbun
International Herald Tribune

Japan Times
Monterey Herald
New York Times
Nikkei Shimbun
San Francisco Examiner
Yomiuri America
Yomiuri Shimbun
Washington Post

Index

42–44, 100–101, 147, 153,
157–58, 161–76
budget, 161, 168, 170
United Nations Protection Force
(UNPROFOR) 163, 169
United Nations Security Council,
161–62, 171–72
Japan's bid, 100, 161, 165, 171–76
nonpermanent members, 175
permanent members, 174–75
reforms, 174–75
United Nations Transitional Authority
in Cambodia (UNTAC), 1, 44,
157, 162–64, 167, 170, 176
UNMOGIP (India/Pakistan), 169
UNOMIG (Georgia), 169
UN Peace Cooperation Bill, 157, 162,
164
UNPKF, 173–74
See also peacekeeping force
UNTAG (Namibia), 162, **163**
UNTSO (Jerusalem), 169
Uruguay Round, 133, 135–37
See also GATT
Ushio, Jiro, 130
U.S.-Japan Mutual Security Aid (MSA)
Agreement, 149
U.S.-Japan Security Treaty, 15–16, 25,
31–33, 42, 59, 131
U.S.-Japan Summit (Tokyo, 1996), 32,
125

U.S. Rice Millers Association
(USRMA), 134–35
U.S. trade representatives (USTR), 5,
36, 135

van Wolferen, Karel, 12
Vogel, Ezra, 12

Wakon Yôsai (Japanese soul, Western
knowledge), 11, 24
Warsaw Pact Treaty, 167
Watanabe, Michio, 1, **73**, 81–82, 87
West Germany. *See* Germany
Western European Union (WEU),
169
World Trade Organization (WTO),
127

Yano, Toru, 10, 68–69
Yara, Chobyo, 122
yokomoji (horizontally-written letters),
61
Yomiuri/Gallup polls. *See* polls
Yomiuri Shimbun polls. *See* polls
Yoshida, Shigeru, 25, 32
Yoshida cabinet, 25
Yoshimoto, Masanori, 125
yunyû taikoku (import giant), 27

zange gaikô (redemptive diplomacy),
68, 70, 87